Tempting the Fates

By the same author

Cordon and Search

Tempting the Fates

A memoir of service in the Second World War,
Palestine, Korea, Kenya and Aden

by

Major General Dare Wilson

CBE MC DL MA FRGS

Pen & Sword
MILITARY

To Sarah, of course

First published in Great Britain in 2006 by
Pen & Sword Military
an imprint of
Pen & Sword Books Ltd
47 Church Street
Barnsley
South Yorkshire
S70 2AS

ISBN 1 84415 435 1

A CIP catalogue record for this book is
available from the British Library

Typeset in 10/12 Linotype Palatino
by Lamorna Publishing Services

Printed and bound in England by
CPI UK.

For a complete list of Pen & Sword titles please contact

PEN & SWORD BOOKS LIMITED
47 Church Street, Barnsley, South Yorkshire, S70 2AS, England
E-mail: enquiries@pen-and-sword.co.uk
Website: www.pen-and-sword.co.uk

Regimental Collects

The Royal Northumberland Fusiliers

O God, our guide from of old, grant that wherever your servants of the Royal Northumberland Fusiliers are called upon to serve, we may follow the example of your servant St George, and ever prove steadfast in faith and valiant in battle; through him who is the Captain of our salvation, Jesus Christ, our Lord.

Airborne Forces

May the defence of the Most High be above and beneath, around and within us, in our going out and in our coming in, in our rising up and in our going down all our days and all our nights, until the dawn when the Sun of Righteousness shall arise with healing in His wings for the people of the world; through Jesus Christ our Lord.

The Special Air Service Regiment

O Lord, who didst call on Thy disciples to venture all to win all men to Thee, grant that we, the chosen members of the Special Air Service Regiment, may by our works and our ways dare all to win all, and in so doing render special service to Thee and our fellow men in all the world; through the same Jesus Christ our Lord.

Contents

Acknowledgements

My thanks begin at home, where my wife, Sarah, in addition to all her other responsibilities, committed herself at the outset to assist with the fulfilment of this book. As well as having all the attributes required of a perfect secretary she has also provided shrewd and helpful comments, often on behalf of those readers without a military background.

In the early stages of my research I was most fortunate in having valuable guidance from the late Professor Sir Harry Hinsley, former Master of St John's College, Cambridge, at which we were undergraduates together before the war. I have since been generously assisted by Sir John Keegan, who has advised me on several complexities in my story, and in a wider sense I have had advice and encouragement from three further academic friends, Richard Field, Russell Lawson and Jeffrey Switzer, the latter having been my supervisor during my second sojourn in Cambridge. Their reactions to passages I sent to them for comment were always helpful and often entertaining. Indeed Russell read every word in draft and was a most valuable sounding-board.

Further help has come from friends whose paths crossed mine and some of whose achievements feature in the narrative. They include Lady Barbirolli, Colonel Ian Battye, Michael Charlesworth, Professor John Crook, Major Bill Derbyshire, Major General Glyn Gilbert, General Sir John Hackett, Harry McCarten, Major Dick Tooth and Dirk Kuipers of Nijmegen, the Netherlands. Other friends have helped unknowingly by stimulating my memory with recollections that have contributed to the story. Should any of them, when reading it, find themselves responding to chords from long ago, I hope they will sense my appreciation.

Valuable assistance has come from the Military attachés and their staffs of the Embassy of the United States of America, the Embassy of the Republic of South Africa and the Canadian High Commission. Through them I have been able to contact sources that have filled gaps in my knowledge of those who were involved in events long past. Numerous other people have helped in their various ways and, in particular, I thank Helen Jones of Exeter University's Geography department for her meticulous care in the production of maps, Lesley Frater, archivist at the Fusiliers Museum of Northumberland, for her unfailing patience in verifying facts and Susan Econicoff, my Pen and Sword editor, for her delightful enthusiasm.

Finally, I thank my sons, Alexander, for his professional interest, and Peter, whose classical background proved invaluable for the major editing task he so capably undertook.

Glossary

AA	Anti-Aircraft
AAI	Allied Armies Italy
AFHQ	Allied Forces Headquarters
ARA	Army Rifle Association
AWOL	Absent without Leave
Bde	Brigade
BEF	British Expeditionary Force
BLA	British Liberation Army
Bn	Battalion
BOAC	British Overseas Airways Corporation
CIGS	Chief of the Imperial General Staff
C.-in-C.	Commander in Chief
CO	Commanding Officer
Coy	Company
CRA	Commander Royal Artillery
CSM	Company Sergeant Major
DCM	Distinguished Conduct Medal
DFC	Distinguished Flying Cross
DI	Dangerously Ill
Div	Division
DP	Displaced Person
DR	Dispatch Rider
DS	Directing Staff
DSO	Distinguished Service Order
DZ	Drop Zone
ENSA	Entertainments National Service Association
FANY	Field Army Nursing Yeomanry
FDS	Field Dressing Station
FLOSY	Front for the Liberation of South Yemen

G1	General Staff Grade 1
GHQ	General Headquarters
GOC.-in C.	General Officer Commanding in Chief
HMG	Her Majesty's Government
HMT	His Majesty's Troopship
IZL	Irgun Zwai L'eumi
JIC	Joint Intelligence Committee
JRBD	'J' Reinforcement Base Depot
KD	Khaki Drill
KGB	Komitet Gosudarstvennoi Bezopasnosti
KSLI	King's Shropshire Light Infantry
LNER	London and North Eastern Railway
LO	Liaison Officer
LRC	Light Reconnaissance Car
MC	Military Cross
M/C	Motor Cycle
MESC	Middle East Staff College
MOD	Ministry of Defence
MT	Mechanical Transport
NATO	North Atlantic Treaty Organization
NCO	Non Commissioned Officer
NDC	National Defence College
NLF	National Liberation Front
OC	Officer Commanding
O Group	Orders Group
OP	Observation Post
OTC	Officers' Training Corps
Para	Parachute
Pl	Platoon
POW	Prisoner(s) of War
PWX	Ex Prisoner(s) of War
QM	Quartermaster
RA	Royal Artillery
RAC	Royal Armoured Corps
RAMC	Royal Army Medical Corps
RE	Royal Engineers
Recce	Reconnaissance
Regt	Regiment
RHQ	Regimental Headquarters
RMO	Regimental Medical Officer
RNF/NF	Royal Northumberland Fusiliers
RNO	Resident Naval Officer

RTR	Royal Tank Regiment
RV	Rendezvous
SACEUR	Supreme Allied Commander Europe
SAS	Special Air Service
S/C	Scout Car
Sgt	Sergeant
SIS	Secret Intelligence Service
SP	Self Propelled
SS	Schutzstaffel
SSM	Squadron Sergeant Major
TA	Territorial Army
Tac HQ	Tactical Headquarters
UNO	United Nations Organization
VC	Victoria Cross
VD	Venereal disease
VE	Victory in Europe
VIP	Very Important Person
VJ	Victory in Japan
VP	Vulnerable Point
WRNS	Women's Royal Naval Service
WO	Warrant Officer
WVS	Women's Voluntary Service

Preface

Memoirs are, on their happiest side, a record of friendships.
B. H. Liddell Hart

For many years a succession of family members and friends, beginning more than thirty years ago with my mother, have urged me to write an account of the eventful times I experienced while serving in the Army, often on Active Service. For a long time I resisted, partly because I was so busy with other commitments, but eventually I made a start and this book is the result.

After joining the Royal Northumberland Fusiliers, or 'Fighting Fifth', in 1939 I soon came to accept its motto,

Quo Fata Vocant – Wherever the Fates Call.

In mythology The Fates were conceived as three sisters who supervised the fate of mortals and some classical poets wrote of them as more powerful even than the Gods. Clotho, the youngest, presided over the moment of birth and influenced the pattern of bright and dark strands in the thread of life. Lachesis, the second, spun and twisted the thread and under her fingers it became now strong, now weak. Finally, Atropos, the eldest and most inexorable, armed with a pair of

shears, remorselessly severed the thread of life at the moment of destiny.

On reflection, the course of my career in the Army was, on the whole, little influenced by personal preference, once I had made my initial choice of regiment. It was events, and decisions made by others, that guided my path. The way in which the pattern fell into place is part of the story and I leave you to judge how The Fates fit into it.

Dare Wilson,
Combeland, 2006

Chapter One

Growing up between the Wars

Child, your life is just beginning;
You must look ahead.
Life, alas! consists of winning
Little bits of bread;
Pause and ask yourself a minute:
How do I propose to win it?
How shall I be fed?

From Wisdom for the Wise by A. P. Herbert

One sunny afternoon in August 1937, when I had just turned eighteen, a fête was held in the garden of Leazes Hall in Co. Durham, barely a mile from home. It was my mother's idea that the whole family should support the event so, somewhat reluctantly because I could think of more enjoyable things to do, I accompanied her, together with my father, my two elder sisters and my younger brother. When we had walked up the hill to the Hall I wandered off to listen to the Silver Band, leaving the others to decide in what order they would visit the various amusements.

A particular attraction was a fortune-teller, a gypsy palmist widely renowned in the north of England at the time. I eventually found myself outside her tent and can remember entering and being bidden to sit, with a little table between us. She had a friendly face, with penetrating eyes and a compelling manner that soon dispelled any idea this was just going to be good for a laugh. She took my hands in turn and examined them at length. Then, looking up, she said with total conviction: 'You know that before long there is going to be another dreadful war, don't you?' Again she looked at my hands with a concentration I can still picture.

This is very interesting; you are going to join the Services, that is clear, but the question is, which one? In most cases I can say whether a young man is going to be a soldier, sailor or airman, but in your case there are things I cannot understand. I see you as a soldier, but you will also fly a lot; that part is blurred, but the rest is clear. You will be in the Services for many years and will come to no harm. You will just have to wait and see how it works out.

She returned several times to the blurred edges, which seemed to fascinate her and part of the time she appeared to be talking to herself. She told me more: that I would travel a lot and see eventful times. She repeated that she thought I would be a soldier, but perhaps I might be an airman, by which I took her to mean in the RAF. How close to the mark she was became clear in later years.

After I returned home, rather more thoughtful than when I had left, I looked up palmistry in an encyclopaedia. I found it described as an ancient art associated with the pattern of the future and widely practiced in the Orient. Moreover, Aristotle and many other learned men through the ages have recognized the art. It all gave me much food for thought and the details of my visit to the fortune-teller's tent have never faded from my memory.

I had spent the happiest of childhoods with my sisters and brother, due largely to the nature and outlook of our parents, Sydney and Dorothea, who brought us up with a sensible blend of love and discipline. Our home was near the village of Burnopfield and here we were introduced to all the delights of living in the country. At the age of six, being too young to shoot and too impatient to fish, I went hunting on Mousie, a Shetland pony of independent disposition. We also played games of every description indoors and out and spent much time 'helping' on the neighbouring farm, particularly at harvest time when there were wonderful rat hunts in the rickyard with a small team of terriers. One day, quite unexpectedly, the farmer gave me a piglet as a reward for my assistance. When it eventually went to market it fetched £6, which I spent on my first Raleigh bicycle.

There was also, of course, the more serious process of learning and after benefiting, or not, from a series of family governesses and tutors, at the age of eight I went to Harecroft Hall, on the far side of the Lake District. Mum took me in 'Jemima', her Austin Seven, and the journey of about 120 miles took most of the day. We were met at the door by the headmaster, R. A .Vallance, who politely made it clear that the time for our parting had come. It was quite a moment. I next saw Mum twelve weeks later on the platform of Newcastle railway station after I had made the return journey at the end of term in company with another boy, little older than myself, who had done it before. It was a memorable homecoming, not least because of the large goose, freshly killed on the school's home farm that morning and still unplucked, which I had won in the Christmas raffle. It travelled with me in the compartment and evoked a wide selection of comments and questions from fellow passengers as the trains from Seascale to Carlisle and Carlisle to Newcastle stopped at every intervening station.

Harecroft Hall was without doubt a remarkable school. In some ways it epitomized the concept of Outward Bound training before Kurt Hahn founded Gordonstoun. The school brochure contained twenty-three photographs of boys engaged in school activities. Ten showed ponies, there were three of boys haymaking (with ponies), two of boys mowing the lawn (one with the assistance of a pony), one of boys fishing, four of sports teams and three of expeditions to the Lakes. It was left to the reader to visualize that somewhere indoors there would be some form rooms, dormitories and other desirable facilities. The school colour was pink, the school song was 'John Peel' and the tradition of the school was summed up as 'Cleanliness, Sportsmanship and Manners'. After three happy years there it was decided that I should devote more time to academic studies and so was sent to Orleton, on the Yorkshire coast near Scarborough. I found this thoroughly orthodox and dull, but it did mean that I successfully passed into Shrewsbury School.

September 1933 saw the beginning of my five years at Shrewsbury and my memories range between resentment in the early days, with occasional moments of near despair, and almost total enjoyment towards the end. It was obvious from the start that life for new boys was not intended to be easy and long after I had left I learned that my house, Tombling's, was regarded by the remainder of the school as having by far the most rigorous regime. However, apart from the isolated case of a boy who ran away home to Switzerland I can recall only one other boy from Tombling's who left the school discontented, while for many of us the latter years were memorable for their enjoyment and lasting friendships were made. Indeed, I have had the privilege on five occasions in recent years of marching with the St Dunstan's contingent past the Cenotaph in Whitehall on Remembrance Sunday, acting as escort to John Painter who was a fellow new boy in 1933 and sadly lost his sight when wounded during the war.

There was a wide range of games and activities at Shrewsbury from which boys were free to choose. Rifle shooting came naturally to me and it was when I was competing in the school team for The

Ashburton Shield that I first visited Bisley. I continued to compete there from time to time with Army teams for more than twenty years. Sixty years after my first visit with the Shrewsbury School team I was there again shooting for the Salopian Veterans, while my elder son shot for the school. However, the activity that involved more boys than any other was 'The Corps', the Officers Training Corps. It was 'not done' to be seen to enjoy the Corps, and those who did were given little credit by their peers. Nevertheless, in 1938 some 450 boys out of 520 in the school belonged to it and some of us found a simple way of making it pleasurable. While the remainder were grouped round dummy Lewis guns, waving semaphore flags or brushing up their section tactics, about forty of us were making our presence felt, and heard, in the band, although we were still expected to be proficient in the basic military skills.

The Shrewsbury School OTC Band owed its existence, and eventually its reputation, largely to two men: H. H. Hardy, the Headmaster, had the idea, paved the way and raised the funds; Warrant Officer Class II W. W. Addison, a former bandmaster in the King's Shropshire Light Infantry, made it work. Some buglers and drummers were converted into bandsmen, and volunteers with the necessary musical aptitude were recruited from within the Corps. Michael Charlesworth (tuba) was appointed Band Sergeant. By 1936 Addison had worked a miracle. With unlimited support from above and mounting enthusiasm from below, the school suddenly realized it had a band that looked and sounded the part. Before long Gilbert and Sullivan selections were being rehearsed for Speech Day and 'Colonel Bogey' and countless rousing marches were echoing round the site. In due course the local inhabitants became familiar with the sight and sound of the entire OTC contingent marching through the town as the martial music reverberated through the narrow streets. This could be on our way to and from the station during 'field days' in various parts of Shropshire or en route to Annual Camp in Hampshire or Yorkshire. It was at the end of one of these camps, when I had been on an exercise crawling through an overgrown wilderness area, that I developed a very painful blistered rash on my chest. I became quite ill and was in bed for a week at home while the doctors pondered over the blisters. Eventually they wondered if I had been in contact with a patch of ground contaminated with liquid mustard gas from chemical warfare tests. No details of such tests were ever divulged and, once I had recovered, nothing more was said. I was just left with a permanent reminder in patches of white skin that steadfastly refuse to tan, even under a tropical sun.

Before I left Shrewsbury I had already made the decision to become a soldier, with a preference for The Royal Northumberland Fusiliers, but had also qualified for entry into Cambridge and had been accepted by St John's College to read modern languages. In those days protocol as well as procedure had to be followed when it came to joining a regiment and among other considerations it was necessary to know the level of private means which many regiments recommended junior officers should have before seeking acceptance. Sometimes mess bills alone would exceed young officers' pay which, before the war, amounted to the princely sum of 10/- (50p) a day. At this stage my father took the unusual step of writing in the first instance to the Colonel of The Regiment to ask for his advice, without prejudice to the final outcome, on whether he would rather see a young officer join his regiment through Cambridge or Sandhurst. Major General W. N. Herbert, a retired officer of the Regiment with a distinguished record, earned my father's respect and my undying gratitude for his answer: 'My advice without hesitation is to send your boy to Cambridge; from there he will enter the Army through the French windows.' I did not realize until much later how untypical this answer was of Herbert's generation, commissioned before the First World War, and I was then all the more grateful to him.

By the time I returned home for the summer holidays at the beginning of August 1938, my father had completed the arrangements for me to leave for Germany within a few days for intensive language study with a family who took one or two English boys for this purpose. I travelled by boat to the Hook of Holland and thence by train to Cologne. My passport contained a visa, stamped with eagle and swastika, valid until the end of September. I was met at the station by my host, Doktor Blasneck, who worked for the Reichsbank, and we drove to his home, a house called Auserka in the middle-class town of Köln Junkersdorf, a suburb of Cologne. My stay turned out to be a useful and interesting experience. Those of my generation whom I met socially were inevitably in the Hitler *Jugend* and it was not long before I discovered that all fit young Germans had no other option. They were often anxious to discuss politics, but only in order to extol the virtues of the Reich and all it stood for. Much of it was in such contrast to the British public school outlook that more than once I made the mistake of becoming involved in arguments. Rule 1 within the Blasneck household was never to criticize, even by implication, the Führer, the Reich, the Party or anything for which they stood.

One day when exploring Cologne by myself I strayed into a Jewish quarter and found myself witness to a small rounding-up operation by troops whom I assumed to be SS, as terrified men, women and children were driven off under escort. At that time concentration camps had been exposed, but not widely reported, and it was a shock for me to get even a glimpse of the system in operation. I certainly registered the fear on the faces of those being taken away, I presumed into captivity. When I returned to Auserka and naively mentioned what I had seen, the Blasnecks' reaction came close to panic and I was told how foolish I had been to stray away from the main streets and to watch something that was none of my business. Thereafter my leisure hours were more closely supervised. It was an interesting coincidence that, within a few days of that incident, a decree was promulgated in Berlin on 25 August laying down that, as from 1 October, foreigners would be allowed to stay in Germany only if, from their past record and the purpose of their stay, they appeared 'worthy of the hospitality accorded to them'. Foreigners who showed themselves to be unworthy guests would be the subject of 'necessary police measures'.

About halfway through my visit to Auserka I was joined by Hugh Feilding, a delightful boy who had recently left Stowe. I welcomed having an English companion with whom I could discuss the strange and ominous things going on around us. In the course of a few weeks of wholly inexperienced observation I was able to get a feel and a picture of what had happened. It seemed that nobody in Germany could any longer express a view or take an action which was out of line with National Socialism. There was unquestioning subservience towards the state and all who acted in its name. The evils of Hitler's psychopathy had penetrated homes, schools, churches and institutions throughout the land. What little I saw was enough to open my eyes and mind for further study. Nothing I have seen or read since has changed my view that the ultimate evil of Hitler's warped mind lay in the calculated way in which he had succeeded in taking over and subverting the youth of Germany.

Early in September, as the Nuremberg rally was about to get under way, I received an enigmatic letter from my father, short and to the point. 'Should you receive word from me, possibly by telegram, to end your visit prematurely, come home at once and without question.' He added thoughtfully, 'All is well at home'. Without showing the letter to my host, I probed for any information he might have about a decline in political relations between our countries. He professed complete ignorance of any such thing and, having been reading the German press as part of my education, I knew this view at least to be consistent with Herr Goebbels' line.

The next day I received a telegram from my father 'Come home now', which I showed at once to my host who expressed astonishment. He asked me if I could explain it and I told him I could only suggest that the political situation had deteriorated and there was now a fear of war. This he disputed: 'But surely you don't see any threat of war in Germany? There is no fear of war here.' There was nothing further to be said. I made the necessary arrangements, bid my hosts 'Auf Wiedersehen' and departed. As it happened this was not to be my only visit to Auserka. The next time, however, would be very different.

When I returned to England I found both interest and apprehension over the quickening tempo of events in Germany. At home my father acknowledged that, whilst he might have acted a little prematurely in recalling me, he felt that in the circumstances it was better to be too soon than too late. My early return had its advantages. I had been in Germany long enough to become convinced that foreign languages did not come easily to me and I felt my time at Cambridge could be put to better use in some other direction. So the beginning of the Michaelmas Term saw me in St John's College, with the good fortune to have as my tutor R. L. Howland. An Old Salopian with a Double First in Classics, he also had the distinction of having represented Great Britain in the shot put event in the 1928 Olympics. Known to the athletic world as 'Bonzo' and in the cloistered precincts of Cambridge as 'Bede', as a tutor he was always helpful, understanding and good-humoured. Having accepted my doubts about Modern Languages he suggested that I might read Economics and arranged for me to meet Claude Guillebaud, another Fellow of St John's, who was an outstanding economist and a pillar of both the College and the University. He supervised my work during the year that led up to the outbreak of war and I could have wished for none better but, despite his encouragement, I found little to inspire me in most of the subjects we studied as I struggled to improve my understanding of Economics.

However, to be fair to all lecturers who had difficulty in holding the undivided attention of their students, university life during that academic year of 1938/39 was considerably affected by wholly abnormal distractions. It was becoming increasingly difficult to isolate the worsening political situation and threat to peace in Europe from the smooth course of academic studies. Even so, outside the lecture halls and the OTC drill halls, life was light-hearted, enjoyable and full of conventional interest. Every evening we assembled punctually for dinner in Hall, suitably dressed and wearing gowns. Audit ale, brewed to traditional college specifications, was readily available and soon became a habit. We frequently tended to cluster together in the same small groups of friends according to our shared interests, which rarely included our studies.

The group of friends with which I spent more evenings than any other comprised a medical student, a law student and Jimmy Edwards, one of the College's choral scholars in the Chapel Choir and already a natural comedian. I believe he was reading English Literature, but I don't think that occupied overmuch of his time. In addition to singing he played the trombone and, as I still had my cornet, before long we were performing together in reviews for charity as members of The St John's College Gadflies. A programme for a revue entitled *Table Top II* given in the College Hall on 1 March 1939 included the following item:

5. Cornet and Trombone: Duets and Solos
Cornet: R. D. Wilson   Trombone: J. K. O'N. Edwards
Accompanied at the piano by A. G. Lee

The College also had a larger instrumental group that rose to such occasions as playing on the roof of the high chapel tower on the morning of Ascension Day and joining the procession through the town on University Poppy Day, using a large brewer's dray as a float. Whatever the occasion Jimmy's irrepressible sense of humour added to the jollity. It was not long before he became one of the stars in the *Cambridge Footlights*, which has produced so many famous entertainers over the years. During the war he became a transport pilot in the RAF and carried out no less than four glider-towing and re-supply sorties to Arnhem. On the fourth he was shot down in flames, miraculously surviving the crash, though he was badly burned. He was later awarded the DFC.

My own principal interests at Cambridge included rifle shooting in the University Rifle Association (CURA), cross-country running with the University Hare and Hounds and inter-college athletics. My interest in rifle shooting soon brought me into contact with Charles Jewell, known to his close friends as Chips, who had just joined Trinity College from Winchester. We had much in common and even prevailed on the Army to allow him to join 'my' regiment during the war. Since then we fished and shot together a great deal, frequently in Scotland.

In the spring of 1939 came news that was of significance to many undergraduates. Late in April the Prime Minister announced to the House of Commons the Government's plan for the conscription of all men between their twentieth and twenty-first birthdays for up to six months' military training. Thereafter they would have the option of entering the Territorial Army for three and a half years or passing to a Special Reserve of the Regular Army. It was anticipated that the measure would ultimately strengthen the Services by 800,000 men. Undergraduates affected by the Act, when it was published, were permitted to postpone their liability to be called up for training until the conclusion of their studies. A few months earlier such a measure would have been unthinkable; it would have conflicted with the Government's appeasement policy. To those of us who were spending more of our time in drill halls, the sense of urgency from above was unmistakeable; war was no longer a matter of 'if' but 'when'.

I also recall, within the wide spectrum of organizations actively involved in student politics, a growing awareness of governmental shortcomings. I had joined the University Conservative Association (CUCA), but had not become a member of the Union Society, although I cannot claim to have been influenced in this by Dr Butler, Headmaster of Shrewsbury School who, in 1817 'thought the Union did "fatal mischief" to men of first rate talents'. Samuel Butler is still regarded as one of Shrewsbury's most distinguished headmasters and one for whom I feel a personal affection, my younger son having been a Butler scholar at the school. At a meeting of the Union Society a vote was recorded against compulsory military service, but many of us afterwards felt that it was unrepresentative of undergraduate opinion in the University. Perhaps with a view to rectifying the situation, CUCA invited Winston Churchill to address a meeting. On 19 May, according to *The Cambridge Daily News:*

> The 2,500 undergraduates and others who packed the Corn Exchange full last night when Mr Winston Churchill made there a striking speech on conscription gave at the end of the meeting a convincing demonstration of the measure of their support for compulsory military training. By an overwhelming majority, estimated by the Chairman (the Master of Clare) to be about ten to one, the audience carried the following motion: 'That this meeting of Cambridge undergraduates gladly accepts the measure of conscription involved in the Military Training Bill, and they express their determination to maintain at any sacrifice England's power to play her part and to do her duty for the British Empire and the world causes that are now at stake.'

From the outset Churchill gave the impression that he was relishing the occasion. The Corn Exchange was packed to capacity and the crowd overflowed into The Lion Hotel's yard, where the proceedings were relayed through loudspeakers. Churchill made an impassioned speech and even before the end would have carried the vote. The mood of the meeting had been transformed from empathy to enthusiasm, but the best was yet to come. No words written in retrospect can convey adequately the great wave of emotion that swept through the vast audience as Churchill spoke his final lines:

> And now to you who stand by yourselves
> Older people can say – 'Go on!'
> But you, the valiant youth of Britain,
> you alone have the right to say to all England,
> to all the Empire, to all the World,
> in the cause of right and freedom,
> 'Fear not! Come on, we will lead the way.'

That is how Winston Churchill helped us so much to win the war. It was by his speeches and his writings – rather than by his strategy or mental capacity. They were good enough but would not have carried the day by themselves.

Lord Denning

Within ten days we were into our exams. That some of us failed to take them as seriously as we should may not be wondered at. Most of us passed, though perhaps not as well as our tutors and supervisors would have wished. I took a week's exeat, returning for the welter of May Balls and parties the like of which were not to be seen again in Cambridge for many years. Those of us who had become identified with the University OTC or Air Squadron left with a strong feeling, if not conviction, that the following Michaelmas Term might start without us. It had been a wonderful year as another world had opened up, memorable for its new interests and friendships, even with its serious overtones. Looking back on it life was never quite the same again.

Chapter Two

Blitzkrieg

We are never ready for war, yet we never have a Cabinet who dare tell people the truth.

Sir Garnet Wolseley, 1833-1913

On that fateful Sunday morning, 3 September 1939, every family with a wireless was glued to it to hear Chamberlain's broadcast to the nation. At home my parents, sisters, brother and I sat in silence listening to the tired voice of a man who had striven for peace with a blind conviction that no price was too high to pay. When he had finished it seemed as if a deeper silence fell over us as we became lost in our own thoughts. Within the family we had all made our decisions; Kitty was in the FANYs , Betty in the Red Cross and Peter was in his last year at the Royal Naval College, Dartmouth. It was probably Mother, whose ideas were plentiful and usually sound, who suggested that we should have a family snapshot taken in our respective uniforms. So the six of us gathered in the garden in front of the house. As the years passed the photograph's interest increased. Soon we four children had dispersed to our various duties, leaving Mother and Father with the universal parental burden of anxiety and foreboding.

By coincidence I was under instructions from the War Office to report to the Depot of The Royal Northumberland Fusiliers at Fenham Barracks, Newcastle, the following morning for my Regular Army attachment, dressed and paid as a second lieutenant. This I did and my Army service began with a greater sense of purpose than I had foreseen. I doubt if even the gifted gypsy palmist could have predicted that nearly twenty years later I would be commanding the same Depot and later still the Northumbrian Brigade, whose HQ was in the same barracks.

Within hours of arriving I found myself on a basic Vickers medium

11

machine-gun course. I had already been introduced to the weapon at Cambridge and the subject soon fell into place. Two further courses followed and in less than two months, while I was still on attachment (which is below the bottom rung of a junior officer's ladder) I was, surprisingly, made an instructor, pending a posting to one of the regiment's four machine-gun battalions. During the previous weeks officers, young and old, had been turning up at the Depot from all quarters. One of these was Charles Mitchell, who had recently joined the regiment from Oxford, having used a parallel route to my own, though he was two years older and had completed his degree. We shared several interests and soon became firm friends. Our paths coincided and crossed over many years until his premature death as a delayed result of wounds received during the Korean War. He had a splendid sense of humour and a highly professional sense of duty; he was also one of the most courageous men I have ever known. His family home near Coldstream I still regard as a sort of earthly paradise; it had all the interests I held most dear and because of Charles's generosity I was a frequent visitor there.

After nearly three months of training, including administration, man-management, regimental history and so on, given by several highly motivated and experienced officers, I received a posting order that, of itself, was no surprise. But instead of going to one of the regiment's four machine-gun battalions I was ordered to join 8 RNF, one of the few motorcycle reconnaissance battalions in the Army, which belonged to the 23rd Northumbrian Division. This unit was at Prudhoe on Tyne where I met the CO (Lieutenant Colonel F. B. Clarke), an elderly territorial who had served throughout the First World War, for most of it as a POW. He was affable and informed me that I was to join 'A' Company. This was situated at Denton Burn, barely two miles from Fenham Barracks, and I was not as amused as my family that my first posting was less than ten miles from home. However, perhaps I did have the last laugh because until then my father had steadfastly refused to countenance any plans I had at home for learning to ride a motorbike.

When I arrived I found that the company consisted of Territorials and National Servicemen who blended well and to whom I took an instant liking. In spite of every manner of shortage they were making the best of what they had and behind the characteristic Geordie grumbles there was determination and good humour. I never lost my affection for 'A' Company (later 'A' Squadron) with whom, after many diversions, I finished the war. But what of those shortages? The Regimental History sums up the situation affecting the 8th and 9th

12

Battalions as being '...considerably under strength, deficient of trained junior leaders and sadly lacking in essential weapons, modern equipment and transport. ... They were two enthusiastic bodies of fine potential soldiers – eager to learn, but as yet almost entirely untrained and lacking all but the simplest equipment.'

The motorcycle battalion I had just joined must have been fairly typical, with a few additional problems stemming from its role. To some extent its situation was analogous to a cavalry regiment full of recruits, most of whom had never been astride a horse, waiting for all but a few of its mounts to arrive before heading for the war. However, although there were insufficient machines for rider training the situation was considerably helped by the expertise of a nucleus of motorcycle enthusiasts who had joined the battalion as Territorials so as to combine their hobby with their sense of duty.

Early in the New Year I was given command of one of the two Scout Car Platoons in the Battalion, yet to be formed and with, as yet, no scout car in sight. This involved me moving to HQ Company at Prudhoe. The men selected for these platoons were chosen with great care and before I got to know them I sensed they were up to something. Every meal there was a repetition of the potato complaint which, at first, I followed up in case more could be produced from the cookhouse. The ringleader was one Fusilier McCarten, whom I suspected, quite wrongly, of having eaten half his helping before making the complaint. His final complaint of 'Please, sor, there's not enoof taties' was made on the day when all his friends contributed one of their potatoes, making a pyramid on his plate which could hardly contain them. The remainder of the platoon had been tipped off and my reaction (whatever it was) produced a roar of laughter.

It was during this period of internal reorganization that Charles Mitchell arrived quite unexpectedly from the Depot and was given command of the other Scout Car Platoon. From that moment all our fortunes became interlinked as the storm clouds continued to gather. Late in March a warning order was received from Div HQ that 8 RNF would shortly be going overseas. It was graded SECRET and all ranks were told 'You may inform your near relatives but no one else'. Exactly a month after receiving the warning order we were on our way to France. The advance party with the vehicles had already left when orders arrived for the main body to assemble at the Prudhoe Drill Hall late on the evening of 22 April for departure on foot for Prudhoe Station. Particular stress had previously been laid on the importance of security whenever the move should take place. This time even families were not to be informed. To assist in putting them off the trail

13

there was a deception plan to disguise all activity as relating to a night exercise. The real intention was to disappear unnoticed into the night, leaving Prudhoe to wake up the following morning without us. In the event it turned out rather differently. As the companies assembled so did the families, friends and a high proportion of the local populace in the guise of unrelated well-wishers. The Police even turned out to control any traffic. It finished up like a carnival with singing and cheering, enhanced by closing time at the pubs which had had an exceptionally active evening. The lads were going to be given a 'reet proper send-off'.

The troop train took us from Prudhoe to Southampton where we embarked in the SS *Finella* for France. The strength of the Battalion was twenty-one officers and 559 other ranks. All wore red and white roses in their headdress in accordance with the regiment's ancient custom, it being St George's Day. We disembarked at Cherbourg the following morning and marched three miles to a transit camp for breakfast, then the same distance back to the station where we entrained for an unknown destination. The French provided the same rolling stock as for their own army, the wagons clearly marked '8 Chevaux – 40 hommes', the only difference between the two species being that the soldiers were deprived of straw. The officers had the benefit of wooden benches in otherwise empty wagons. Some comparisons were made between the two railway companies involved thus far, the LNER emerging a clear winner on all counts. We eventually drew out of Cherbourg at 1800 hours on Wednesday, 24 April. Just over five days later, and seven since leaving Prudhoe, we arrived at our destination, an idyllic village by the name of Dieval between St Pol and Bethune. Why a journey of this limited length took a week never emerged. Not unnaturally there was plenty of 'rhubarbing', but soldiers in such circumstances are remarkably patient. As we formed up for the final march into camp I overheard one of my Fusiliers remark, 'I wonder what the 'osses think o' them bloody wagons when its theor torn?'

The camp of bell tents had been pitched by the advance party on the outskirts of Dieval among a scattering of small orchards and it was indeed an attractive setting. However, a short distance away was the airfield awaiting our labour. Almost without pause we fell into our new routine. Four days each week were to be spent on airfield construction duties that involved physical labour between 0800 hours and 1730 hours. It was back-aching work for those not used to it, but produced useful dividends in terms of fitness when the fighting began. Two more days were spent on training and one was set aside for 'rest and other purposes'. The latter was variously interpreted, with a not insignificant proportion of the troops heading for the brothels of Bruay. When the subject came up for discussion at a higher level, Hugh Gass's (the RMO) advice was that the choice would appear to lie between the adopted practice or unlicenced premises with the inevitable rise in VD. The matter was allowed to rest. I cannot remember how the officers spent their days off, but as there were only two between the date of our arrival in France and Hitler's next initiative I suspect we enjoyed our serene surroundings among the orchards of Dieval and unlimited champagne at 5/- (25p) a bottle.

As we settled into our new surroundings we began to get the benefit, in terms of training and cohesion, which comes to every battalion when it leaves its barracks, forsakes its wives and families and finds itself able to concentrate on 'serious soldiering'. Even the Colonel seemed to shed his part-time Territorial mantle and assume his full authority, perhaps strengthened psychologically by the proximity of battlefields associated with his earlier war. I do, however, recall wondering, young and inexperienced as I was, whether he had moved with the times and which war he was preparing to fight when the time came. In spite of our shortages it was a great stimulus to be in France at what became known as the 'sharp end' of the war. Most of us were young and keen and the significance of our deficiencies did not, at this stage, weigh heavily with us. The half dozen officers in the battalion who were veterans of the First World War were not, on reflection, taken as seriously as they should have been by the score of us who lacked their judgement and experience. In somewhat muted tones they voiced their concern about training, equipment and general fitness for war without taking the edge off our enthusiasm.

At dawn on 10 May 1940 the waiting ended. Hitler had chosen this day to attack Belgium, Holland and Luxembourg. Our own introduction to the blitzkrieg was gradual. It would be a little while before the tide of war would seriously affect the village so we continued with our labours on the airfield. There was even time to write home and this was one of the earliest of several hundred written on active service that my mother kept and handed back to me more than thirty years later.

In the Field, Friday May 10th, 1900 hrs.

Just a line, while there is time, one never knows quite what is going to happen next and I may be busy shortly. ... We don't get all that much sleep and as a result sleep rather soundly, so this morning very early I woke up cursing what I assumed to be another thunderstorm and it was sometime before I realised that it was a bit more than a thunderstorm, i.e. an air raid. It was exciting while it lasted, but no damage was done on our doorstep. We had the satisfaction of seeing, however, two Boche planes crash out of control. ... We just took it as a routine visit till we heard on the wireless a few hours later about the invasion of Belgium and Holland. I am glad it has come in a way as we now know where we are and it may shorten the war – I think it is a mistake on Hitler's part. Up to the present news is good and the wireless makes hopeful listening.

... I'm sorry I can't tell you more but there it is so don't worry as everything is OK.

Our battalion spent the first week of the blitzkrieg labouring, last minute training, following up reports of enemy parachutists and scrounging for additional arms, ammunition and equipment to reduce our deficiencies. We were still, officially, without entrenching tools of any description, though, with so many Northumbrian miners in the battalion, we probably had the best 'entrenchers' around.

17 May. 8 RNF received its orders in the usual way, by dispatch rider, because we had no wireless communications. This First World War system had its limitations in a blitzkrieg, as we soon learned. We were to move forthwith to concentrate at St Leger, a small village some thirty miles distant, between Arras and Cambrai. 11 Platoon was the first in the battalion to leave and, in spite of one or two diversions due to severed roads and some civilian congestion on our route, we reached St Leger to discover, with satisfaction, that we were the first to arrive. The journey was memorable because it was our introduction to the refugee problem with which the whole of the British Expeditionary Force had to contend throughout most of the campaign; sometimes we found ourselves moving against the flow and sometimes as part of it, overtaking as and when we could. On this occasion we were advancing, so naturally the refugees were moving in directions counter to our own. It was less natural to meet groups of disorganized French soldiers walking, weaponless, among them. From then on we became ever more familiar with the vast tide of humanity which surged, generally westwards, with pitiful bundles of possessions.

As night approached without further arrivals from 8 RNF I began to wonder if the good St Leger was venerated elsewhere in the locality, but there was no one to whom I could put the question. Eventually, as I was about to send off patrols on the few motorcycles we had in search of the nearest divisional unit, a DR arrived with orders to rejoin the Battalion which was now at Croiselles, a few miles away. Now, it is impossible to belong to a reconnaissance unit for long without becoming sensitive to criticism where navigation is concerned. To start a regimental move as the leading sub-unit and to arrive some hours after all the others have gone to bed can be difficult to laugh off at the best of times, but when it happens as one's regiment is advancing to meet the enemy in the early stages of a war it can be highly embarrassing. Fortunately the Regimental War Diary fills in the vital gap:

17 May DIEVAL Bn ordered by 23 Div to move to ST. LEGER. Later orders received from 23 Div to move instead to the neighbourhood of CROISELLES.

18 May. Early in the day I was sent for and given a task for which, at first, I doubted I was qualified. A detachment of Auxiliary Military Pioneer Corps (later to become The Royal Pioneer Corps) was encamped some miles to the south of us and had requested tactical advice on how to defend the forward airfield on which they were working. I was told to visit them at once by motorcycle and to offer such advice as I could. On the way I was to keep my eyes skinned because I should be passing through a 'grey area' in which, so rumour had it, enemy tanks were soon expected. I set off on my Norton and did my best to scan the landscape ahead while avoiding potholes, occasionally stopping to listen. Happily my journey was without incident.

I arrived at the airfield to find a scene of intense activity, as a force of between 100 and 200 pioneers were changing their role in order to fight. There was no mistaking the urgency and commitment that marked everything they did. There were in France by then more than 20,000 officers and men of their Corps, who had been brought in to work on the lines of communication, in the ports unloading the supply ships and on the forward airfields. They included old reservists, mostly with service in the First World War, and young militiamen who had been drafted in. Most of the officers were in their forties or fifties and many had seen war service in the trenches. My impression was that up to this stage few had sung their praises and they had received little acknowledgement for the Herculean work they did during that long, hard winter. Their OC soon appeared and together we did a circuit of the airfield, while I explained the need for all-round defence with interlocking arcs of fire and a quick plan so that further trenches could be dug without delay. I advised him to deploy his sub-units so that between them they could cover all the main approaches and take advantage of the adjacent higher ground. This was a second lieutenant who had not yet exchanged shots fired in anger giving advice to a senior major, but he seemed genuinely grateful and went off to make his plan.

On my return journey I was going quite fast when I saw approaching me a British Bedford 15-cwt truck going flat out. We both braked hard and I nearly finished in the ditch. After the truck had skidded past and come to a halt the driver, taking me for a dispatch rider, shouted a warning that enemy tanks had been seen in the vicinity. Perhaps it was then that I first experienced the peculiar sensation one gets when knowingly approaching the enemy, either alone or as one of a small group, without protection, in broad daylight and clueless as to their whereabouts. It became quite familiar in later years. On this occasion it was a case of 'nothing to report' when I arrived back.

That evening 8 RNF received its next order to move, as usual without warning, this time to the village of Cherisy, two miles to the north, where it arrived around 2000 hours. My surviving notes contain the entry :

> 2200 hrs. Spent the night with Charles in village carpenter's house. Two very recent graves just outside the window next to a large bomb crater.

19 May. In fact it turned out to be rather a short night because at 0200 hours the Battalion was ordered to move at once to Mouchy le Prieux, two miles closer to Arras. We were established there by 0600 hours. As at every new location, we would organize our defences, start digging-in and probably send out patrols to discover what was happening around us. By now the supply system was already in a shaky state and following each of these moves the Quartermaster might or might not have the rations for the next meal. If we had a meal at Mouchy we were lucky, because nine hours after we arrived we were on the move again.

It requires little imagination to picture some of the consequences of this pattern of events. Soldiers get used to short rations and irregular meals in war; in battle they will not even be aware of when they last fed, but their performance sooner or later will be affected, particularly when their level of sleep over a period of days or weeks drops below the minimum required. The combined effects of prolonged shortage of rations and sleep become cumulative and lead to physical and mental exhaustion. In this condition soldiers may fall asleep on sentry duty at night and this is one of the most serious offences on active service. Fortunately, it happens rarely among good soldiers, whose sense of discipline and duty helps them to resist the compelling urge to sleep when exhausted.

In the afternoon came the orders for 8 RNF to conform with the divisional plan to fall back under cover of darkness to Thélus aerodrome, four miles north of Arras. Though we had not yet had to contend with the German Army, there had been a marked increase in the *Luftwaffe*'s activities and any movement by day now resulted in bombing and machine-gunning. We moved off well dispersed and all went well until we reached the River Scarpe, east of Arras, where, in the dark, we found the bridge mined for demolition by French engineers, thus making it impassable. The marching column changed direction and crossed the canal at the next bridge some two miles away. The transport had a breathtaking diversion along a very narrow canal towpath, creeping without lights and at times with inches to spare as it followed those on foot. As a result of this detour the battalion was not established in Thélus until 0500 hours the following morning. A couple of hours later we were bombed and machine-gunned from the air, but no casualties were reported.

20 May. At 0900 hours, four hours after our arrival, the dreaded DR from Div HQ was back again; 8 RNF would move at once to Arras where it would come under command of the 1st Battalion Welsh Guards. Some of my Fusiliers observed pithily that this would be our sixth move in less than three days, but though we were all by now tired and hungry there was no grumbling. On arrival in Arras we soon discovered that it had already been heavily bombed the previous day, when the railway station was destroyed, together with two trains filling with refugees, many of whom were killed. The Welsh Guards had also suffered their first casualties. Our three companies took over some of their positions on the east, north and west perimeters where they had been stretched, because Arras is a large town. Enemy mortar fire and sporadic air attacks by the *Luftwaffe* provided all the incentive necessary not to waste time. For the first time we felt a sense of purpose and direction as we were fitted into the garrison defence plan and learned something of the general situation. The enemy were now closing in on all sides and had already been repulsed on several of the roads leading into the town. There was also a strong awareness that, here, the Welsh Guards were in charge and any Germans who thought otherwise would be seen off at the double. The Guards were an inspiration to all of us, however weary, who were gathered into their fold. No time was lost in making every possible preparation for the assault on the town which was now considered inevitable; road blocks were

erected, fire positions protected, mines laid and a host of other arrangements made, all with a sense of urgency.

21 May. Little seemed to be going on around us in Arras that evening, apart from sniping, but our hopes of an unaccustomed quiet night were shattered at midnight by the arrival of an advance party from the 6th Battalion Green Howards, also part of the 23rd Division. They would be taking over from us within a few hours. By the time the changeover took place B Company was briefed to move off to another part of the perimeter and we, 11 Platoon, were given a detached task. Initially this was to take over, from No. 4 Company 1st Battalion Welsh Guards, the defence of two road bridges over the River Scarpe – St Nicholas's and St Catharine's – several hundred yards apart on the northern side of the town. It seemed rather excessive for one platoon, but fortunately before long 10 Platoon under Charles Mitchell arrived to defend the latter bridge and I was able to concentrate my platoon in support of St Nicholas.

By the time we arrived at the bridge, No. 4 Company had been withdrawn to stiffen the defences elsewhere on the perimeter where the Germans were making determined efforts to breach the roadblocks with armoured fighting vehicles. We therefore arrived at St Nicholas Bridge without local knowledge or the benefit of taking over from the previous defenders. Before deciding on a layout I needed to find a good view of the approaches to the bridge, see what protection the river would offer and take a quick look at the lesser approaches from the rear. Before leaving I told Sergeant McGregor, my Platoon Sergeant, to disperse the platoon because of the enemy aircraft in the offing and to find out what two soldiers were up to digging, stripped to the waist, not far from a recently-bombed house.

In the course of my circuit of the area I followed a well-used path between gardens where bombs had destroyed a garage. Picking my way through the rubble, around a corner I suddenly found myself looking down at a body. It was that of an elderly postman. He had been heavily struck on the head and blood that had not quite dried had trickled down his face into his large waxed moustache. His distinctive postman's helmet was lying crushed beside him and out of his postbag the letters had cascaded on to the ground. I guessed that no one would know what had befallen him. His family would be missing him. Who could I tell? Then I realized there was no time for such thoughts, so there was nothing to be done. Sooner or later most young soldiers have their own equally abrupt initiation into this aspect of war when, for a few seconds, they may be caught off balance. This was mine.

When I returned to the Platoon I called up the section commanders and gave them their orders. This done, Sergeant McGregor said: 'Those two soldiers are from the Welsh Guards; they belong to a platoon which got a direct hit from a bomb last night on that house over there. Half of them were either killed or wounded and those two are digging the graves.'

'Then I think we should offer them some help,' I said.

He had already done so: 'They thanked me but said they would rather finish the job themselves.'

There was so much else to do that this sad episode went to the back of my mind until, some hours later, I saw the two Welsh Guardsmen approaching. They had washed, cleaned their boots and uniform and now, with their rifles at the slope, they were immaculate. They halted in front of me and gave a cracking butt-salute before one of them took a pace forward and announced: 'Guardsman Morgan and Guardsman Evans reporting for duty – SIR.' I was unaccustomed to this standard of Guards discipline, but hope I didn't show it as I asked whether they had been given any further orders. The answer was equally precise: 'This was our post and we cannot leave it without the order to do so from an officer.' I thanked them for their readiness to remain with us and had a few words with them before directing them to where I was confident they would find their battalion. I found this little incident highly impressive and cherish its memory as an example of the Welsh Guards' standards. I recall, too, that their professionalism as fighting soldiers was matched by their morale and good humour.

22 May. The alarums and excursions since our arrival had been fairly continuous, with a high degree of alertness by day and night. We were tired when we arrived and we were certainly no less tired now. The first entry in 8 RNF's War Diary for today was timed 0400 hours and read 'Town reported to be completely surrounded by enemy'. There was a daily schedule of enemy air raids which were noted in the Welsh Guards' War Diary as taking place usually '...at about 6.30 am, 11 o'clock, 4 pm and just before dark'. These main raids, which were augmented by fighter aircraft operating singly, were always carried out by massed formations of Ju87 dive-bombers, usually referred to as *Stukas*, though that is the German term for all dive-bombers.

Surprise played no part in the *Stuka's* performance; on the contrary, its purpose was to contribute the maximum noise by every means possible. It had a very loud engine with a distinctive howl in a power-dive and attached to a leg of the landing gear was a siren which added its own piercing note. The *Luftwaffe* pilots fittingly christened the Ju87

21

'The Trombone of Jericho'. On one raid I estimated there were 120 aircraft orbiting above us. The noise was tremendous and the effect almost theatrical. When the leader decided that the moment had come he waggled his wings and peeled off with aircraft in cloverleaf formations of three following in succession. This was the point at which the performance was apt to become personal. The pilots achieved their accuracy, which far exceeded that of bombers in level flight, by aligning their aircraft on to their targets and holding this course in an almost vertical power dive of several thousand feet. It was easy to imagine in the early stage of any dive in our direction that the pilot had his eyes fixed on our trench – this one is coming at us. They pulled out of their dives at about 700 feet, sometimes lower, and just before they did so we would see the bombs leave the aircraft. Any bomb landing within 100 yards or less would certainly produce a lot of blast and debris, but it had to be very close to be dangerous.

After the best part of a week, in spite of many near misses within our platoon area overlooking St Nicholas Bridge, the bridge itself was still intact and we had sustained no direct hit on any of our trenches, but it was a challenge to all and a test of discipline, particularly the first time. It is a tiring business being bombed four times a day, quite apart from all the other things going on. The situation was not helped by various shortcomings in administration within the Battalion, which were not surprising in view of the low level of experience among the majority of officers and NCOs. As a young officer I was learning much from trial and error, now and again from my own mistakes, no doubt at the expense of others. But mistakes made under such conditions are rarely repeated and one learns fast. During the week we were in Arras my platoon was never visited by a company commander, the CO or the second in command. Fortunately Charles Mitchell and I kept in close touch and shared such knowledge and experience as we had. Every now and again the 'fog of war' returned, occasionally from unexpected directions. One contribution came from the BBC in a news bulletin when it was announced that Arras had fallen to the enemy. A number of units were tuned in at the time and the report was soon causing more mirth than consternation throughout the garrison.

I forget when the rations in Arras gave out, or when the water supply was bombed and we got orders to stop drinking any until it had been either boiled or sterilized. There were no water trucks and we had no cookers or sterilizing tablets so we had to seek alternative sources. We were close to what had been, before the bombing began, some smart houses with well-stocked cellars and storerooms and there was no need even to break into them because many of them were already partly demolished. Foraging parties went further afield in search of bottled mineral water, which was scarcer than wine. During one of my visits to the house we used as a base, I noticed a number of empty brandy bottles (including liqueur) among the mounting pile of wine bottles and began to read the Riot Act, concerned about intoxication. I was soon interrupted by the corporal in charge who assured me, 'Oh, ye needn't worry yoursel about that sor, it's only been used for washin' wor feet in; and mind, it's champion for the job!'

23 May. The Battalion war diary notes '...intermittent but severe enemy aerial machine-gun and dive-bombing all day'. During the afternoon I was told that the CO wished to see me immediately at Battalion HQ. When I arrived I sensed there was something in the air. 'Dare, the General wishes to know as soon as possible whether this village, Ecurie,' pointing on the map, 'is occupied by the enemy. I want you to go there, find out and return with the information.' Pause. 'Have you any questions?' Ecurie looked to be about two miles due north of Arras. I thought and then asked, 'What size of patrol shall I take, how long have I got and is there any information which might help?' His answer was not what I expected. 'There's no information and no time to set up a patrol; take a motorcycle and do it yourself, there's a good chap!'

I had not come across one-man patrols before, but I managed to refrain from voicing any doubts. I returned to my platoon to collect binoculars and then, just short of the edge of the town, stopped to observe. I could see the village in the distance; the intervening area was a patchwork of open fields with a marked lack of cover. Setting off again I had just passed the last two houses when I heard a sharp crack, as of a rifle bullet passing close by. I slowed down and looked over my shoulder to see a British soldier behind cover, aiming his rifle at me. As I turned he lowered it and by the time I reached him he had been joined by a sergeant. They belonged to the Welsh Guards and as I glanced round I realized I had driven through one of their defence posts. As soon as I switched off, feeling angry, but relieved to be in one piece, I was saluted and addressed by the sergeant.

He: 'Good afternoon, sir. May I enquire where you are going?'

I: 'I'm on a reconnaissance.'

He: 'And where to, sir?'

I: 'Ecurie.'

He: 'I would like to see your identity card, if I may, sir.'

As I produced the BEF ID card, complete with thumbprint, recently issued by the Provost Marshal, the sergeant apologized, but explained that they had been thoroughly briefed about the fifth columnists who were moving about in disguise and while he did not think I was likely to be one of them he was not happy about my mission.

'But why was I shot at?' I interposed.

He: 'Excuse me, sir, you were not shot AT; that was only a warning shot. Now sir,' he continued slowly, 'you are on a reconnaissance – by yourself – on a motorcycle – to the village of Ecurie?'

I: 'That is so.'

He gave me that look one used to get on occasions from the best and most experienced NCOs, in which respect for rank was blended with the conviction that you, the second lieutenant, had it wrong and they knew it, God bless them!

He: 'On whose authority are you doing this, sir?'

I: 'On my Commanding Officer's instructions.'

He: 'Then I must ask you to return to him and ask him to put the order in writing before I can let you pass. And if it is of any interest, sir, we reported this morning that we have observed enemy movement in and around that village.'

There was nothing further to be said. The Sergeant was not only acting in accordance with his orders, but was being helpful. I thanked him and with mixed feelings returned to report to the Colonel.

'Hello Dare, that was quick', he greeted me. 'I'm glad you're back because just after you left we heard from the General's staff that Ecurie has just been reported as occupied by the enemy.' Then, almost as an afterthought, 'How did you get on?' I told him what had happened, to which he replied, 'Well, perhaps you were lucky, eh?' I never met the Welsh Guards sergeant again, but I have a feeling that if he is still alive I owe him more than a drink.

At about 1900 hours that evening General Franklyn, commanding the Arras garrison, received Lord Gort's order that the town was to be held 'to the last man and the last round'. It reached those on the ground later that night, where it duly made its sobering impression. One or two scrawled a quick note to Mum or the girlfriend. Most of us were too tired to write to anyone.

Chapter Three

Deliverance

We have discovered riding along the coasts of France and Dunkirke an English Navy.

Thomas Heywood 1570-1641

24 May. Not long after midnight, in what might have become known as 'the Arras tradition', a further message arrived. We were no longer required to fight to the end, but to evacuate the town immediately. Companies were ordered to abandon all transport, except one 15-cwt truck per company, and proceed independently to Douai (about fifteen miles to the north-east) via St Nicholas Bridge. As the enemy had been sighted recently at many points on the perimeter, the importance of moving quietly was stressed. My platoon was already there, so we were able to move as soon as the CO arrived. An order of march had been circulated, but to save time he changed it and told me to lead off. Charles' platoon was next, followed by the CO with his tactical headquarters.

We set off at about 0230 hours, in the moonlight and a heavy mist. At first we had to pick our way round bomb craters and other obstacles, which slowed our progress until we reached open country. As dawn was breaking we had covered about three miles and had reached a demolished viaduct over a railway line, which we had to circumvent before we resumed our route to Douai. It was now lighter, but the mist was still thick in places as we marched in single file along a slightly sunken road with open fields on either side, keeping our eyes open for trouble, whether on the ground or in the air.

Shortly the mist began to lift and I suddenly noticed an open formation of dismounted enemy troops converging on us from our right. I halted the men behind me and gave them a signal to lie down; within a few seconds those further back followed suit, by which time all had seen the advancing troops. We were in an ideal fire position

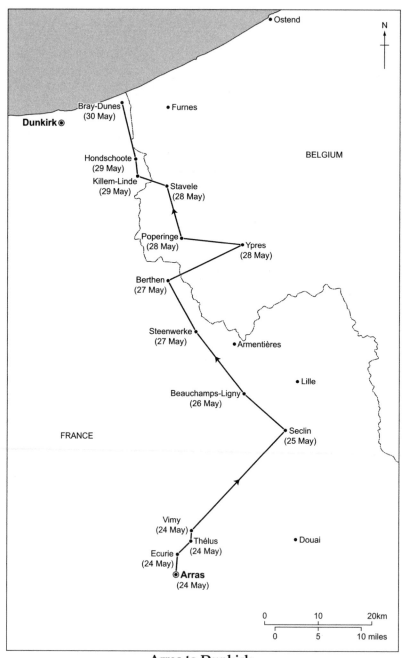

Arras to Dunkirk
24 - 30 May 1940

behind the bank at the roadside; the enemy had not seen us and were still approaching. I guessed there was up to a company of them and already we could make out their distinctive German helmets and long greatcoats. I was struck by their size; every man looked well over six feet tall. Whether this was in fact the case, or whether it was due to the mist, there is no means of knowing. By now the closest of them were only fifty yards from us and gave the impression that they were totally unaware of our presence. There was no need for a procedural fire-order, every man was ready and all that was required was the single word 'Fire'. Those of the advancing infantry who were closest to us had no chance and I saw the officer who was leading them crumple up and lie still; a number of others also fell, killed or wounded, and the remainder crawled back into dead ground or were swallowed up by the mist. Our moment of satisfaction, I would not describe it otherwise, was one of very few we had during these few weeks of bitter punishment at the hands of an enemy who was incomparably better equipped and prepared than we were. But, even on this occasion, our advantage was short-lived; soon we came under light automatic fire and a machine gun on a haystack to our left opened up, while we fired back with our rifles. Our only advantage, having lost our surprise, was in our fire-position, which gave us some protection, but already the enemy were regrouping and only needed to move a short distance before they would be shooting at us in enfilade.

The exchange of fire had only lasted for a minute or two when we heard some tracked vehicles approaching on the road behind us. They were three Bren carriers of the Welsh Guards and the leading one stopped by me as I stood up. It was the platoon commander's and he, Lieutenant the Hon Christopher Furness, wanted to know what was going on. I told him all I could, to which he replied, 'Right, we'll see if we can sort them out'. While we were talking, three light tanks had joined us and took up a position of observation on our right. As soon as he had seen as much as the remaining mist permitted, Lieutenant Furness had a quick word with his Sergeants in command of the other two carriers and they set off, accompanied by the light tanks, at a good speed heading directly for the enemy. Almost at once the enemy's fire increased, as they brought further weapons to bear, including one, if not two, anti-tank guns. At first the tanks appeared to take the brunt of it and one by one they were put out of action, with at least two of them going up in flames. The carriers pressed on and I saw them circling, firing on the move but unable to penetrate the enemy defences. Apparently they inflicted heavy casualties on the enemy, but their armour plating had been penetrated by enemy anti-tank fire and before long one of the carriers returned to us with two wounded men, whom the Sergeant wished to leave with us. As we had no means of dealing with them I told him to take them down the road until he could get them into a vehicle. This he did and was soon back with only his driver in the vehicle, but not before it seemed to us that the other two carriers had been knocked out. He stopped to see what was happening and on the spur of the moment I said: 'Don't go, they've all been knocked out.' He hesitated only for a moment and then said: 'It's my duty, sir. Mr Furness is in trouble', and without pause they sped off to join the others. In the mist and the smoke from the burning tanks I could not see clearly, but I think his carrier was knocked out before it reached the others. Then the firing from that direction stopped and I became aware that Charles was by my side. He had closed up his platoon and it was now just behind mine. We were still under intermittent fire, all the carriers and tanks had been knocked out and we had to decide what to do. We agreed there was only one course open, which was to take to the fields on the left of the road and go cross-country in order to find a way round the enemy in front of us. We decided that Douai should remain our destination, though it was necessary to set off in the opposite direction, and we would move independently in order to attract less attention. We managed to disengage without too much difficulty, going back along our semi-sunken road before the two platoons headed off on slightly divergent northerly courses. After a mile we came to another road and made use of it, hoping the enemy had not yet reached it. They had, but fortunately we saw them in time and took to the fields again, breaking into the double when they machine-gunned us at long range. I then realized we were heading straight for Ecurie and wondered how far I might have got on the previous afternoon, had I not been prevented by a certain NCO. We made an abrupt change of course and headed towards Thélus, which we gave a wide berth, and soon found ourselves on Vimy Ridge, where we came under machine-gun fire. Without realizing that we had sustained two casualties, who were later taken prisoner, we doubled to the only cover within reach, which turned out to be a British First World War Cemetery. We did not look for a gate, but jumped the wall and sank to the ground among the graves in a state of exhaustion.

Inside the cemetery it was so peaceful I decided we would take a short break. If the enemy had seen us enter and planned to flush us out that would be too bad. We were now very tired and hungry. Water bottles came into use, though I doubt if anyone dared to mention breakfast; we had missed so many, together with other meals, that no one could remember when we last had eaten properly. But now the sun was shining and the larks were singing. Over the wall, on Vimy Ridge, 'our' war was in full swing; inside it the headstones we were leaning against belonged to 'theirs' and they and their setting were contributing to the peacefulness of which we were so conscious. The two wars seemed to have become entwined and I was tempted to stay longer, but there was no time for contemplation and we made our departure. I was keen to find another way to Douai; suppose all the others who had escaped from the enemy's net were now converging on it? I need not have worried; before long we met a party from another unit coming from that direction, who had also been evading the enemy, and they advised strongly against Douai, though they had no alternative in mind. I felt that Lille, some twenty-five miles to the north-east, was unlikely to have fallen, so we set off towards it on our own. We met no further opposition and made good progress until late in the day, when we met a staff officer from 23rd Division HQ, who was on the lookout for such parties as our own. He directed us to a wood near Seclin, six miles short of Lille, and here we found some other early arrivals preparing to spend an uncomfortable night. It was a long time before I was able to piece together the whole story and it was nearly six years before the posthumous award of the Victoria Cross to Lieutenant The Hon Christopher Furness, Welsh Guards, was published in *The London Gazette*.

25 May. Those who had become separated from their companions following the evacuation of Arras renewed their efforts to rejoin the battalion at our woodland RV. There was no word of the Colonel, so General Herbert appointed Major John Challoner to take command. The list of those missing was not closed for several weeks, by which time it had stabilized at rather less than 150 including five officers.

Within our own limited view of events we had little knowledge of the problems facing the higher command, as the confusion swelled around us and disaster threatened. Movement by day was impeded by the chaos on the roads, as countless thousands of refugees sought to escape from the advancing German columns, only to be harassed and attacked from the air. By comparison, our own problems were puny, though not altogether insignificant. We had received only occasional ration supplies through normal channels for nearly a fortnight, mainly due to the fact that, except while we were in Arras, we had been almost continually on the move and, in effect, the system had been unable to keep up with us. Otherwise we were dependent on windfalls from abandoned vehicles and/or foraging. Another worsening problem concerned the condition of the men's feet and their boots. The former were, in many cases, badly blistered and, in some cases, bleeding. The latter were either worn out or in need of repair. Lack of sleep was one deficiency above all others for which most soldiers remember this campaign. Discipline and morale were now the forces upon which performance and, in due course, survival would depend.

26 May. By now we were back under the command of the 23rd Division and it heartened everyone to have General Herbert around once more. He was always cheerful and encouraging and at this time was following up every report concerning parties of stragglers that had not yet homed in.

Our day began early when orders arrived at 0100 hours to move to Beauchamps-Ligny near Lille. We left at 0200 and arrived at 0630, having been met by guides and directed to lie up in another wood. After a few hours' rest we were heading north again, starting in the middle of the day, with Steenwerke near Armentières as our destination. It was a long and tiresome march, during which we moved well spaced out, keeping alert for enemy aircraft. They had already targeted the road, killing many refugees by low-flying attacks, and the dead were mostly lying where they had fallen, though some had been moved to the side of the road. At one point a fighter approached from behind, flying low and fast so that it was almost upon us before we saw it. My platoon dived for the nearest cover and I was not the only one to land on a corpse, concealed in the roadside ditch. The burst of fire raked up the road, scarring the surface and raising a ripple of dust. We were lucky and resumed our journey, sickened by the stench of bodies but glad to be intact.

All these enemy air attacks increased our resentment at the total lack of air support we had from the RAF, which thus became the target of much abuse. I think it was on this particularly hot and sticky day that we noticed a figure approaching us across a field, whom we soon recognized as an RAF pilot. He had just stepped out of his parachute, after being shot down. He was very young, that is perhaps a year younger than most of us, cheerful and fortunately uninjured, though slightly shaken by his experience. Having been parted from his Hurricane, he now had to face the problem of how to get home. After asking if we had any objections, he joined us because, it appeared, we were 'going his way'. As we got to know him over the next few days we found him good company and, perhaps more important, he seemed to know far better than we did what was happening across the front and something of what was going on at home. For some days past, large numbers of our troops working in the ports and supply depots and on the lines of communication had been arriving back in England from Boulogne, Calais, Dunkirk and Ostend, but now, it seemed, only Dunkirk was open. As we later learned, by the evening of that day nearly 30,000 men had been evacuated.

When we got to know our pilot better we asked him what the RAF had been doing, because he was the first representative of that Service we had seen, in the air or on the ground, since the blitzkrieg started. He was able to assure us that those squadrons that were committed to support the land battle had been hard at it, and, indeed, had suffered quite high losses. As, at this moment, he represented one of them, we were in no position to argue. A few days later, when it appeared we were heading for more trouble, being unarmed and anxious to return to his squadron, he sensibly detached himself and set his own course for home. He had helped, at least partly, to restore our confidence in the Royal Air Force and I hope he made it safely back to England.

Many of us at the time resented the lack of close air support and, having no wireless communications, had no understanding of the whys and wherefores and could only draw our own conclusions; the RAF had let us down – we had not even seen them. This of course was unfair, but in the circumstances not surprising. As things turned out, it was fortunate that those at the top set a limit to the number of RAF squadrons committed to support the land battle. Had they not done so the Air Defence of Britain would have been jeopardized later in the year. Their mistakes, as far as the BEF was concerned, lay in the planning and organization. From these flowed the inability to provide close air support, whether or not they realized what its absence meant to those facing the *Luftwaffe* with total freedom of action. Soon we were to see the other side of the coin as the Royal Air Force threw themselves into the task of covering the evacuation.

27 May. We reached Steenwerke at about 0200 hours and rested for a few hours. At 0800 the Battalion was ordered to move on to Berthen, about ten miles to the north, and on arrival was met with the order to keep moving. 8 RNF crossed into Belgium, heading for its final destination of the day. It was another wood, this time between Poperinge, now almost deserted, and Ypres, which it reached between 1700 and 2000 hours. The *Luftwaffe* was again active. Here, on ground bitterly contested during the previous war, we remained for the night, again without sustenance; to miss the main and probably the only meal of the day, following a march of some twenty-five miles in quick succession to the previous one of comparable length, was considered a little more than unfortunate, even on the form of the preceding weeks.

28 May. That morning we left our wood near Poperinge and

continued our march for a further fifteen miles to Stavele on the River Yser, to the north-west. By now stocks of ammunition were limited, virtually all infantry and armoured units were depleted and some were defunct due to battle casualties; tank strengths were even lower. Rations were generally short and frequently, as in our own case, all issues had finished. While the spirit of the BEF was unbroken, exhaustion was affecting efficiency in many units – almost certainly in the majority. This was a major factor and throughout 8 RNF, which had two gruelling weeks without a day's respite, there was now cause for concern over the ability of some men to keep going. In more specific terms I can only tell of my own platoon, which may not have been quite typical because its members had been hand picked for their specialist role. From these men and their performance, individually and collectively, I was learning about the deeper side of man-management. When conditions become almost unbearable, as by now for us they had, men have to draw on their reserves and good soldiers are always mindful of the needs of their comrades. They will never let each other down and will often conceal their own ailments, which may be of medical significance. If an officer is doing his job properly he will not accept assurances from good soldiers that all is well if he has reasons to doubt them. We were fortunate in having an outstanding RMO, Hugh Gass, who did wonders in keeping the physical condition of many such men in the battalion above the survival level during the latter days of the retreat. I was also lucky in having no member of the platoon on whom I could not depend. In such a happy position what one sees are the essential qualities which enable men to contribute to, and draw on, a corporate inner strength which increases determination to keep going, despite the exhaustion which feels irresistible long before it is.

On the line of march we were now overtaking stragglers from units ahead of us. They mostly responded to encouragement and a few kept going with us until they met their own companies, possibly taking a roadside break. I also learned the true importance and value of discipline, which is so often misunderstood outside the Army, and how it can be both effective and humane. In situations such as the one I am describing, in the last resort it is discipline, the maintenance of high standards under all conditions, which lies between success – i.e. survival – on the one hand and failure on the other. Without discipline the BEF would unquestionably have perished. From what we saw with our own eyes, the lack of it must have played some part in the downfall of our allies.

One of the many things I learned on that journey was that when

Geordies stop grumbling they mean business. And who was among the first to show this trait but Fusilier McCarten. He came to my attention in Arras, quite undaunted by dive-bombers and ready to undertake any task. After our engagement on Vimy Ridge, hardly a day passed without him confronting me with a question on the same theme: 'When are we gan te torn roond, Sor, and feace the buggers?' or, 'Isn't it time we stopped marchen away, Sor, and began to de some proper fighten?' My own theme in answer was limited to 'Keep your powder dry; the time will come'. I was right in due course, but not as soon as he would have wished. By way of change, on the line of march McCarten would fasten on to some comment up or down the column, such as 'Must be about a week since we had any proper grub but ah'd settle for a mug of tea'. Such self-pity cut no ice with him: 'Caal yoursel a sowlger? Ye bugger, ye should be asheamed o' yorsel!' This sporadic banter opened the way for the others to join in. But not all members of the platoon were able to respond, for one or two were now marching with the dull eyes, expressionless faces and stiff joints of men who are approaching the limits of their endurance. These were under close observation and would be given every encouragement and assistance to keep them going. There are many sides to these situations and humour is one of them, because it strengthens those who can assimilate it, whose duty it is to assist those who cannot. By this means it helps to maintain the level of determination for all to keep going, whatever the pain, disability or conditions.

Before long we caught up with the rear of a company marching in file. In a number of cases a soldier was being assisted by the one next to him and we watched how they were unable to march straight, but would wander out of the column, as though unable to control their legs, until they were guided back into line. Then we reached a fork where a minor road offered an alternative route, without any congestion, and this we followed. It seemed there were more British troops ahead of us, because soon we came across a soldier at the side of the road, whom at first we thought was dead, but found to be unconscious. He had not been wounded and we concluded he was suffering from exhaustion, so tried to revive him using every means known to us. We failed completely and, being ourselves too tired to carry him, left him with heavy hearts. After a while we came across another, and another; I forget how many there were.

At Killem-Linde, according to a note I made later, we had lunch. If it really deserved that description it was the first for weeks. During the afternoon, orders arrived from 23rd Division to destroy all our transport and I was put in charge of the drivers for this purpose. There were nineteen assorted trucks that had been recovered here and there by the enterprising MT Platoon. My instructions were not to set fire to them, but to make as good a job of it as we could by other means. Sergeant Clarke, the MT sergeant, came up with the answer, which was to start and race the engines and then remove the engine oil drainage plugs. While some of the party were doing this others slashed the tyres and canopies and took hammers to the instruments, windscreens, windows and lamps. It was a disagreeable job, made easier by the knowledge that at least they would be of no use to the enemy. We finished it at 1800 hours and at 1815 the Battalion was ordered to hold a defensive position, together with 5th Battalion East Yorkshire Regiment, to cover the withdrawal of the Division until 1945 hours. We were then ordered to move independently to Furnes, twelve miles east of Dunkirk.

It was another difficult march, as we found ourselves repeatedly held up by transport blocking the road and French troops, many of whom were drunk, wandering about aimlessly, most of them without officers. We know now that many French units fought courageously on their coastal sector of the perimeter, but those we encountered gave every impression of being deserters. Some, still armed, were threatening all and sundry as they lurched drunkenly in any direction. But the particular picture that has remained in my memory is of a single *poilu* lying unconscious, on his back in the middle of the road, beside a large horse-drawn Army dray bearing the largest barrel of red wine I ever saw. He had fired his rifle into the side of it, causing a thin but powerful jet, which formed a parabola on to the road. At its extremity he had positioned his face, before passing out. We assumed he was the driver, who had anticipated soon being out of a job, and his horse was still standing patiently in its shafts. It all looked like a grotesque cartoon in the Bruce Bairnsfather style and perhaps what I appreciated most were the expressions of my Geordie soldiers as we paused to take in this memorable sight.

At Hondschoote, a few miles further on, we were told by a staff officer not to go to Furnes, but to make for Bray Dunes on the coast, six miles north-east of Dunkirk. From him we also got the confirmation we had been waiting for, that a large-scale evacuation from Dunkirk, and the beaches to the north of it, had been in progress for some days. As we moved off to cover the last five miles it sunk into our debilitated minds that, however events worked out, this was likely to end our long march. By now my map, which had served me so well, was in poor condition and though I kept it I never worked out the distance we had covered since we left Arras, all of which was on foot. However,

Neville Gill, another platoon commander, who was a solicitor in his civilian life with a penchant for accuracy, is on record with an estimate of 150 miles. We travelled by similar routes, with 11 Platoon's slightly the longer, and it took us exactly six days.

So, in the early hours of 30 May, we finally met the sea on the extensive beach of Bray Dunes. The moon was in its last quarter and we could faintly discern the outlines of ships lying off in deeper water, beyond the shallow approaches to the beach, and a number of wrecks, that had been sunk by bombs. As we came closer we saw the orderly columns of men, stretching out into the calm sea. Soon a guide appeared, who took us to the waiting area on the edge of the dunes, from which we could watch much of what was going on. From here we awaited our turn, with Charles and his platoon next to us, as had so often been the case. Then, at intervals, further platoons and Battalion Headquarters arrived, with John Challoner, the acting CO, looking extremely tired, if not close to exhaustion. I had been carrying rum in my water bottle since we left Arras, as also had Neville Gill. Both were now well depleted, having helped to revive many other flagging spirits during the long march. I offered mine to John, who reprimanded me for having seriously violated King's Regulations, meanwhile seizing it and taking a good swig. He was one of a distinguished band of survivors from the trenches of the Great War who rallied to the Colours in advance of the Second World War, rejoining their regiments in preference to taking a staff or administrative appointment. I greatly admired him and those like him.

We had been told by our guide to hold ourselves in readiness to join one of the lines of troops stretching into the sea and Charles and I realized that we were so weary it would be as well if one of us were to stay awake. This we ensured by taking it in turns to remain on our feet, as we kept an eye on the progress of the nearest line preparing to embark. While we waited we could hear artillery fire in several directions from the steadily contracting perimeter, but it was only sporadic and the bombing, too, could have been very much worse, for although, fifty years on, Harry McCarten remembered the conditions then as being 'a bit warm', the Royal Air Force was being very effective.

It was my turn to be 'on watch', when an embarkation officer who was passing by said: 'That line [pointing] will soon be moving again and it will then be your turn.' I immediately woke Charles and we went together to tell John Challoner. He responded by telling us both to move as soon as we had the opportunity. We took our platoons down to the beach and waited for orders. Eventually we were told to join different lines and did not meet again for several days. It was a long wade out to join the waiting line and when we reached the tail we were waist deep. Progress was slow and I suppose we were in the water for about an hour, by which time we were in as deep as the shortest men could stand without having to be supported. The further the troops could wade the quicker was the Navy's turn round of pinnaces taking men out to the ships. It became bitterly cold, but I never heard one word on the subject. At last it was our turn and helping hands were heaving us into the boat. A few more minutes and we were clambering up a ladder into a Royal Navy minesweeper, the name of which we were all too tired to enquire. All my men were given spaces to lie down somewhere and I was led by an officer to his own cabin, where I took off most of my wet clothes and was asleep almost before I was horizontal.

It seemed only a few minutes before we were awakened as we were about to enter Dover Harbour and assembled for disembarkation. A most efficient military organization then took over as we were relieved of our weapons, asked for number, rank, name and unit, given a mug of tea and marched over to the railway station. I believe some effort may have been made to sort us out by regiments or formations, but the whole emphasis was on speed, so as to avoid bottlenecks. Before long we were marched on to a platform where an empty train was waiting. My party was early into it and I had the strange feeling of wondering what I should be doing for my men and slowly reaching the conclusion that I no longer had any responsibility. My brain would not accept that the war was now, for us, in abeyance, though my body ached all over and protested at every command.

I looked out of the carriage window, gazing at the dishevelled appearance and degree of exhaustion of all who passed by, as they made their way up the platform. I wondered if I looked as bad. Then my confused brain began wrestling with one question after another. Where is all this calamity leading? Have we lost the war? Can we now defend ourselves? What are they making of it all at home? I thought of asking one of the WVS ladies if she had a postcard with her; my parents would like some news, however brief. Then I noticed a telephone box and my thoughts changed. 'At a time like this every operator will be busy. Anyway, when could anyone hope to ring Burnopfield in County Durham from Dover? I don't even have any money.' It took a while before I got up and made my way over to the kiosk. I dialled 0 and at once an operator replied.

'I haven't any money', I blurted out, 'but I need to ring home.'

'Where is your home?'

'In County Durham.'

36

'And what is the number?'

'Burnopfield 241.'

'I'll try it for you.'

I waited and then heard my mother's voice. 'It's Dare,' I said. 'I'm at Dover.'

'You're back? In England? How are you?'

'All right – only tired – very tired. How's everyone at home?'

There was no answer.

'Are you still there?'

There was a stifled 'Yes' and I realized Mum was crying, which I had never ever known her do. Unthinkingly, I asked what was the matter. Then I realized nothing was the matter; all the worries she had been bottling up for three weeks had disappeared and soon she would be wanting to share her joy – with Father, the family and goodness knows who. I started again:

'I don't know where we're off to from Dover, but I'll let you know all I can as soon as possible. I must go now – someone else may want to use the phone. I'll ring again soon. Goodbye.'

It was echoed indistinctly and I returned to the train with the intended message 'That phone box is working, if you want to use it'. There were no takers. As I walked from carriage to carriage there was only silence; every man was asleep.

We travelled for several hours and stopped at least once at a station, so I learned later, for the WVS to give us food, for which there had been no time at Dover. Their efforts passed unseen, but they were understanding; though most of us had not eaten a square meal for a fortnight we were all asleep. The train eventually reached Tidworth on Salisbury Plain, where we were 'taken into care' by the garrison. The small and motley collection of officers was bidden to gather 'over there by the group of ladies who will look after you'. I was seized by a brigadier's wife and taken by staff car to a house very like the one I was to occupy in the same road thirty years later. Here I was made to eat and then taken to the bathroom, where the bath was ready and the brigadier's batman on duty to prevent me, at all costs, from going to sleep in it. I was then given a pair of the brigadier's pyjamas and put to bed where I sank into instant oblivion. I slept for nearly two days.

As I look back on those last days before Dunkirk I still marvel at the fortune we had, and I shall always remain convinced that, had it not been for the guiding hand of an Almighty Providence, the BEF would never have left the shores of France.

Field Marshal Viscount Alanbrooke from *The Turn of the Tide* by Arthur Bryant

Chapter Four

Defence of the Homeland

An island fortress, England is fighting a war of redemption not only for
Europe but for her own soul. Facing dangers greater than any in her
history she has fallen back on the rock of her national character.
                                        Arthur Bryant, *English Saga*, 1940

Regaining consciousness, after the longest sleep I can recall, did not
bring with it an instant return to normality. The weariness lingered
and I was aware of the odd gap or two in my memory of recent events,
but these were of little account and within a few days I was very fit.
Nor do I recall a single member of my platoon, several of whom had
been close to battle-exhaustion, suffering any lasting effects. Later in
the war, in various battles, I observed men in advanced stages of
exhaustion, but by then medical knowledge had progressed and regimental officers and NCOs knew what to look for. Most cases
responded to hot food, a short spell of rest, relaxation and understanding. Most senior commanders understood the need to relieve
units that had been heavily involved in protracted operations before
battle-stress became widespread. On occasions this was just not
possible and then it was up to regimental officers and medical officers
to ease the conditions of those who were worst affected. Had we had
to contend with the modern practice of pressing counselling on all
who have been subjected to battle-stress including, it appears, the
encouragement to discuss problems which may not even exist, I
wonder what the effect would have been on the performance of our
armies and the outcome of their campaigns.

Back in Tidworth we were soon in the hands of quartermasters, pay-
masters and medical officers who attended to our needs. The main
and easiest requirement was rest, and then information. For weeks we
had been unable to distinguish between reliable reports, by word of
mouth, and rumour. Now at least there were newspapers and the BBC

and these provided the means of catching up with aspects of the war beyond the narrow limits of our own ken. My most vivid memory connected with the cascade of dramatic events during these critical weeks as we counted our losses, France tottered and then sued for peace, Italy entered the war and Russia grabbed her spoils, was the comfort of knowing that, at last, we had a leader of great stature at the helm. Already Winston Churchill was not only inspiring the government and the country, but coordinating the whole Empire's war effort with authority and a deep understanding of what was at stake. Certainly he made his mistakes, but they were dwarfed by his courage, energy and grasp of events.

Following the wholly uncoordinated return of the BEF, which was now scattered in emergency accommodation throughout much of the United Kingdom, there was at once an urgent need for a total redeployment to meet the invasion threat. There were nearly 500 miles of beach on the south and east coasts suitable for the landing of armoured fighting vehicles, much of which lay within the range of *Luftwaffe* support.

After a few days at Tidworth those of us who belonged to 8 RNF left by train for Launceston in Cornwall, which was the selected assembly location for the Battalion. From there most of us were sent on seven days' home leave, which was a great morale booster.

It was a little while before the country as a whole fully understood the gravity of the situation; few were in a position to know that even before the evacuation of the BEF from Dunkirk had been completed, the Chiefs of Staff had warned the Cabinet they thought it highly probable that Germany was now 'setting the stage for delivering a full-scale attack on England'. Nor was the full extent of the heavy losses to all three services in men, ships, aircraft, tanks and guns during the blitzkrieg and the evacuation from Dunkirk known to the public. Nevertheless, Churchill made it quite clear that Britain had suffered a colossal military disaster.

Many felt that England, at that critical time, shone as a dearly beloved country for which no sacrifice could be too great. Nothing excelled the sanctity of freedom and truth, of which by now most of Europe had been deprived. To me, more than sixty years later, these two pillars of civilization, which evil men continue to abuse, remain the principal issue over which war is justifiable and can be necessary. Such were the thoughts which passed through our minds as the storm clouds gathered over England during that otherwise exquisite summer of 1940.

In the meantime, there was no let up in the succession and suddenness of events. During the early hours of 3 July I was one of several junior officers ordered to move at once to Plymouth railway station for escort duties. During the night the Royal Navy had boarded all ships of the French Navy lying in Plymouth harbour. They included a battleship, two destroyers, three sloops and three submarines. While most of the boardings had been unopposed, some resistance had been met and in one large submarine, the newly-built *Surcouf*, there was bloodshed on both sides, including several killed. The crews of these vessels had been escorted ashore and some were entraining as we arrived. The Royal Navy had the whole situation well in hand, although the high level of Gallic excitability among thousands of matelots was audible from afar. After reporting, we were briefed and then paired off to carriages as officer escorts with one of us at each end; we were all armed. The carriage for which I had joint responsibility happened to be the one allotted to the most senior officers and, though I was unfamiliar with their ranks, it seemed there were several admirals among them and, I guessed, all the ships' captains. This I verified later. Our destination was Liverpool and thence to Aintree racecourse, where a tented camp was being prepared to provide temporary accommodation for as many as 10,000 men. There were no farewells or other courtesies when we parted company at Aintree; others were waiting to take charge of our unhappy guests and we left them with a sense of relief to have seen the last of them. The thick smoke from hundreds of Gauloise cigarettes in such a confined space throughout the journey had not helped our empathy and I must admit it was a little while before my outlook on these unfortunate sailors became worthier.

Soon after that interlude 8 RNF entrained at Okehampton for Falmouth, where our re-equipment programme gained momentum while we assumed a dual role of coastal defence over more than forty miles from Penryn to Praa Sands, coupled with mobile reserve for use against enemy seaborne or airborne landings.

On 10 July, barely a week after bidding the French Navy adieu at Aintree, another naval engagement came my way, this time to take my platoon to Padstow where we would come under command of the Resident Naval Officer, Gordon Campbell, a retired Admiral who had volunteered for re-engagement with the rank of Commander. I can remember thinking it sounded like a platoon commander's dream. Here was I, aged twenty, about to leave on an independent operational mission to the north Cornish coast, with the rest of the battalion fully occupied on the south coast, at a time of intense activity and excitement, with invasion in the air. Apart from the deeper implications of a

German invasion, the rest of it seemed too good to be true. Just before leaving, however, I was given the locations of our campsite and the RNO's HQ, noting that they were on opposite sides of a road over-looking Padstow, within less than 100 yards of each other. This, I felt, was far from ideal and wondered if it was the hidden snag. It does not take long in the Army to learn that, in general terms, the further one is separated from one's superior headquarters the less complicated and more peaceful life is likely to be.

On arrival at the RNO's headquarters I was met by a flag lieutenant, who led the way to the Admiral's office, introducing me formally as 'Second Lieutenant Wilson, sir'. After shaking hands I found myself looking at a man to whom I took an instant liking. Somehow I sensed from the start that all would be well. Stockily built, in his mid-fifties with a friendly smile, I think it was his eyes which struck me first, clear blue and penetrating; his ruddy, weather-beaten face, keen expression and alert manner conveyed an impression of strong leadership. His greeting was breezy and memorable:

Hello, Wilson. Welcome to Padstow. I'm glad to see you, we badly need a soldier here. There's much to be done and very little time; decisions to be made which are not in my line. Ever worked with the Navy? Probably not at your age; I hope you won't find it too strange. Your job will be to see to the landward defences while I look after the seaward problems. Come back, if you please, at 10 o'clock in the forenoon, but first have a good look round the harbour and down the estuary on this shore as far as Gun Point. Between us we shall have to guard the approaches to the harbour.

The landmarks he pointed out on a well-thumbed chart; I do not recall ever seeing him with a map.

While this quick-firing introduction was in progress I was able to take in the rest of him. He was, as expected, dressed as a Commander RN, with three very new stripes on the sleeves of a well-worn reefer jacket. They had taken the place of the older and broader stripes of a vice admiral, the outlines of which were still visible. On his chest were more medal ribbons than I had ever seen, starting with the Victoria Cross, followed by the Distinguished Service Order with two bars and then a host of other decorations, both British and foreign. Altogether he made a wonderful picture, not only impressive but also inspiring. This first of many meetings lasted only a few minutes, but when it ended I was fired with enthusiasm as my platoon commander's dream came into focus.

The following morning I rose early and set off on foot for my first visit to the small town and its capacious harbour, before making my way northwards. By the time I reached Gun Point I realized I was exactly one mile from the southern end of the harbour. What a frontage for one platoon. If the Germans were contemplating even a diversionary landing in the Padstow area, what impression could my small force make against them? I made my way back to what the platoon already referred to as HMS *Padstow* full of doubts and wondering how to explain them to a very senior and determined sailor, to whom all obstacles were part of the game. When I arrived he was waiting and I was shown in at once. So far he had done all the talking, but this time he began with a question of substance from which an interesting discussion developed. I was greeted by 'Well, Wilson, what do you make of Padstow's land defence problems?' I suggested that, to begin with, we should ignore the possibility of enemy airborne landings, because we had too few rifles even to defend the harbour and estuary. I was then asked what I thought was needed to improve matters and explained that most of the problems were related to the extent of the beaches within the Camel estuary and the impossibility, with one platoon, of adequately defending them as well as the harbour. We needed, first, automatic weapons to increase our firepower, second, protection, if possible by means of pillboxes, and third, more manpower, even if it had to come from the Home Guard. The Admiral's response was immediately positive:

Interesting you should mention pillboxes, they seem to be in vogue. I was at a conference a few days ago when they came up in discussion. Everyone seemed to want them so I said Padstow could do with some too. I'll follow that up. Now, additional weapons. You say the whole Army is short of Bren guns and we'll have to wait our turn. Quite so, but are Bren guns the only sort of machine guns in use? What were we using during the last war? May there not be some in store somewhere?

My thoughts switched to the Vickers medium machine gun with its sustained rate of fire, greater accuracy and longer range; happy memories of my initiation in Fenham Barracks returned. As soon as I had made the suggestion I felt I had to point out that they were bound to be in even shorter supply than Brens, because they were ideal in a coastal defence role. The Admiral was undeterred:

Leave it to me; I have a friend in the Admiralty who may be able to help. Back to the pillboxes. Let me know as soon as you can how many you think you need and can justify. Now, manpower; I think we'll have to be careful about calling for more troops at this stage. Wouldn't the Army consider a larger force called for a more senior officer to command it and where would that leave you? And I don't think the solution lies with the Home Guard. They are full of retired senior officers including, so I have been told, at least two Generals. Putting you too close to them could lead to difficulties! Let's leave that problem until we have solved the others; because there are insufficient soldiers the 'powers' may be more generous with pillboxes. If we ask for everything at once we might overplay our hand and mess things up.

Soon Padstow became a hive of activity. I reported to the Admiral daily and additionally was summoned as necessary. Within a day or two I met a small group of Army officers, accompanied by a contractor, to discuss the requirement for pillboxes. I requested six, all of which were approved and most of which have survived, including one at the harbour entrance that, sixty years on, was still being used as a store. A few days later came the news that, by some means which I never discovered, one of the Admiral's friends had achieved the impossible; two Vickers machine guns with spare parts and a generous quantity of ammunition had been released for immediate delivery to No. 11 (S/C) Platoon 8 RNF for the defence of Padstow.

Before long I was asked if we needed any land mines for our beaches and fortunately, in the light of the problems which they later caused elsewhere due to tidal disturbance, I declined them. Instead, we undertook a major operation involving a vast series of barbed wire obstacles designed to delay, if not deter, the enemy. Day after day the platoon toiled in the summer heat, as though the fate of the south-west peninsula hung on their efforts. There was, however, an important consolation; at intervals throughout the day all work stopped long enough for a good bathe, often without having to move more than a few yards. The fact that fencing gloves were unobtainable meant that every cut sustained provided a sharp reminder, each time it was reintroduced to the sea, that barbed wire requires handling with care. Nevertheless, bathing for most of us became part of a long-lasting memory of 'Happy Padstow', which survives, like the pillboxes, to this day. It could not be otherwise; we arrived on a Wednesday and within four days every soldier had been adopted by a local family for Sunday lunch.

By the middle of July the coastline of Britain was rippling with activity, as hundreds of thousands of men and women strove to complete within days and weeks what in normal times would have taken months and years. Padstow was probably typical among isolated defended areas where problems were transformed into achievements by determination and a total absence of obstruction; the only constraint was imposed by the hours of daylight, and they permitted the equivalent of two days' work in one. What was so encouraging was the support from above; our requests for almost anything, providing it was available, were accepted on the assumption that they were valid and necessary.

In the knowledge that invasion remained a strong possibility, if not a certainty – the view was widely held that it was not a question of if, but when – preparations continued unabated. Nor did Admiral Campbell relax for a moment. As soon as our pillboxes were completed the one with the best view of the channel connecting the harbour with the open sea (several hundred yards wide and nearly two miles in length) was designated as my platoon command post. From here a series of large sea mines (provided by the Admiralty) could be detonated individually, on known bearings, by remote control. Soon after the mines came the artillery. By means of some tortuous joint-service initiative, prompted by the Admiral, it was agreed that a battery of field guns would be mounted in a coastal protection role at Gun Point, so named and defended, it is believed, during the American War of Independence against privateers attacking our merchant shipping using the British Channel. The Admiral was at pains to assure me that, although the battery would be commanded by a major, I would remain OC Troops, Padstow.

The next two months were punctuated by a series of false alarms, sometimes preceded or followed by code word OLIVER (state of emergency exists) or CROMWELL (invasion of Britain is imminent). One day towards the end of August Admiral Campbell called me into his office for a briefing and explained that he had received some secret intelligence from naval sources indicating the likelihood of the anticipated German invasion being launched within the next few days. By now he was totally convinced that Padstow and the Camel estuary would be among their objectives and had been studying the tide tables from which he had identified the tide most likely to meet the enemy's requirements. His briefing continued:

By last light on Saturday I wish you to post your coastal lookouts and put the remainder of your force in camp on short notice. By 0200 hours on Sunday I wish a full scale stand to. I shall appreciate it if you will provide me with some form of transport, more suitable than my staff car, to negotiate your barbed wire entanglements in the middle of the night, because I intend to join you in your pillbox at 0400 hours. I shall issue orders to the Home Guard and artillery later; in the meantime please keep all this to yourself.

In the early hours of Sunday my BSA motorcycle combination, ridden by Fusilier Charlton, being the only suitable transport available, called for the Admiral who, on arrival, admitted that he had never before been in a sidecar, but had enjoyed the experience! Then, inside the command pillbox, our vigil began. The Admiral positioned himself by the embrasure next to the row of levers for detonating the sea mines laid on the bed of the tidal channel in front of us, for which he had been responsible. Little was said as we waited, alert in anticipation and straining our eyes to pick up any movement within our field of vision, which extended towards the open sea with the scant assistance of a quarter moon. As the land and seascape very gradually clarified in the dawn light, with the only movement visible confined to estuarial birdlife, no one showed an inclination to break the silence. Once more the Admiral looked at his watch and in vain searched the distant waters with his binoculars, then suddenly, and almost to himself, burst out with great feeling: 'The buggers – they're late.' I don't recall finding a suitable response, although the humour escaped none of my men present and we often laughed about it later. As Aristotle had observed :

War, as the saying goes, is full of false alarms.

It turned out to be a fitting end to an enjoyable sojourn in Padstow, because soon I learned from the Admiral that the Army had called for my platoon to return to the battalion. The evening before we left, I called on him to say farewell and to thank him for all his help and encouragement during the two months we had been under his command. I took with me the remains of a decanted bottle of vintage port which my father had laid down twenty-one years earlier to mark my birth and which he had entrusted to the wartime post for me to enjoy. Part had been consumed on my birthday and the Admiral and I shared the remainder. A day or two after we left Padstow I received a thoughtful and charming letter from him ending:

Although not strange to me to work with the military, I expect you have found it strange (but I hope not too difficult) to work with the Navy. Anyhow you have done it well and I thank you. I am extremely sorry that you have left – especially on this tide – but may be you will have better luck where you are. Please let me know if you are coming this way. All best wishes,

Yours very sincerely,

Gordon Campbell

I loved his characteristic closing wish that, having been deprived of the opportunity to deal with an invasion with him on the north coast we might have 'better luck' in the south. Later in the war, I was able to obtain a copy of his book on the Royal Navy's Q Ships (later known as mystery ships), which were converted tramp steamers introduced in 1915 as a means of decoying German U-boats. Campbell commanded three mystery ships, all of which were either sunk or heavily damaged, while he and his crew sank three U-boats; among approximately thirty ships' captains he was the most highly decorated and the only one who stood the strain of mystery ship service for more than a year. His crew were awarded more than seventy decorations including four Victoria Crosses.

On 31 August we rejoined 8 RNF, who were occupying strong positions on a stretch of Cornish coast to the east of Penzance, and spent six weeks in defence duties there until, on 11 October, we suddenly moved into Seaton Barracks, Plymouth. Here we remained for several weeks, during which we were privileged to see glimpses of what became known as 'The Spirit of Plymouth'. There was an air raid the night we arrived, as there had been the previous night, both causing casualties. They were just two of the fifty-nine air raids that Plymouth endured between July 1940 and April 1944. Service casualties were never published, but there were nearly 5,000 civilian casualties and 70,000 homes were destroyed or severely damaged.

Towards the end of our time in Plymouth, the Battalion received news that went far beyond the rumours that had been circulating for several weeks. The War Office had made significant strides in planning a reorganization, based on the concept of close armour/infantry cooperation, to provide the groundwork to enable the Army to take the offensive when the time came. The New Model Army, as it became known to some, would include a number of new armoured divisions, and such cavalry units as were still employed within the current divisions would be switched to these. The gaps they left in what would become known as the infantry divisions would be filled by regiments from a new corps yet to be formed, the Reconnaissance Corps. As part of this process, 8th Battalion Royal Northumberland Fusiliers was selected to become the new 3

Reconnaissance Regiment (RNF), integral to the 3rd Division – the only Territorial Army unit within an all-Regular division. The Battalion remained in Plymouth for a month and then, in preparation for our new role as part of the Recce Corps, we were suddenly moved over 100 miles to a cluster of sleepy towns and villages in north Somerset, where we went round in circles, like a lot of nesting rooks, looking for our prearranged billets. My own platoon eventually came to rest in a haven of peace named Hallatrow, some ten miles from Bristol where, in due course, I was admitted into the vicarage. It was from this locality that during the following night (24 November) we watched as the *Luftwaffe* flew overhead, and listened to distant explosions as Bristol was heavily bombed. Then the sky reddened and boiled as it reflected the bursting bombs and fires caused by incendiaries. It happened that we had been in the area just long enough for the quartermaster's staff to collect up the accumulated backlog of clothes for laundering and had delivered it earlier in the day to the only laundry in Bristol capable of handling the large quantity. None of it was ever seen again and it threw kit inspections into chaos for years, as the excuse 'lost in the Bristol laundry, sir' was repeated ad nauseam. There seemed to be no way of catching up with the accountancy between moves and exercises. Every fusilier, it appeared, had missed some critical check due to a course, leave, sickness etc. and there were always excuses for the gaps in their kit layouts. At least two years later dire threats were still echoing down corridors and within hutted and tented camps on the lines of 'The next man who mentions the Bristol Laundry will be shot!'

Late in January 1941 some of us had our first experience of the series of 5th Corps exercises that Monty planned and directed with such effect in the south of England that winter. Our first exercise involved some 30,000 troops, including the 3rd Division and Corps troops, in a seventy mile approach march by night followed by a crossing of the Thames using bridges built by the Sappers. Into this, 8 RNF was initiated at reduced strength while still only partly re-equipped and semi-trained. However, my platoon was included and we enjoyed our introduction to training as part of a battle-experienced and highly professional force. As in all Monty's exercises, it was meticulously planned, faultlessly directed and umpired in such a way that nothing went unobserved. Plenty of scope was left for decision making at all levels and mistakes made were later exposed and discussed in public, so that all could benefit from them. So far as I can remember from several of these exercises, military training areas, such as Salisbury Plain, played little more part than the rest of the countryside, across which streamed thousands of vehicles. Although efforts were made to limit damage, much was inevitable as freedom of access across agricultural land and within private woodlands was permitted when judged to be necessary. Compensation for damage was paid to landowners later, but the way in which they uncomplainingly accepted such damage, often by tanks and artillery deployed in open formation, as part of their contribution to the war effort was beyond praise.

Early in the New Year the Battalion moved to Dorset where 'B' Company settled peacefully into the charming village of Child Okeford. By the time the second winter of the war receded 8 RNF was rapidly becoming merged into the Recce Corps, although there was a period of uncertainty during which we faced the possibility of complete severance from our county regiment. However, due to General Herbert's intervention, it was eventually agreed that we might retain (RNF) after our new title of 3rd Reconnaissance Battalion. Our training continued, influenced by Monty's exercises, as reflected in part of a letter home dated 29 June:

> We were on the move for 24 hrs without a minute's rest or a wink of sleep, in which time we drove about 125 miles in the carriers [armoured tracked vehicles with a crew of 3 or 4]. The men were all tired out and we were fortunate to have none going to sleep at the wheel – in a carrier weighing 4 tons it can be a serious matter. One driver was almost too tired to stand so I brought his carrier back for him. The crews were flat out in the back and when we got into Child Okeford the vehicles closed up and switched off and there was no sign of life at all as the drivers subsided over the wheel and the crews continued to sleep in the back!

In September I was promoted to captain and posted to the newly formed Recce Junior Leaders School at Annan in Dumfriesshire. I had only thirty-six hours to pack up and head north, and departed with a certain amount of regret, particularly in leaving my platoon after nearly two years. However, I realized that it was a definite step up and there were other compensations, not least of which was the opportunity to enjoy the best wildfowling of my life. Because I was occupied as an instructor only by day, much of the remaining time was my own and it became my practice throughout that winter to set off from Annan to my favourite stretches of foreshore whenever possible, using whatever mode of transport was available. Gradually I built up a network of friendly farmers who would let me know the latest flight lines of the Greylag and Pinkfoot geese as they flew at dawn from their roosting sandbars, often far out in the estuary, to inland feeding areas and then back again at dusk. By night duck, mainly Widgeon, would traverse the salt marshes below the high watermark and when the moon was favourable these would keep any keen fowler out of his bed. My companion on all such occasions was Dinah, a black Labrador given to my mother in 1936 and soon handed over to me as a shooting dog. She was the first of a line I have maintained to this day and was one of the finest dogs I have ever known. I do not recall my conscience ever being uneasy about such frequent forays to the foreshore, but I could have argued that my recreation was subjecting me to conditions far more rigorous than those of any Special Forces training programme, and also made a very welcome contribution to the cookhouse.

In May 1942 I returned from Annan to rejoin 3 Recce, who had temporarily settled in Buckinghamshire with a new CO, Eric Bols, and a new second in command, Hugh Merriman. (Eric Bols subsequently commanded 6th Airborne Division in the Rhine Crossing and later in Palestine.) In November, while the whole country was rejoicing at the news from El Alamein, I was told by Colonel Bols to hand over the running of the regimental training cadres, in readiness to attend a Squadron Commanders' course at The Royal Armoured Corps Tactical School, which had taken up residence in Brasenose College, Oxford. The course lasted for a month, finishing just before Christmas. Until then I had had no opportunity to study the tactical handling of tanks or joint infantry and armoured warfare at any level and it proved most valuable. While I was at Oxford I saw a newly-released film, *Mrs Miniver*, and recommended it to my parents.

By the time I returned to the regiment, Colonel Bols had been posted to GHQ Home Forces and Hugh Merriman, having completed only six months as second in command, had taken his place, retaining this position until the end of the war and proving to be an exceptional CO.

One day not long after Christmas he asked me if I would like my name to be put forward for another instructional appointment, this time as chief instructor to the 3rd Division Battle School, then located at Hythe in Kent. He explained that due to my age, or lack of it, there was little prospect in the short term of getting command of a squadron, but he was prepared to recommend me to the Divisional Commander for consideration for the vacancy at the Battle School of which he had been notified. I was delighted at such a prospect. Before long I was called to Div HQ for an interview with Major General William Havelock Ramsden. At less than half his age, I found him somewhat formidable. After questioning me at some length about myself, he went on to outline his ideas on the need for fresh thinking and innovations in our training for war. He particularly wished to see more realism, with plenty of live firing, including artillery, mortars, machine guns and the demolition of enemy defences by the Royal Engineers. Above all, our training must be designed to develop the offensive spirit. How all this was to be achieved in Kent was not at the time clear, but probably he knew what I did not, that the Division was soon to move to Scotland where all these ideas would make more sense. After this discourse, it began to look as if the job was mine, though he almost caught me off guard towards the end:

> As you know, Wilson, there's been quite a turnover in the Division since Dunkirk and many men have never heard a shot fired in anger. They don't know what it's like to be frightened in war. Your job at the Battle School will be to provide the experience – battle inoculation and lots of it. Of course, if the training is to be effective you're bound to have casualties. What percentage do you think I should authorize so that you will know where you stand?

This approach was quite new to me and, after a pause for thought, I suggested that we should aim to avoid all accidents without defeating the purpose of the training. His response was quite firm:

> Now let us be realistic about this. You cannot train for war properly without accepting risks. To be effective, battle inoculation necessitates men coming under fire and in the nature of things some rounds will go astray or drop short, just as they do in battle. There will also be ricochets.

It was then his turn to pause for thought, after which he announced that as long as my training casualties due to realism did not exceed five per cent I would have his support. I thanked him, without expressing my hope that I should not need his support in this direction. To have done so, I thought, might have caused him to wonder if he had the right man in front of him. On this note the interview ended and the job was mine.

On the day I arrived at the Battle School early in February, now promoted to major, I found a court of enquiry in session on the death of a sergeant who had been killed a few days earlier by a training grenade. Although the casing of these grenades was made of plastic, they all contained a spherical steel ball that could fly at high velocity in any direction. The risk of striking anyone within range was thought to be small and was accepted, but problems arose when they were used like thunder flashes and thrown among troops. As soon as I had taken over as chief instructor, and had seen everything I needed to of the training methods and safety procedures, I made it my business to study every instructor's approach to his duties. I found that most of them, officers and NCOs alike, were excellent men and every one of them highly regarded within their regiments. But, I also found grey areas of doubt within attitudes, techniques and procedures and there was an acceptance of the inevitability of training casualties, which were being incurred as part of the price of realism. I then better understood the General's outlook, though I was far from willing to take advantage of it. I decided that changes were called for and introduced a code of practice backed by safety procedures, which would also identify the causes of training casualties and set out ways of minimizing them without reducing realism. The most interesting outcome of this step became apparent during the following year, when we learned that, without having had a single training casualty, the realism of our training, far from being diminished, had been dramatically increased.

Within weeks of my arrival we received the order from HQ 3 Div to close down the school at Hythe and reopen it at Moffat in Dumfriesshire. Quicker than might have been thought possible, our various courses took shape. They changed from time to time, but all were designed for a division which at this stage was expecting to go to war within months; indeed 3 Div had been sent to Scotland in order to train for an Allied invasion of Sicily, the decision having been made in January. Then came the frustrating news that our place had been given to the Canadians, who had become restless with their insatiable appetite for action, and they, not we, took part in the Sicilian landings on 10 July. Our exercises involved battle inoculations in a variety of settings. One was an extended assault course in a natural setting with mainly natural obstacles; an unpleasant bog, which had claimed several sheep, on the fringe of which Sappers had laid charges, had to be crossed under small-arms fire. To achieve this safely, we devised a system of using machine guns on fixed lines (using stable mountings) in order to bring sustained fire power within a few feet of students, not with the purpose of frightening them, but rather to introduce them to the sounds of close-quarter fighting. Another was a woodland night patrol which came under fire and activated booby-traps on its route. Penetrating woodland by night under these conditions raises the level of tension for most men even if it is not in war. By contrast, the urban training took place in a requisitioned street of terraced houses in the Gorbals district of Glasgow, where all the rear doors and windows had been bricked up. Along the length of this street, demolition and small-arms firing with live ammunition, including hand grenades, was carried on with no restriction on noise. In the adjoining streets life continued normally, despite the daily simulation of full pitched battle just the other side of the wall.

Such training sharpens reactions and saves lives. Many of the issues were fully discussed with the students; they were under no illusions about the unpleasantness and dangers of an infantryman's war and accepted the need to experience at least some of its effects beforehand, in order to be better prepared both physically and mentally for the real thing. All were agreed that they were far more confident of their ability to respond instinctively to enemy action by the time they had completed their Moffat course than they had been before it.

Towards the end of 1943, by which time I had been at Moffat nearly a year, Hugh Merriman called in one day for a chat. He explained that as there was still no vacancy for me as a squadron commander he wished to suggest that my name should go forward for consideration to attend a four months' course at the Middle East Staff College in Haifa. I readily agreed, particularly when he offered to have me back in 3 Recce if I was not required to take up a staff appointment at the end of the course. When I left the Division I knew, perhaps better than most, what a magnificent force it was. Morale could hardly have been higher; at last the men knew the end of their long wait was close and they wanted to get on with the job. They were in the process of moving north into the area around Inverness and there, on the Moray Firth, they would soon be involved in a series of intensive exercises with the naval task force which, before long, would lift them in their assault on the mainland of Europe.

Chapter Five

Prelude to Battle

We are living in one of those rare epochs of history when once again we see that mankind has struck his tents and is on the march. When and where it will end we have yet to know.

Jan Christian Smuts, Italy, June 1944

My embarkation leave, which coincided with the festive season, provided a heady mixture and, with all the shooting included that time permitted, the days flashed past. I know of no county to rival Northumberland for the enjoyment to the full of both Christmas and the New Year, even in wartime. My orders were to report to the London District Assembly Centre on 8 January 1944 and it was several further days before those of us who had foregathered from the Home Commands en route to the Middle East Staff College were on our way to Liverpool. Part of this time my father was in London on business, staying at his club, and it was here that I had the pleasure of meeting once again the redoubtable Admiral Campbell, by now finally retired, but still full of interest and good humour. I also twice had a meal with Hugh Merriman, on leave from Scotland, who hoped to see me back with the regiment in due course.

We eventually got our movement orders to Liverpool, where we embarked in HMT *Stirling Castle*, a fine ship of 25,000 tons, which had been built to carry 780 passengers but, following a wartime refit as a troopship, could take 5,000. In addition to the 27 Lancers, there were several minor units and sundry draft reinforcements. Nor did it take long for our small party of seven officers, all of whom were single, to discover that there were about 120 WRNS on board, most of whom were bound for Alexandria to undertake cipher work and other confidential duties. They were young, intelligent, full of life and quite delightful. Moreover, notwithstanding their juniority, for practical and common sense reasons they were treated as first class passengers, though their mealtimes were earlier than ours. Their three officers, with whom we shared a table, I recollect as mature, responsible and very protective, i.e. fairly formidable, whereas I noted in my diary that 'the ratings are terrific'.

After a short while at sea we headed out into the Atlantic on a circuitous route to Gibraltar, in a slow convoy heavily escorted by a naval force of destroyers. On the fifth day we watched sudden activity as they sped off dropping depth charges, which diversion continued for some time and underlined the need for our daily boat drills, for one station of which I was responsible. Within a few days the ship's entertainments got into their stride and everyone began to mix more freely. There was some high quality sound reproduction equipment, with a good library of excellent gramophone records on board, and soon daily record concerts were packed out, with classical music for the upper deck and progressively lighter music the further one descended. One day, by chance, I found myself sitting next to one of the prettiest Wrens, whose musical taste was in line with my own. The following day I visited the first-class passengers' ironing room at the right moment with a shirt I proceeded to maltreat. In no time it was taken from me with a smile, soon to become familiar, and given more care than even the best batman could have bestowed on it. How easy it can sometimes be; we were away! Her name was Pamela and she came from Lincolnshire. Soon she was featuring in my letters home.

It was not long before I made the acquaintance of Doc Martin, the ship's medical officer, who was a delightful Geordie. Through him I got to know the members of a concert party drawn from the Covent Garden Opera Company, who were also heading for the Middle East to entertain the troops under the auspices of ENSA. Because the ship, in common with all troopships during the war, was 'dry', the hospitality which some of the ship's officers were able to offer was doubly appreciated and it was largely by this means that I met the individual members of the concert party. Until then they had been keeping a very low profile and were never heard rehearsing, though they spent much time doing so in a secluded part of the ship and eventually staged a quite magnificent concert of the very highest quality. The only further excitement occurred during a violent storm in the Mediterranean when the convoy became split. Otherwise our eighteen days at sea, with dancing on deck in the warm evening air, were more like a peacetime cruise than a wartime interlude.

After disembarking at Port Said we began a weary train journey to Cairo, taking all day. In a subsequent letter I related diverse impressions from 'different varieties of horrid smells, mud villages along the

Suez Canal, hundreds of wild duck in the marshes and the miraculous way in which I haven't so far (Abbassia Camp, Cairo) managed to lose any of my baggage'. The next day there followed another long journey to northern Palestine, with a pause for dinner at El Quantara on the Suez Canal and further stops at Gaza (0300 hours) and Lydda (0600 hours). Soon after it was light enough to see, we were passing through miles of orange and grapefruit groves, broken here and there by Arab villages and Jewish settlements, with their characteristic family and collective systems of farming. As we continued on our northerly course, the mountains of Samaria to the east stretched into the distance, while to the west lay the blue Mediterranean, often close to the railway track. Long before we reached Haifa, the Carmel range had shown up on our right, rising towards 2,000 feet. We arrived at our destination after a journey of nearly twenty-four hours, in a most uncomfortable, semi-upholstered, second-class compartment, and were very weary. The Middle East Staff College stood on high ground above the town, overlooking the sea, and first impressions were very favourable. We were given a friendly welcome, but for a while the seven of us were at a disadvantage, having arrived in Haifa three days late because, I imagine, there was no choice of sailing dates from the UK. This meant that the other members of the course, more than 100 who had arrived from Italy, North Africa and the Middle East, had a good lead over us which, it was made clear, we must make up somehow and the sooner the better. The advantage the earlier arrivals enjoyed was that most of them had been fighting with the First or Eighth Armies in North Africa, or more recently in Italy and elsewhere, while we in Home Forces had still been training, albeit at full stretch, for the approaching Allied invasion of north-west Europe. Initially, we had to accept that those with the brownest knees would be best placed to divine the 'DS Solution' to the succession of indoor and outdoor exercises that comprised much of the course programme. (The Directing Staff, having planned all exercises, were obliged to present the DS Solution at the conclusion of each problem.) It was the policy that there would be six very full working days each week, with a brief mid-course break. However, even with evening studies continuing to a late hour, the tempo of work was acceptable, partly because of the attractiveness of the Palestinian landscape within which our outdoor studies took place, but more so for the endless interest associated with this fascinating small country. As the weeks passed, it became almost impossible to go anywhere without a conscious awareness of Biblical and historical events, with the latter spanning most of a millennium from the early Crusades to Allenby's masterly

Palestine Campaigns of the Great War. Indeed, such became the level of interest among a proportion of our course members that, once each weekend, recreational transport was provided to take those who wished to places of interest throughout most of the country. By this means we were able to visit the city of Jerusalem, together with a host of smaller places and features associated with Biblical times. We were fortunate, too, in finding that the small parties into which we tended to split later on were almost invariably the only sightseers in evidence, because tourism throughout the war was virtually at a standstill.

Our introduction to what Palestine had to offer occurred on the first Saturday, when the whole course was treated to what, for most of us, turned out to be a memorable afternoon of discovery. We set off to the south-east in a small convoy of trucks, climbing to the ridgeline of Mount Carmel and following a narrow, twisty road which connected several isolated Druze villages of mountain dwellers. After about an hour we arrived at the highest peak on this remarkable seventeen-mile-long massif, where we alighted and walked a short distance to a small chapel belonging to the Carmelite Order. Here the DS dissected the most breathtaking panorama, feature by feature. If ever, before the end of my days, I was offered the opportunity to revisit any point on earth for the last time, this would be my choice. It was explained at the outset that we were standing on the traditional place of Elijah's Sacrifice, known to the Arabs as *El Muhraqa*, the Place of Burning. It is a formidable climb, as I discovered some years later when accompanied by a Druze *mukhter* (village headman). Out of sight because of its depth below sea level, even from our wonderful vantage point, was the Sea of Galilee, but there was no missing the snow-capped Mount Herman of nearly 10,000 feet in the far distance.

A letter home dated 4 March reminds me of how it came about that I should find myself giving a lecture to the assembled College, including members of the DS, within just over a month of our arrival. Soon after we assembled, all students had been told to submit a subject on which they would be capable of lecturing for forty-five minutes, to be followed by questions. Some, no doubt, had the sense to choose a subject sufficiently obscure to stand no chance of being selected, for only six were required out of a field of well over 100. However, I sealed my fate by submitting as my subject 'The training of the assault divisions for their role in the anticipated landings on the mainland of Western Europe'. For security reasons I had to write my lecture first for the Commandant, who approved it, but gave me strict instructions to stick to the text and not to answer sensitive questions. Even within this brief, I learned afterwards that what had made some impact was my report of the scale on which the preparations were being made. Without quoting any figures of significance, a picture must have emerged of something far bigger than the audience had visualized. It is interesting now to read that when, at about the same time, the Naval Orders of Operation NEPTUNE (the code name for the assault phase of the Allied invasion of Normandy) were published, for the use of those who had a need to know, the introduction included:

This is probably the largest and most complicated operation ever undertaken and involves the movement of over 4,000 ships and craft of all types in the first three days.

Towards the end of March came the four-day mid-course break and, together with four others, I shared a taxi to Beirut. We were certainly impressed with the city and enjoyed ourselves throughout our stay as five, admittedly young, majors behaving like the youngest of subalterns and making the most of superb cuisine, cheap wine and exotic entertainment. In our more serious moments we even admired its layout, splendour and orderliness, certainly outwardly, as an example of all that was best in French colonialism.

On return to Haifa we plunged into the second half of the course, conscious of the fact that before we reached the end we should all know at least the theatre we would be heading for, though at that stage we had only been told it could be anywhere in the world. Interestingly, as things turned out, I mentioned in my letter of 16 April that I had just heard Charles Mitchell was serving in a Recce Regiment in Italy and added:

If I were superstitious I should say now that I shall go to Italy after this course because Charles and I have followed each other about since 1939 with the most surprising regularity.

Shortly before the end of the course about half of those attending it, including me, were told that we had been selected for employment in Italy.

Most of those destined for Italy chose to take their week's end-of-course leave in Egypt, making the journey by rail. However, as an attractive variation, and with the help of a naval friend, I was able to arrange passages from Haifa to Alexandria for Ian Battye of the Middlesex Regiment and myself in a Free French corvette, which left early the same Sunday morning on convoy escort duty. It was a small ship with, as we soon discovered, a marked tendency to roll. The following day it received orders to turn round and proceed to a port some several hundreds of miles in the opposite direction, but, when our predicament was realized, we were lowered into a small boat and rowed, with our baggage, to a British warship for safe passage to Alexandria.

The rest of the week was spent in sightseeing and parties, two of which included Pamela, then on to Cairo with its well-known tourist attractions, also without tourists, and more parties. Then it was time to return to Alexandria to embark, on 5 June, for a five-day voyage to Taranto, at the heel of Italy. The next day turned out to be D-Day for the long awaited Allied invasion of occupied north-west Europe, codenamed OVERLORD, which began with the Normandy landings. Throughout the day my thoughts were with the 3rd Division and 3 Recce. I had been hearing regularly from many of my old friends and most recently from Hugh Merriman, Peter Carse and Tom Bundock. My letters home had reflected my uneasiness, as well they might; the last two of this trio were both killed, one in Normandy, the other later on. The following day I wrote a letter home to be posted at our destination:

I rather naturally feel terribly out of it as my old Division will now be up to their necks in it. Had I not gone to MESC I should still have been with them. I am not looking forward to hearing about their casualties as I knew nearly every officer in the Division. Guy [Thornycroft] was an Assault Company Commander and I hope he will have better luck than his two brothers, one of whom was killed in the Middle East and the other is a POW. ...Last night we heard the King's message, it was 10 o'clock and some of us were on the top deck listening to the loudspeaker up there. It was a glorious night with a full moon shining so brightly that I read by it for a short time. All the ships of the convoy could be seen quite easily. The King's voice seemed to draw us much closer to home, coming so clearly over the air.

We reached Taranto on 10 June and travelled by train overnight to Naples, where we were taken to a reinforcement holding unit from which, it was hoped, we would soon be on our way to our various appointments. The next day I had to report to the Royal Armoured Corps (RAC) branch of Central Mediterranean Forces because by then the Recce Corps was part of it. Here I was given a black beret to take the place of my khaki one, before being interviewed by Brigadier Watkins, a large officer nicknamed 'Boomer' because of the pitch of his voice. He explained that his staff were checking to find out if there

58

was either a suitable staff appointment or a recce squadron commander's post vacant. Until then I was asked to report daily, rather like a prisoner on parole, except that it was all very gentleman-ly.

When I look back on the course of events during the following few weeks, as they affected me personally, I have mixed feelings, some of which come close to guilt. I have to remind myself that my circum-

Italy 1944
The Allies penetrated the Gothic Line
from the south in late August

stances were not of my own seeking and were largely imposed on me while the Army tried to find me suitable employment. It was as though the war and I were momentarily in different worlds, leaving me with nothing to do but enjoy the Mediterranean summer, with all the joys flowing from the perfect weather, good wine, fresh fruit and swimming, first in one sea, then in another. For entertainment there was opera of such choice and quality as are rarely available to most music lovers in a lifetime. As far as I can remember, much as I genuinely sought to do something useful, my conscience did not at the time trouble me and now I look back on this heavenly interlude as my 'divertimenti in Italia'.

When Italy had signed an armistice with the Allies, as heavy fighting continued with the Germans, the Allies found various ways of helping to stabilize the Italian economy and maintain the morale of the population, partly to lessen the likelihood of a Communist revolution, of which there was much fear. One imaginative decision made by the British was to support the world famous San Carlo Opera Company and its theatre in Naples, for the benefit of the local population and for the provision of entertainment for soldiers on leave. The seats were *very* cheap; the equivalent of 7/6 (less than 40p), secured a seat at a performance as good as any available at that time anywhere in the world. The standards were so high and the productions could be changed daily because of the number of opera houses that had closed down during the previous year. As word spread, singers and musicians flocked to the San Carlo. My first evening in Naples I saw *Aida* and the following day attended a performance of *Rigoletto*. I was just beginning to fancy my chances one day as an opera critic when the Brigadier found something more suitable to occupy my time. He had decided there was enough liaison work to make a full time job, visiting any armoured units with problems of concern to him that needed investigation on the ground. They mostly involved personnel, equipment and training and I soon became a go-between, working in both directions to save time and paperwork.

However, after less than two weeks on my liaison duties I was sent for and given the background to another temporary job further afield. In November 1942, when the Anglo-American landings had taken place in North Africa under command of General Eisenhower, the Allied Forces Headquarters (AFHQ) in the Mediterranean theatre had been located in Algiers. Following the Allied invasion of Italy, the command centre of gravity had shifted to the Italian mainland and very soon AFHQ was due to take over the vast and impressive Palace of Caserta in Naples. In the meantime the rump in Algiers contained elements of all British Army arms and services that would soon be on the move to Italy. The RAC element was under command of a Major Neilson, due to return to the UK, and I had been nominated as his relief. Before leaving Naples, I wrote to Hugh Merriman to keep him informed of my movements and then, on 23 June, joined a Service aircraft from Capodichino airport to Algiers. There, at AFHQ, over the next two days I took over my job in a very relaxed atmosphere. Neilson had everything under control and was assisted by a small staff of efficient and willing other ranks, also very relaxed. It did not take me long to realize that there was little to do, partly because most of the administration was in the hands of others, and it was therefore a relief to find that my opposite number in the Infantry, one Tiny Dolman of the Loyal Regiment, was in the same situation. His routine was to visit his office early and late in the day and to spend the rest of the day swimming. I soon followed his example and together we enjoyed the best conditions either of us had ever known, usually on Palm Beach near Sidi Ferrouch to the east of Algiers, which had a number of islands offshore, offering swims of up to a mile or more. Apart from our small groups, which usually included our drivers and clerks, the beach was often deserted, though from time to time locals would visit us, offering fresh fruit and coffee.

In less than a month the time came to join the rear party of AFHQ on its move to Naples and, on 21 July, we embarked at Algiers on the *Ville d'Oran* for a two-day voyage. The following morning I reported to my HQ in Caserta, where I found they still had no long term plans for me, but forecast there would be plenty more liaison work before long. The same day, however, there was much excitement in Naples of a totally unexpected nature, when we were visited by the King. There was tremendous appreciation shown throughout his ten-day visit, during which he travelled round in jeeps and open cars for considerable distances on roads inches deep in dust, with the object of seeing as many of his subjects as possible in the time. Many nights he spent in a caravan and he certainly got within the sound of the guns, and on one occasion to within sight of enemy positions.

For a while, Tiny Dolman and I were both without our transport, which was following us in a later ship from Algiers, and there was little we could do without it except, in my case, take advantage of the opera, which I attended daily throughout the week. Then I heard that John Barbirolli had made arrangements to conduct resident orchestras in Rome, Naples, Taranto and Bari. I bought my ticket for the first concert in Naples and then was prevented from attending it by the best of reasons. I learned during a routine visit to AFHQ at Caserta on 5

August that I was to report to Brigadier Watkins at HQ Allied Armies in Italy, in Rome, the following day. By now I was reunited with my driver and the old desert-model Ford from Algiers and, having risen in the small hours, we had a wonderful trip north to Rome, rather over 200 miles in perfect conditions, arriving around midday. I learned from the Brigadier that as there was still no vacancy for me as a squadron commander in Italy he had arranged for me to be posted as a Liaison Officer to Eighth Army HQ for employment in the RAC Branch. It was a new appointment and he forecast that before long I should have plenty to do, which turned out indeed to be the case.

This brought to an end an embarrassingly enjoyable interlude of semi-active service. The following morning I left Rome with the Brigadier, who was making one of his periodical visits to Eighth Army. Unfortunately his car broke down and, in view of the uncertainty of how long it would take to sort out, I was lucky in being able to hitch a lift with my kit for a mere 120 miles.

Eighth Army HQ, near Poggibonsi, was under canvas, as was its custom 'in the field', and there I found several friends from the Staff College. The following morning, Tuesday, 8 August, I reported to Brigadier Ivor Moore, who held the appointment of Brigadier Armoured Fighting Vehicles, and it was to him that I remained responsible for the rest of my time in Italy. I soon discovered how lucky I was, first because he was such a capable and delightful person to work for and second because my job turned out to be one of the most interesting and stimulating.

My initial briefing was detailed and thorough, as if the Brigadier were visualizing the situations I would meet as well as the information he would require during the forthcoming operations, as the Eighth Army closed up to the Gothic Line, with the prospect of a battle to follow of greater magnitude than any which had gone before. His responsibilities were by no means limited to tanks and armoured cars, as his title suggested, but also included shared responsibilities for the personnel of most of the armoured units and formations within the Eighth Army. Of constant concern to him was the prompt replacement of battle casualties, particularly among officers who sometimes had to be transferred from other units. Experience had shown that it could take days for accurate and detailed particulars of battle casualties to pass through all the intervening stages between the battlefield and the Army HQ. Moreover, the larger the scale of operations, the longer the passage of reports would take. For this reason he had asked to have a liaison officer on his staff, with the task of gathering information.

After giving me the background to the job, the Brigadier warned me that the modus operandi would have to evolve through trial and error. Although, at this stage, operations were mostly of low intensity, he mentioned a number of formations then in the line that he wished me to visit in order to get to know them and become familiar with the work. He also stressed the importance of putting observation before liaison, while units were in action, and the need to judge when to time my visits so as to assist COs, rather than interrupt them when immersed in post-battle reorganization. This was easier said than done, and would call for luck as well as judgement if I was to get information into the hands of the Brigadier ahead of normal channels. He wished to see me every other evening for debriefing, unless I had important information to pass on earlier. To enable me to operate on these lines I was to be provided with a Jeep, a driver-operator (a driver also trained in operating the radio and RT procedures) and all we needed to be self-contained for two days each time we left HQ. The wireless was mainly to enable me to 'read the battle', with such codes and frequencies as I might need; only during lulls or in an emergency was I permitted to transmit.

After this briefing my driver was sent for and it was not without some interest that I waited to meet the man who would contribute so much or so little to our joint task. Before long a smart, young soldier, who looked no more than eighteen, came up to me and introduced himself as Trooper Lyons. He belonged to the Royal Tank Regiment (RTR) and had been in Italy only a few months since finishing his training, which had followed several years' service as a band boy. As time passed, I realized what a good choice someone had made, when asked to nominate a soldier who could be relied upon to do what was required of him, at times without supervision, in a job which was likely to be exacting. As I soon discovered, he also had a healthy zest for action, which was satisfied sooner than either of us might have expected. In due course we came under fire not infrequently, and he never put a foot wrong or lost his cheerful disposition.

As soon as Trooper Lyons and I had drawn our rations and stowed reserve fuel and water, we set off on 9 August on our task of visiting and assisting those at 'the sharp end'. I was soon to learn the valuable lesson of the importance of listening to niggling problems, which most units hesitate to mention to senior officers, and then taking them back to those at HQ who were best able to deal with them. I had been given a list of units to visit and the subjects to raise with them. According to my diary, which I never took with me for security reasons, but used as a record of where I had been and what I had seen and done, I left Eighth Army HQ at 0830 hours on my first day of visits. Twelve hours and 270 miles later I had completed the day's work, by when it was time to find a convenient spot to pull off the road, have a meal and spend the night. It was not entirely coincidental that at the end of the day Lyons and I found ourselves well forward, in the area held by 44 Recce Regiment of the 56th Division where, though not expected, we were welcomed, fed and entertained until the small hours, before turning in. My host, whom I took completely by surprise, was my old friend Charles Mitchell, whose tent I shared, which was just as well because it rained all night. The next morning I was greeted by Fusilier Watson of my platoon in the BEF and Sergeant 'Snakey' Cardwell of Charles's platoon of those days, whose favourite recreation in Arras had been shooting at dive-bombers from the top of a water tower with a First World War Lewis gun he had acquired 'by irregular means'. The day followed the same pattern of visits, though I did take advantage of pausing in Assisi to look around, and then visited the 4 New Zealand Armoured Brigade of the 2nd NZ Division, which was out of the line at the time. Many of those who were familiar with this division judged it to be the finest they saw in action anywhere; I found them friendly, relaxed and confidently awaiting their next battle.

The previous day I had visited the 6th South African Armoured Division which, at the time, was resting after liberating Florence the week before, together with the 2nd New Zealand Division, though they beat the latter into the city by a short head. It had taken them ten days of fighting, while exercising all possible restraint from causing damage to the city during the engagement, in contrast to the Germans who destroyed four of the five bridges spanning the River Arno in Florence as they withdrew.

The next phase of this unrelenting, grinding-down of German resistance involved the preparations for a major offensive against the Gothic Line itself, described by Alexander as '...the most formidable of all the defensive "Lines" built by the Germans in Italy'. The C.-in-C. Eighth Army, General Leese, had managed to persuade General Alexander at the last moment to jettison the first, well matured concept of forcing the centre of the Gothic Line, in favour of a wholly undeveloped plan, subsequently codenamed Operation OLIVE, in which the Eighth Army would cross the Apennines and attack on the Adriatic Coast, while the Fifth Army would make subsidiary attacks on the Florence-Bologna axis. And this is exactly what happened, secretly and swiftly, just out of sound and sight of the enemy, who remained in total ignorance of the passage of an army, almost under their noses, until it was too late. Only two suitable roads were available across the Apennines in the right directions and all their bridges had been blown by the enemy rearguards, so both had to be completely re-bridged, one to 30-ton standards for tanks on tracks and the other to 70-ton standards for use by laden tank transporters. Notwithstanding these and many other difficulties, the entire programme was completed on schedule, but the change of plan delayed the opening of the Gothic Line offensive and reduced the period of good campaigning weather before the rains came early in September. As part of this large scale flit, I was covering a lot of ground. My diary entry for 17 August records:

> Another rather tiring day's driving. We reached our destination just outside – at teatime. The whole journey of 250 miles along some of the twistiest roads in the country is most misleading, being half an hour's flying time I should say in a DC3. Our new camp is in an orchard next to a farm. The farmer seems quite a good fellow and I have handed a bundle of washing in to his wife. I hope she does them as well as the last woman did, and the patching too.

We met quite a lot of the country folk, mostly simple farmers and villagers who were friendly and helpful, particularly with information about enemy activity in the forward areas, where we spent much of our time. I had already discovered that Lyons had a remarkably useful grasp of the language, which got him much further than my Latin-based smattering. I asked him how he had come by it and was rather impressed by his answer: 'When I was in the band we had a very strict bandmaster who made all the boys learn the musical dictionary by heart and, when you know that lot, all you have to do is fill in the gaps.'

In the middle of August there had been an inconclusive flurry of signals concerning my employment, which had by then been on a temporary basis for over two months. Brigadier Watkins sent one to the War Office and another to 21st Army Group in Normandy, confirming that I was still available to the 3rd Division if required, as there was no vacancy for a Recce Corps temporary major in Italy. A week later I had an air letter from Hugh Merriman, telling me that the War Office had turned down his request for my return. This I showed to Brigadier Ivor Moore, who immediately sent a further signal to the War Office, repeating that I was still available. This was followed by silence. In the meantime my temporary work as a liaison officer continued to provide me with a high level of interest. On 21 August I visited the 2 Polish Armoured Brigade, near the Adriatic coast, and was able to observe them in action at close quarters. At some stage, during a lull in the proceedings, I was taken to Brigade HQ and welcomed with courtesy, then permitted to remain while information from their forward units came in by wireless and was entered in the log of events. It was during this period of waiting that I had the opportunity of conversing with some Poles and observing and listening to others. There was considerable tension and emotion in the air, which ran much deeper than the strain of battle could account for, that in any case was clearly going in their favour. It was not long before I realized that they were also immersed in the tragedy of the second Warsaw rising which, by then, had been in progress for three weeks. Altogether I found my brief visit to the Poles quite a profound experience. Of the twenty-six nations that contributed forces to General Alexander's army group, none were of greater interest or commanded more respect than the 2nd Polish Corps under its outstanding, eight times wounded commander, General Anders.

When I had the information I needed from the Polish Brigade HQ, Lyons and I had a quick swim in the Adriatic to get rid of caked dust and then made the long trip back to our HQ. By the time we got there we were just as covered in dust as we had been before. There was little time to tidy up, because the Brigadier wanted what information I had as soon as possible after my return. I went in search of him and, not for the first time, found him having a bath. I must qualify this. Nowhere in the HQ, or even within the 'mobile bath unit' which was equipped with showers, was there a proper bath, other than that perhaps of a general; certainly, so far as I knew, none for brigadiers. However, somewhere along his route through the Middle East or southern Europe, Ivor Moore had acquired a baby's bath. It was made of tin, circular, about three feet in diameter and some nine inches deep. Into this, with remarkable dexterity, the Brigadier would manoeuvre his portly self. There was little room left for water, but, with the use of a bucket, his batman would slowly raise the level to within an inch of the rim. The clarity of the image, set in the open Italian countryside at sunset, has remained undimmed in my memory ever since.

Several days before this, the Brigadier had told me that in the early stages of the battle he wished me to work with the Canadians, and had arranged for me to attend the Army Commander's pre-battle address to the senior officers (COs upwards) of the Canadian Corps on 24 August. It turned out to be a memorable tour de force, which greatly impressed all those present. I recorded at the time:

He spoke brilliantly to a crowded opera house full of senior officers and we heard the whole plan of attack. It is impressive but essentially simple as the best plans are. The move across has taken 3 weeks and is one of the most magnificent bits of staff work of the whole war. The coming attack is to be the biggest in the history of the Eighth Army.

Oliver Leese's talk lasted all of eighty minutes, during which he spoke with confidence and clarity, explaining, phase by phase, how his troops would be deployed, their tasks, objectives and timings. The outline plan was to attack with three corps abreast, with the Poles on the right, the Canadians in the centre and the Fifth British Corps, consisting of five divisions, on the left, through hilly country. The ten divisions at his disposal would be supported by 1,200 tanks and over 1,000 guns.

25 August (D-Day). After fitting an improved wireless to our jeep, drawing supplies and marking maps, Lyons and I set off to visit the British 21 Tank Brigade west of Ostra, about twelve miles from the Adriatic, and found them completing their preparations. The Brigade comprised the 12th and 48th Battalions of the Royal Tank Regiment and 145 Regiment Royal Armoured Corps and I planned to remain in touch with them during the next few days. I discovered too late on this occasion that Tony Kingsford, a Salopian friend in Tombling's House, was at the time serving in 48 RTR. Though we have met again at intervals over the years, it was not until very recently that I found myself admiring the relaxed hand of whoever had the responsibility for maintaining his battalion's War Diary (not known for light reading) at this time in Italy. Tony's name appeared twice on the page which included the day I visited his battalion; one with a routine connection, the other being the eye catcher:

> 23 August. All tanks had arrived at Iesi. Captain A. F. Kingsford now with 'C' Squadron [ex Adjutant] travelled with the tanks. 'JOE' the mongrel Italian sheepdog he picked up at Presenzano, wouldn't go near the tanks, and had a ride in Major Haigh's Jeep instead.

During my visits that day to 21 Tank Brigade I noted the usual concentration on last minute adjustments, checks and inspections, which go on in all good units before battle is joined. One came to sense the mood of men before an impending operation of this kind and the bigger the occasion the greater was their awareness of what was at stake; but there would be no bravado, no feigned or excessive humour, no overconfidence. When one knew them well, by virtue of sharing their problems and many of their feelings, one would know much of what they were thinking. Not far below the surface, regardless of where in the British Isles they hailed from, one would usually be aware of a determination in the ranks not to let the side down. Depending on whether they belonged to a Cavalry Regiment, the Royal Tank Regiment, a Foot Guards Regiment or a County Regiment – or more simply the Royal Armoured Corps or the Infantry – a soldier's loyalty on the battlefield embraced his crew or section, his troop or platoon, his squadron or company and his regiment or battalion, almost invariably in that order. This sometimes comes as a surprise to those who have never taken up arms, but it is the men who are closest to the action who give most, and expect most from their comrades, when, as a group, they are put to the test. No comradeship surpasses that of the battlefield and soldiers have acknowledged this down the ages.

As the evening drew on and H-Hour approached, Lyons and I left the tank crews and made our way forward, through the gun lines and far enough on to reduce the inevitable ear-splitting noise of gunfire on a scale rarely heard and which, if too close, would have saturated the senses. We soon found suitable cover in which to harbour for the night, not far from the Metauro, well aware that sleep would be out of the question when the barrage began. This is the stage when there is nothing left to be done, and one can only wait, watch, listen and ponder.

Chapter Six

The Gothic Line

In war it is not always possible to have everything go exactly as one likes. In working with allies it sometimes happens that they develop opinions of their own.

Winston S. Churchill

Some miles away, in the direction of Florence, a distinguished guest had arrived at General Leese's Tactical HQ to live in the field and sleep in a caravan, just as the King had done the previous month. The Prime Minister had timed his visit to the Eighth Army to coincide with the attack on the Gothic Line. Within a few hours of his arrival he was enjoying himself, smoking one of his large cigars while watching the barrage that started at midnight.

The following morning revealed that the enemy had been surprised by the weight of the Canadian 1st Division's assault, which had taken the village of Saltara, a mile north of the Metauro, almost unopposed, though later it became the hub of considerable reaction. To their right were the Poles, to their left the British, and by dawn a total of five divisions were across the river. My own plan, made the previous day, was to wait south of the river until the tanks of the 21 Brigade had married up with the battalions of the Canadian 1 Infantry Brigade on the north bank and were resuming the advance, before we crossed and followed them into open country. This would take us through Saltara and northwards on to higher ground, where I would look for a suitable observation post (OP).

It was about midday, when I judged from what we could see and hear, that the tanks were all across the river and heading for their respective RVs north of Saltara. With the infantry and armour now well clear of the river, there should be much less congestion in and around Saltara, so we set off to watch the battle, snatches of which we could already hear in the distance. We crossed one of the recently completed bridges, reached the main lateral road beyond and then followed the narrow, twisty road to the village, which was sheltered by raised ground. Beyond its entrance, the road turned sharply and we were surprised to find ourselves at the tail of a number of stationary tanks. A few heads protruded from turrets, with attention on what lay ahead, and I doubt if we were noticed, but above the noise of their engines we soon heard more tanks approaching from behind, which closed right up, sandwiching our jeep within the extended column. Suddenly, and without warning, the whole of the centre of the village around us erupted in a heavy concentration of rapid and accurate artillery fire: 'Were heavily shelled in Saltara and the houses came crashing down. We were trapped behind our tanks and couldn't get out of it.'

That was the succinct entry in my diary, which had more important things to cover. What also gets a mention in a letter home, written two days later, was the thoughtful action of the driver of the tank behind our jeep, who had driven so close that we were afforded a measure of protection from exploding shells and flying masonry. The tank in front, unknowingly, was doing the same, but we were completely exposed on either side as the houses continued to collapse around us. Suddenly the tank driver behind signalled frantically for us to dismount and seek shelter under his tank, which Lyons and I did with alacrity, though it is not the sort of thing one does uninvited. Such thoughtfulness at that precise moment added another face to the gallery of Good Samaritans who appear out of the blue from time to time and solve a problem, offer water, give a lift when broken down in the back of beyond or even save your bacon under fire.

With the Saltara bottleneck behind us I was able to search for a suitable feature from which to observe the battle that, though not yet in full swing, was beginning to warm up. We soon came to an ideal spot about a mile north of the village, on the road to Cartoceto. Here a track left our road and ascended a small, well-elevated feature, with a short escarpment from which there was every prospect of a full view of the rising ground facing the Canadians, with their objectives clearly visible. As we reached the top, already aware of the need to drive with caution and minimize dust, we were met by a Gunner OP party who, I think, were the only troops on the feature at the time. They stressed the importance of keeping a low profile, by telling us that the feature had already been shelled since their arrival half an hour earlier. I thanked them and we tucked the jeep out of sight, before moving off towards the other end of the flat-topped ridge, where there was a small, unoccupied farmstead. Sizing it up as a possible target for enemy artillery, who might identify it as one of our likely OPs, I chose a spot about 100 yards short of the farmstead from which to observe, behind some cover alongside the path leading to the building. From there I was able to identify the units we had come to watch, using knowledge of their objectives, routes and boundaries. Already there were signs of stiffening resistance from the German rearguards and the 48 Highlanders to our right were having problems. It was during the afternoon that my attention was suddenly diverted by the incautious approach of a jeep, containing some rather unwarlike soldiers. I remember asking Lyons what the hell was going on and, when he replied that it was a jeepload of redcaps, I told him to go and give them a rocket and remind them what follows dust on a skyline. There was a pause, before he returned with a broad smile, which I may have misinterpreted because few troopers get the opportunity, even on active service, to tear a strip off a quartet of military policemen. But there was more to it. Lyons explained that they were on escort duty. He waited for my question as to the identity of those being escorted, before revealing, 'Mr Churchill and General Alexander, sir'. He had a splendid sense of humour and my face must have been a study; I had been outranked by about as far as his imagination would stretch.

I got up to go and explain to the military police what was the likely outcome of their prominent arrival, but I was too late. The VIPs had also arrived and were just getting out of the C.-in-C.'s jeep. Soon they were heading in our direction and all sorts of thoughts were passing through my mind, the principal one being: 'Can General Alex not realize the dangers of bringing Winston this far forward on such an exposed feature?' However, as we stood to attention, waiting for them to pass, my indecision was resolved, though my fears remained, as I caught the worried expression on Alex's face and heard a snatch of his conversation, which went something like: 'I shouldn't have given in to your insistence to come up here; we must make it very brief.' Winston, in total contrast, was clearly enjoying himself, as was his wont on these occasions. 'Nothing is more exhilarating than to be shot at without result', as he wrote of his days with the Malakand Field Force, nearly half a century earlier. They disappeared in the direction of the building beyond us and re-emerged some twenty minutes later, Alex still anxious and Winston still beaming with satisfaction.

Finally I come to the remainder of my own diary's entry about the day's events:

In the afternoon after the shelling had just stopped we looked up when shaking the dust off us and saw Winston and Alex.

Heartening in a way but far too far forward for the PM. They had come forward against General Alexander's wishes and better judgement to see the attack go in on Point 393. I for one was relieved to see them go. Have seen too many of our fellows blown to various degrees of smithereens today on mines to make for absolute peace of mind. Spent part of the afternoon directing operations on clearing the road from Saltara to Cartoceto. Demolitions on large scale and lots of mines. Appropriated a tommy-gun from a Canadian who was beginning to get high. May come in useful. An Italian gave me much information about mines and booby-traps.

I might have summed it up as quite a day.

Writing retrospectively about the presence of a Prime Minister and a Commander-in-Chief on a Second World War battlefield, I realize that many will hold conflicting views. British and Canadian soldiers who saw them, within sight and sound of infantry, tanks and artillery in action, were greatly impressed and survivors will never forget the boost to their morale. But, had it gone seriously awry, what would have been the effects on the Allied cause? Before passing judgement, perhaps one should remember that such decisions and actions are determined by human nature. Both these men had established reputations for courage, but prudence does not always come easily to old warriors.

On 27 August, the enemy continued his methodical withdrawal to the next river line, that of the narrow Arzilla, and thence to the broader Foglia, beyond which lay the challenging Gothic Line. Because my own role at this time was closely linked with the Canadians, who played such a prominent part in breaching the Gothic Line, I learned much during this battle, mainly from watching various actions, but also from listening to command wireless nets and conversations on the ground during lulls in the fighting. I soon observed how close was the relationship between the units of the 3 Canadian Infantry Brigade and the 21 British Tank Brigade. There was a period of just over seventy-two hours, later in this battle, during which 'B' Squadron, 48th Battalion Royal Tank Regiment, was in action by day and night almost continuously, switching their support between three Canadian battalions.

In the meantime the largely one-sided air war continued, to the almost constant advantage of the Allies. By now the *Luftwaffe* was largely confined to hit-and-run raids and late one day, when I was returning from Army HQ to rejoin the Canadians, a minor incident occurred, of interest only to two Englishmen enjoying their evening meal, and a passing German. My diary entry, written a day or two later, was descriptive:

I purposely leaguered South of the R. Metauro hoping for a quietish night and said to Lyons – we'll stop here and have a safe and peaceful sleep. Not a bit of it! Just as it got dusk a Jerry plane came right down on us and let go full blast. Luckily he didn't drop bombs but his 20 mm cannon kicked up our camping ground good and proper. Very spectacular if unpleasant. I think it was my mosquito net, which is white, which attracted him!

P.S. I have dyed my mosquito net!! [P.P.S. With a strong brew of tea.]

When I recall this incident of a few seconds' duration as the light was failing, what comes back is still vivid; the peaceful little valley with a narrow stream flowing through suddenly erupting as a lone aircraft flew straight at us fast and low. We could see its guns blazing as an animated carpet of flying earth and debris flashed towards and past us, leaving a trail of smoke, a campsite looking as if it had been instantly cultivated and the two occupants without a scratch between them. Fortunately, too, the jeep had been camouflaged and was well clear of the beaten zone. As soon as we realized we had sustained neither injury nor damage we had a good laugh and returned to our supper without undue resentment.

On 29 August, with the Metauro behind them, the Canadians were advancing through difficult hilly country towards the River Foglia. By now my attention was focused on their 5 Armoured Brigade, under Brigadier Ian Cumberland, with Lord Strathcona's Horse, Princess Louise's Dragoons and the British Columbia Dragoons, all of which I was able to observe in action during the next few days. Two qualities which struck me from the beginning of our short acquaintance were their effervescent high morale and determination. A third dimension, which before long transcended all others, embraced their fighting qualities, which soon spoke for themselves. Distinguished by a maroon patch on their dark grey battledress and nicknamed 'The Great Maroon Machine', their confidence and readiness to get to grips with the enemy were deep and striking. But, had one been able to make the same evaluation on 'the other side of the hill', I believe one would have found a similar outlook within the German 1st Parachute Division, whose reputation for professionalism and courage was second to none.

Some may have foreseen the violent, bitter and often close-quarter nature of the fighting which followed, but I must admit I was not expecting the intensity with which these aspects characterized the battles, as August gave way to September. At some stage of the battle every Canadian armoured regiment became involved in close-quarter fighting, often as crews of knocked out tanks fought hand to hand against parachutists who had remained concealed until tanks came within the short range of their *Panzerfausts* (hand-held rocket launchers). Casualties mounted on both sides, with the enemy paying the higher price. There were several possible reasons for this, one of which was known to the ancient Greeks: 'Willing obedience always beats forced obedience.' (Xenophon, 430-350 B.C.)

Attacks by infantry of both Canadian divisions began during the afternoon of 30th, but it was the following day, from an excellent viewpoint on high ground south of the River Conca, six miles from the River Foglia, that I watched the seemingly slow and painful advance of the British Columbia Dragoons. Already, by about 0930 hours, they were being delayed by artificial and natural obstacles, and from an early stage came under anti-tank and artillery fire, which increased as they advanced. We watched one tank after another stop, some unmistakably hit and 'brewing up', others obviously under fire and returning it, and some immobilized by thrown tracks or bellied on rocks. It was a grim spectacle and drawn out over more than three hours, during which numerous contests occurred between individual tanks and concealed anti-tank guns. I still feel privileged to have watched their progress, though I recall no elation, even when they reached their objective, for they had suffered much and their problems were by no means over.

I withdrew before darkness fell, but some hours later became aware of further fighting and accordingly we rose earlier than usual and set off in search of Brigadier Cumberland's Tactical HQ. After crossing the Foglia I took the road through Montecchio, which had only finally fallen into our hands during the previous afternoon. My diary records: 'Montecchio hadn't one house wall standing. Dead and burning tanks on all sides.' It was the same story from here northwards for the next mile, all of which lay within the Gothic Line; the remains and debris of the previous day's fighting were widely scattered.

Just short of the Dragoons' intermediate objective, we came to 5 Armoured Brigade's Tactical HQ. I introduced myself to the Brigadier, explaining my interest in his battle on behalf of Army HQ, and found him to be one of those who go out of their way to make even junior staff officers welcome in such circumstances. He was just off to visit the Strathconas, who had been involved in fighting for much of the night, and invited me to accompany him, so I followed for half a mile before we left the road and headed steeply up the slopes of the hill that had just seen nearly twenty-four hours of fighting.

We found Lieutenant Colonel McAvity by his tank, still reorganizing his regiment after the battle. The wounded had all been taken care of and the dead were being searched for and counted. Some tanks were still burning and most of the others were showing their scars, but everywhere there was activity, as crews went about their many tasks. Though I had not seen him before, there was no mistaking the CO, his eyes still ablaze with excitement and everything about him in need of unwinding. His RHQ, next to 'B' Squadron, had been in the thick of the fighting during most of the hours of darkness, as enemy para-troops in large numbers had infiltrated within the Strathcona's laager, fired by a suicidal impulse to sell their lives as dearly as possible. McAvity had shared responsibility with the CO of the Perths through-out the night from his command tank, shouting into his wireless headset above the din of battle, and was now exercising command by hoarse whisper. By this means he described to the brigade commander the course of events during the night. It was a moving and inspiring account, unforgettable mainly, perhaps, because of the way in which not only his own spirit, but that of the regiment, came through. No man can, from the inside of a tank in the middle of the night, inspire others to risk their lives unless they are already motivated. On this occasion the motivation was mutual and, as the account unfolded, the Brigadier interposed from time to time with a question or note of appreciation, as he sought to relax the tension with understanding and good humour following such a testing experience.

Such a night of sustained counter-attacks by enemy infantry, who fought as though their own lives were of no account, would impose mental and physical strains on the most resolute defenders and when talking to some of them later I was not surprised to notice that a few faces had hardened. In that short period, the Gothic Line saw some of the most brutal fighting of the campaign, during which the spirit of the contestants had more effect on the outcome than the equipment and support at their disposal.

The previous three days had provided a multiple experience which probably left Lyons and me as tired as many of those who had been engaged in the fighting. I had found that observing, moving around and keeping in touch with events from the fringe of a constantly moving battle, though in itself a privilege, was at times not without the temptation – sometimes the necessity – to assist, or at any rate to become involved, if only on the periphery. Sometimes neither privilege, temptation nor invitation had much to do with it; we would find ourselves at the 'receiving end' like everyone else. In addition to being tiring, it was occasionally emotional, as is understandable when one is fully committed. As Lyons drove me back to HQ I felt as if I, personally, had been through much of what I had seen. We were both, I think, exhausted.

The previous day, Eighth Army Main HQ had moved forward and was now only about a mile from the Adriatic, midway between Ancona and Pesaro. I was aware of this and as we approached the new location, late on 1 September, I had nothing in mind beyond making my report and getting some rest. First, though, I had to find my tent in which to make myself more presentable, before meeting the Brigadier. When I found it, I was surprised to see most of my kit still unpacked. I saw my batman approaching, as if he had something to say, and was about to have a somewhat terse conversation. I can hear him now, retorting in response to my displeasure about the total lack of preparation:

'But haven't you heard, sir?'

'Heard what?'

'You're leaving early in the morning – back to the UK!'

The duty officer in HQ RAC confirmed that a signal had arrived that morning, posting me to 3 Recce Regiment in Normandy. I was to move as soon as possible and to report to my personnel branch in the War Office after arrival in London. In the meantime, I was to leave early the following morning for HQ AAI in Rome, where I would be given further instructions. My memories of the next few hours are blurred. I reported to Brigadier Ivor Moore to discuss the various actions I had observed during the battle and I hope I thanked him adequately for all he had done on my behalf. After that I had much more to do and only had a few hours sleep before rising at 0600.

Tired though he was, Lyons offered to drive me to Rome and, according to my diary '...in spite of a hold up when we ran into 1 Armd. Div. and one puncture we did the 200 miles over the Apennines in 6 hrs and a quarter. A very fast trip.' [The state of all roads in Italy at this time varied between poor and almost impossible.]

In Rome I was relieved to find that all arrangements had been made for my departure by air to the UK. When dismissing Lyons for his return journey across Italy I could hardly have failed to show my appreciation for his services. He was always cheerful, had done remarkably well – often in tricky situations – and was a talented and very promising young soldier; I hope he survived the war and flourished in later life. Years later I tried to trace him, but had left it too late to do this through regimental channels.

On Sunday 3 September, the anniversary of the Anglo-French declaration of war, I had another early start in order to catch my flight. The route for the day was Rome-Naples-Tunis-Oran-Casablanca, which we reached at 2300 hours. My diary adds: 'Flew all the way in a Dakota – plenty of room. A long and tiring day covering nearly 2,000 miles.' The following day it continues:

> Weather bad but just good enough for flying.
> Dep Casablanca 1040. Arr St. ? Cornwall 1640. Rather a more pleasant trip, this time in a Liberator. The sight of Cornwall on this sunny but windy day was most inspiring.

After a short pause I continued my journey overnight by train to London, arriving early the next morning. One priority was to find a barber for a long overdue haircut, before visiting the War Office. I was still in KD (Khaki Drill) as worn in the Middle East, and it certainly confused the barber whom I remember as being in a talkative mood:

'You look as if you've seen a lot of sun lately, sir. Been on holiday?'

'Not exactly; I've been in Italy,' I replied.

'How interesting. I didn't know you could do that these days – it must be a nice place – peaceful too,' he added thoughtfully. 'You know, London's becoming quite dangerous with all these flying bombs about.'

I sympathized with him and we parted on the best of terms. After that I missed breakfast and my sense of duty faltered, as I reversed the remaining two priorities. My diary records:

> ...as I was in such a hurry, I visited Jeffery's and talked guns hard for ½ hour. Eventually I left with a nice pair on trial (£200). Then I visited AG 17 WO [War Office] and was granted 7 days leave. They seemed to expect me which was rather surprising and my opinion of them generally went up quite a bit. I caught the 12.15 and was met at Newcastle at about 7.15 by Father.

I omitted to note in my diary that, having missed breakfast, I thought I would treat myself to a meal at the Savoy Hotel, but was refused entry by the maître d'hôtel because, being in KD shirt and trousers, I was, in his view, 'improperly dressed'.

To start with I was not sure that I needed leave; by now the Allied armies were bursting out of Normandy and there was excitement in

77

the air. The last thing any keen, young officer would be looking for at such a time was home leave, but, having said that, I certainly enjoyed it and before long was even prepared to admit that it made sense. My father, who until lunchtime had no idea I was not still in Italy, reacted just as I would have hoped by organizing, with the help of the keeper, a partridge shoot the following day around Beamish Hall, where he often went. Situated six miles from the centre of Newcastle, today, where we shot partridges, you will find the North of England Open Air Museum. That day was an ideal antidote to the lively times of recent weeks, and by the evening the two of us had shot seven and a half brace of grey partridges and two 'various'. Dinah excelled herself, the Jeffery gun I used was a great success and we returned home after walking many miles in open countryside, with our tails up and good appetites. Five days later I caught the overnight train to London, on my way to France.

Chapter Seven

Normandy and Beyond

For they had learned that true safety was to be found in long previous training, and not in eloquent exhortations uttered when they were going into action.

Thucydides – of the Spartans
at the Battle of Mantinea, 418 BC.

From London there was a well-trodden reinforcement route to France, via Lewes and Newhaven, which I followed as one of a group of some thirty officers heading for the British Liberation Army. At Newhaven I sensed a hint of flexibility in the system, though my diary notes that, '...a lot of persuasion was required to get me on today's "Skylark" draft'. However, having completed all the formalities, I embarked that evening and landed in France, close to Arromanches on the Normandy coast, where I was not surprised to find a shortage of direction when it came to 'onward routing'. The first move was to find out what was happening and, then, what means of movement might be responsive to diplomatic approaches.

The uncertainty was symptomatic of the military turbulence then sweeping through this part of northern France, as armoured columns radiated north and east in pursuit of the vast German forces in full retreat. It was an exciting time for everyone involved, and newcomers had to catch up with events as best they could, while the BBC provided continuous coverage, sometimes anticipating the fall or liberation of towns well before they happened. For the past few weeks the situation had been changing, as the Allied armies finally broke the stalemate and restored mobility to the battlefield. There was an atmosphere of excitement everywhere, with the enemy on the run and talk of an imminent total collapse. Attention centred on what, at the time, was referred to as the 'Falaise Gap', later known as the 'Falaise Pocket', a small area that had assumed immense importance some

79

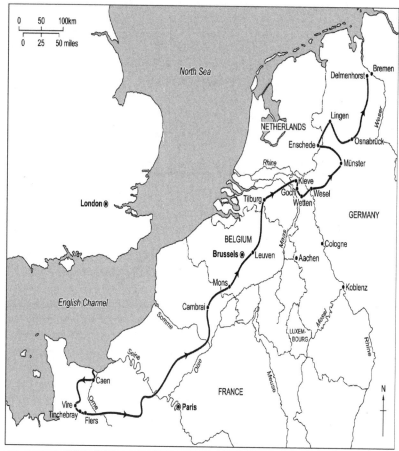

Third Reconnaissance Regt (RNF) Centreline
6 June 1944 - 8 May 1945

thirty miles south of where we were. This proved to be a vital battle, where the Germans showed the fatal tendency to stand and fight when logic demanded a strategic withdrawal. Even so, although for the Germans it was a disaster, the 'Falaise Pocket' yielded, at the most, only 60,000 men, compared with the nearly quarter of a million who had escaped across the Seine, denying the Allies the opportunity to strike the final blow. But now the whole log jam was on the move and there was a jubilant sense of relief, as the Battle of Normandy was decisively won.

Observing their well-established Geordie motto, 'Bash on, Recce', my own regiment had the good fortune to liberate a number of small towns and villages south of Caen and, in the face of significant oppo-

80

sition, had taken Flers, following which General Whistler, GOC 3 Div, had authorized a rum ration to the whole division. This was followed by a congratulatory visit to the regiment by Lieutenant General O'Connor, the Corps Commander. In Normandy, in towns and countryside alike, the people had been unforthcoming, although there was no hostility, but when the Allies pushed deeper into France the enthusiasm for their arrival increased and they were indeed greeted as liberators. After a brief rest 3 Div joined in the Allied pursuit from Normandy, which was spectacular and, to those involved in it, elating. There was widespread rejoicing, verging at times on euphoria, as Allied columns swept along their allotted routes, liberating millions of people who had suffered so much during more than four years.

From my own point of view it was a wonderful moment to arrive as the Second (British) Army, much of it still in Normandy, was strung out in a north-easterly direction over more than 300 miles. Somewhere along this axis, within this massive exodus, was 3 Div and, presumably, 3 Recce. My diary picks up the story:

> I started off to find an airfield from which I could fly to Brussels. I tried three without success and then planted myself down at one from which I caught a 'Sparrow' to Amiens, which is halfway. [Sparrow, shortened from Sparrowhawk, was the nickname for the US Army LS Sentinel, a four-seater communications light aircraft.] On the plane is a colonel who is also bound for Brussels and we plan to move off tomorrow in his borrowed Jeep.

The following day's entry begins purposefully *In the Field*:

> Made a very early start in the Jeep as soon as it was light and passed through Doulens, Arras, Cambrai and on to Brussels. From there forward to Louvain and eventually to Div HQ where I met Col Merriman who took me back to 'C' Squadron where we spent the night. Today I passed our old battle grounds of 1940. I stopped and thought it is all still so vivid I could write a book [!].

My first night back with 3 Recce was memorable because, not surprisingly, they were on the top of their form, following several days of stimulating exploitation in a traditional cavalry role, a brief rest and a trouble-free 'march' of nearly 300 miles to catch up and overtake those in front of them. As I had feared, there were many missing faces, including those of two majors that partly accounted for my arrival. Among the other ranks I missed were Charlton and Frazer, my former driver and batman, who had both been wounded, but among the old

81

friends still flourishing were Chips Jewell and George Fox, our padre, who was tireless in attending to his many duties. In an early letter home I also mentioned: 'I am the senior squadron leader, the oldest inhabitant by some considerable time, and the only officer in the Regiment now who was in France with it in 1940!'

In the days to come, as we went about our various tasks, I had opportunities to catch up with the news of other regiments, in most of which I knew, or had known, a number of officers. I was much saddened to find how many of them had become casualties.

The following day was 17 September, by when most of 3 Recce had concentrated near Peer, a small Belgian town on the border with Holland, south of Eindhoven, in readiness to assist in an opposed crossing of the Meuse-Escaut Canal. During the morning there was intense air activity by some hundreds of Allied heavy bombers, softening up targets ahead of us. This was followed by a lull, during which came a distant throbbing of more aircraft. As the sound rose in a slow crescendo, we saw the head of a mighty armada of transport planes approaching on a wide front, with no end in sight. By the time they were passing us, the sound had swollen to such a climax that conversation was impossible. As they receded, we were left guessing where they were bound, and with what purpose, though obviously an airborne drop was imminent. Before long we learned that we had been watching the United States 101st Airborne Division, one of the three divisions of the newly formed 1st Allied Airborne Army, engaged in Operation MARKET GARDEN. All were contributing to what Field Marshal Montgomery, as 21st Army Group Commander, referred to as '...the laying of a carpet of airborne troops' over five major obstacles: the Neder Rijn at Arnhem, the Waal at Nijmegen, the Maas at Grave and two major canals between the Meuse-Escaut Canal and Grave. It was an ambitious plan, surprisingly bold and, as it turned out, injudicious, which was not in keeping with Montgomery's style or reputation. Equally surprising, it was enthusiastically supported by General Eisenhower, who had recently assumed full command and had made the Airborne Corps available. Together they must share the responsibility, not only for the limited success of the operation but, as is now widely accepted, for getting the strategic priorities wrong.

As 3 Recce advanced into Holland, like everyone else we kept in touch with the news of the airborne landings ahead of us, and became familiar with the voice of, among others, Stanley Maxsted, on the BBC Home Service. After landing with 1st Airborne Division he reported from Arnhem, in tones that carried more meaning than he was

82

probably conscious of, but to his listeners he had the rare gift of conveying atmosphere, and I am just one of those for whom his voice remains unforgettable. No one who heard it could have failed to grasp the strain under which those men were fighting, or to be as moved as we were, closer, but not close enough to come to their aid.

As soon as we crossed the Dutch border we felt we were among friends, as people of all ages poured out their hearts to us, as if they had been counting every day since their army had been instructed by their leaders to lay down their arms, nearly four and a half years before. Now every face had a smile on it and every child was so overcome with excitement it was difficult for us to keep our minds sufficiently on our work. In the background, usually, but not always, out of sight, grimmer things were happening as rough justice was meted out to Quislings who had sided with the enemy and betrayed members of the Resistance and other patriots; lampposts in Hamont and doubtless in other towns were used for summary executions.

Soon, by remarkable coincidence, I found myself commanding the squadron I had joined when it was a motorcycle company in Newcastle in 1939. Apart from the very sad circumstances that led up to it (the death from meningitis of Major Terence Greenall), I immediately felt that of all possible outcomes this was the one I would have preferred, and I remained with the squadron for the rest of the war.

A few days after most of our airborne survivors had made their way back from Arnhem across the Rhine, some of them swimming, I wrote my second letter home from BLA. My aim was, as usual, to convey impressions of what was going on in the background to our work. Most of my letters were written at the end of a long day and the sense and clarity of writing often suggested haste and fatigue, so this one is probably a fair reflection of how I felt on the night of 18 September 1944. It begins with due greetings, including thanks for a splendidly warm jersey my mother had knitted, before picking up earlier strands:

It is wonderful being back in the Regt and I have not been so happy since I was last in the old Div. There are great changes and most of my old instructors are killed or wounded. I have seen Guy [Thornycroft] who is now 2nd in command of his Battalion. He is a great leader and quite unshaken. He takes a captured German shotgun round with him and shoots partridges when he is not shooting Germans. He is shooting both very well I hear.

The Regt is doing well and has already avenged Dunkirk and Arras which to us was so much more important. I can give you more details later on but our reception in this country [Holland] has been quite wonderful. The people are so genuinely glad to see us that their joy and rejoicing does one good to see. The troops love them and there is a great feeling of warm friendliness between us that I have not met in our relations with any of the other allies.

Today I went up a long drive well off the main road and came into a clearing in the wood at the end of it. In it was a lovely pretty little bungalow. The children came running out; they hadn't seen any British soldiers being so far from the road and they couldn't believe it was true what they had been told. They had to come up to my jeep and touch me one by one in order to convince themselves that it was true. It was very touching. The older people are just as moved and nothing is too much trouble.

The tenor of my account then changes. What follows is still a matter of historical fact and, as such, should not, in my view, be glossed over or ignored because in some eyes it may today appear distasteful, vindictive or irrelevant. I therefore reproduce it as the other side of the same coin, although I would not express my feelings retrospectively in the same terms:

> Their hatred of the Germans will never die and they loathe them with a bitterness that is very great. The Boche burns their farms as he goes back very often and pillages their homes and steals their cattle and hens etc. He is doing worse things, too, which will all be remembered on the day of reckoning.

Hate is an ugly word and, many would say, unchristian, regardless of circumstances but it crossed many lips during this stage of the war, as we became surrounded by evidence of how the Germans had ill-treated their neighbours during the previous five years.

After crossing the Meuse-Escaut Canal, 3 Recce pushed northwards, with several successful engagements while reconnoitring in open country, and had reached beyond Helmond before stronger forces of both sides joined in, including the US 7th Armoured Division 'who announced their intention of sweeping down through Overloon and Venraij'. However, during the next twelve days the US 7th Armoured Division failed to dislodge the Germans from Overloon and were relieved on 9 October. It was then that a unique story began.

Overloon was a medium-sized village in a sparsely populated area, four miles west of the River Maas and about twenty miles south of Nijmegen. Its population had already been forcibly depleted by the Germans to work on their defences east of the river and now the remainder, including women and children, became widely dispersed, as their homes were enveloped in violent fighting.

Concurrently our patrols were providing information that suggested there were at least two enemy battalions between Overloon and the river, but there was no means of knowing how many more there were to the south. 8 Infantry Brigade of 3 Div were entrusted with the attack on Overloon and Venraij, code named Operation AINTREE. The attack was planned from the start as a set-piece infantry operation, with all the other 'Arms' in support and 3 Recce was employed in holding the villages to the north-east, and maintaining observation on the river. For us in 3 Recce it was the beginning of a long association with the River Maas.

8 Brigade crossed the start line at 1200 hours on 12 October, supported by fifteen regiments of artillery, but before that there were extensive air attacks by American Marauder bombers and RAF rocket-firing Typhoons. However, although Overloon was virtually destroyed, many of the enemy defenders had sought refuge in the cellars and some emerged fighting as our Infantry confronted them. That day ninety-eight wounded men of 3 Div passed through its chain of advanced medical units, which were operating under most difficult conditions, including poor facilities, heavy rain and deep mud. But worse was to come during the battle of Venraij and the clearing up operations to follow; in nine days the number of wounded totalled 856 and cases of battle exhaustion 219. Close to 200 were killed.

Following most battles, and certainly those as hard fought as this one, there is time to reorganize and reflect. A soldier does not have to be physically wounded to be scarred, and there is much in the mind as well as the body that requires rest. Part of this process is in the hands of company officers, whose responsibilities include understanding symptoms of troubled minds, and behind them are the medical officers with specialist knowledge and experience. More difficult to define are the duties and expertise of the chaplains, referred to and addressed within the Army as padres. There is no precise definition of their duties, but, within broad guidelines, they minister to the needs of those associated closely, remotely or not at all with their own faith. George Fox, to whom I have already referred, was one of the best, with energy, understanding, compassion, humour and sense of duty. He also kept a diary, which has been reproduced for private circulation, and I quote, with permission, an entry he made only a few days after AINTREE:

23/10/44. We are still on the outskirts of Oploo [next village to the north of Overloon]. These last few days life has been very hectic in contacting all my units. Yesterday I had perhaps one of the most impressive evening services I have ever held, this one was held in a barn with straw on either side, the men fixed an electric light in one corner, and from the candles on the altar we all worshipped God – God was there and refreshed we went away.

Several of my letters home during this period referred not only to the friendliness of the Dutch people, but also to their stoicism, as they came to terms with the worst of misfortune: the loss of relatives, friends, homes, farms, stock and indeed the whole fabric of their lives. All this they bore during one of the most severe winters for many years and in the face of starvation unknown in their country in modern times. Yet they never sought pity, but continued to voice their gratitude for their liberation, leaving us at times lost for words, though often soldiers would exclaim, 'They are the heroes!'

Late in October the tide of war receded from Overloon, as 3 Div forced the Germans eastwards across the Maas and southwards beyond Venraij. Gradually the displaced inhabitants of the village, who had become widely scattered, began to return and some reoccupied what fragments remained of their homes, where they started to rebuild their shattered lives. It was a hard and sombre time for them because many of the younger men were still working under duress on enemy defences across the river and there were all the problems of caring for the young and elderly with no facilities and every manner of shortage.

Little more than six months after the war ended, restoration work began and was soon in its stride. In 1946 the Overloon Council announced, in the name of the community, that they had included in their reconstruction programme the building of a War Museum 'as a monument to honour the memory of the British soldiers who sacrificed their young lives at Overloon'. Over the years the museum prospered and expanded, though always retaining its original purpose. As it became more widely known, visitors came from all parts of the Netherlands and further afield including, as would be expected, pilgrimages by veterans of the regiments which took part in the battle. It was therefore of little surprise to learn in due course that it had been renamed the National War and Resistance Museum. What did come as a much appreciated surprise to the Old Comrades of 3 Div were the invitations, received by their associations and by individuals known to the museum, to attend the Commemoration of the 50th Anniversary of the Battle and Liberation of Overloon in October 1994. We, with our wives, were all bidden to join in a four-day visit to include ceremonies, social events, entertainments and the all-important visit to the enlarged museum. On the Saturday there was a 'Solemn Commemoration Session' in the 'new' church of Overloon, designed to take our thoughts back to the battle and then to span the achievements of the intervening years. Two speakers, one Dutch and one English, reminded us of the background, and gave résumés from their respective viewpoints. I made one or two notes from our host's address: '90,000 artillery shells were fired against targets in Overloon. The village was almost wiped from the face of the earth.'

On the final day, Sunday, 16 October, there was an uplifting service in the church, followed by a silent walk to the British War Cemetery where wreaths were laid, before the children of the village decorated each grave with a large red poppy made by them in school. Our own special host was Dirk Kuipers from Nijmegen who had been 'adopted' by 3 Recce during the campaign in Holland as its sole irregular. He belonged to Sergeant McCarten's troop and fought with them until the end of the war, dressed and equipped as a British soldier, though he did not receive any pay.

Our four days in Overloon could not have been more enjoyable and we made many new friends, but the highlight of the visit for both me and my wife was a quite outstanding play called *That Village does not exist any longer*, written in Dutch for the occasion and performed by a talented and committed cast, which included many children, drawn mainly from the neighbourhood of Overloon and Venraij. The story of what happened to Overloon and its inhabitants was movingly and, we felt, accurately portrayed, almost as if all those who were involved in it had pledged themselves to honour the faith, spirit and courage of a previous generation. It was an inspired performance and for over two hours we sat transfixed by the suspense, as the inhabitants of all ages reacted to every development, while their village was destroyed. The final scene opened with a stage empty save for a single chair set against the backdrop of the ruined village. A young man from Overloon stepped forward to conclude the play:

I have not lived though all this. In 1943 I was picked up by the Germans. In May 1945 I was set free in Sauerland, Germany, by the Americans. After the liberation I returned to Holland with some people from Dachau who could still travel. When I left the station in Deurne I stopped somebody and asked him:

'How did Overloon get through the war?'

'Overloon!' the man answered, 'that village does not exist any longer!'

I didn't know how to get to Overloon quickly. I ran more than I walked. In Merselo I borrowed a bike. I didn't recognize Overloon. I found our house, because on a wall destroyed by gunfire I saw the steel ring of the pump in the manure-pit. I walked around the wall to the part of the house that was still in use and knocked on a door. When the door opened I saw my complete family at table. I was the last to return home. My chair was ready.

It was not revealed until later that the young man was playing the part of his own father, fifty years before.

Chapter Eight

Winter Vigil on the Maas

From camp to camp, through the foul womb of night,
The hum of either army stilly sounds,
That the fix'd sentinels almost receive
The secret whispers of each other's watch.
                    William Shakespeare, *King Henry V*, Act IV, Prologue

Beyond the ruins and rubble that, until recently, had been Overloon, lay a scattering of peaceful villages closer to the River Maas, which the tide of war had not yet reached. Sadly, but inevitably, their turn would come. Among them was a trio, situated in a line parallel to the river and within a mile of it, called Vierlingsbeek, Groeningen and Vortum, all of which now lay in the path of 3 Recce Regiment. When 'B' Squadron reached Vierlingsbeek, they encountered stiff opposition and had to employ considerable effort and resources to capture this large village. Having done so, they were finally held up by strong enemy defences on the line of the Molenbeek, a tributary that joins the Maas within a few hundred yards. This became our southern boundary and constituted an open flank, of which the enemy did their best to take advantage, though their incursions were usually heavily punished.

3 Recce became closely identified as the custodians of these villages during that winter. A slow exodus began before we arrived and, sad though it was to watch, there was nothing we could do to influence it in any way; one side or the other was bound to be in occupation while the situation remained as it was. Moreover, having secured the villages, it became necessary to fortify them against all forms of attack and infiltration. It was a heartrending business and particularly so when in the presence of families who had the courage to stay and take their chance. They remained allies on whom we could depend, though their numbers lessened as we watched the trickle of people

89

moving west. As usual the farmers were among those who remained, many indefinitely, in order to tend their stock and show ownership to enemy foraging parties.

No sooner had we settled into our new positions than we were confronted by enemy fighting patrols, which were well led and aggressive from the start. For a week or more their identity remained a subject for conjecture, until we learned, through the Dutch Resistance, that we were facing the German 2 Parachute Regiment. It became clear, as soon as we learned who we were facing, that the challenge would require from our assault troops the highest standard of training, infantry skills and cunning, with continual emphasis on weapon handling, physical fitness and night craft. Thus we became involved in a succession of deadly serious games of hide and seek, played almost entirely at night, during which each side strove to outwit the other. Gradually the pattern of winter operations on the Maas took shape and our long winter vigil began. Here we would test our adversary and in turn would be tested by him. Not a yard would change hands until after the enemy eventually retired from the Molenbeek, and the Maas, whatever its height and mood, remained neutral. For many with the zest and stamina for what used to be rather quaintly referred to as 'proper soldiering', that bitter winter turned out to be one of the most challenging and interesting periods of the war.

By day it was all quite different, almost orthodox, with our own armoured car troops and supporting gunners providing continuous observation from OPs across the whole front. The higher these OPs were, the better and further they could observe, so both sides made full use of church steeples, which were closely watched and frequently engaged by the opposing artillery. One of the tallest was that of Afferden church on the right bank of the Maas, opposite Vortum, which was widely believed to be in use by day as an enemy OP. On 9 November self-propelled guns of 20 Anti-Tank Regiment RA from 3 Div removed the steeple, while observed by 'A' Squadron OPs in Vortum, just over a mile away. Without doubt there were always feelings of uneasiness, if not genuine regret, when a church was damaged, but, in the circumstances, hearts had to be hardened in the interest of the lives of our own troops. I feel quite sure that some Germans regarded it in the same light.

At the beginning of December, while the Maas was running at a high level and little was happening on our front, 'A' Squadron handed over its stretch to the 2nd Battalion the Royal Warwickshire Regiment as the first stage of a move out of the line by 3 Recce for a period of rest, recuperation and training. It was to prove a welcome respite, with just the right blend of work, play and the unexpected, that included a change from winter to 'winter plus'. The bitterly cold weather was reflected in letters home:

November 11...Winter comforts are going to be very difficult this year and much scarcer than usual though even more necessary. Can you do all you can to get people to make (a) Woollies (b) Gloves (c) Scarves? They [soldiers] can get socks from the Army and they wear well. But scarves are not issued at all and only one pair of gloves and one pullover are issued to each man.
December 15...Your wonderful parcels are arriving in swift succession.
December 27...The comforts really are appreciated. ...The cold has been bitter with the hardest frost I think I can remember. In an officer's room last night his bottle of TCP (large size) was frozen into a solid block and the bottle shattered. The vehicles are so cold that we have to take blow lamps to the brake drums of many of them every morning before the brakes will function; we have never had that before.

The highlight of Christmas 1944 for me, and I suspect for everyone who shared the same experience, was a concert for which George Fox had obtained three tickets. I described the evening to my parents:

Last night 3 of us went haring off at high speed in my armoured car to Eindhoven where we listened to the most wonderful concert by the Hallé Orchestra conducted by John Barbirolli. It was a real treat and how they were appreciated. Long after the end of the advertised programme we kept them playing encore after encore and still they kept playing for us. They were quite inspired by the appreciation shown and gave us nearly a whole extra hour of wonderful music.

When Barbirolli had managed to hush the applause, he explained that, much as the orchestra would love to go on playing, they would finish after one final encore. He raised his baton and paused. Then, from the first bar, every soul in the hall became entranced, as the orchestra surpassed itself, with a performance of such feeling and beauty that not a muscle twitched; tears rolled down faces that had not known them for years, as we listened enthralled to the *Londonderry Air*. There was a long, long pause after the music had drifted into total silence, then came one final rousing cheer, followed by clapping which continued, until eventually conductor and orchestra, smiling and waving, left the platform. Once outside, we all dispersed back to our units, many with hours of travel on potholed roads ahead of us, but everyone uplifted, thoughtful and less conscious than usual of that coldest of winters. Fifty years later I was able to discuss this tour with Lady Barbirolli and, from her, learned that J.B. had regarded it as one of the highlights of his twenty-seven years as conductor of the Hallé Orchestra. (Evelyn Barbirolli gives J.B.'s own account of this concert in her book *Life with Glorious John*.)

Nothing seemed to have changed as the New Year came in and we resumed responsibility for our stretch of the Maas from the Royals who, as an Armoured Car Regiment, had been caretaking for the last two weeks; enemy patrols were still active and the weather was no less demanding. Before long, however, Hugh Merriman called on me with some exciting news. He felt the time had come to take on the Paras on the other side of the river at their own game and outlined his ideas of how he intended this should be achieved. Moreover, the infantry battalions of 3 Div had been equipped with boats early in December 'for training with a view to patrolling at a later date across the Maas'. He forecast that shortly I should hand over command of the squadron temporarily to Andy Brough, my second in command, with the exception of three assault troops and a command element which he wished me to train comprehensively for river crossings and raiding operations by night. From the outset, he recognized the river itself as the major challenge, as the Germans must have done; it was fast flowing and wide – 250 yards at least on our part of the front at the time. He therefore wished every man who might be involved with river crossings to be fully proficient and confident under all conditions. When the time came, two experienced Sappers would assist us in boatmanship and aids to low level amphibious operations at night. Security was a major factor that precluded us from being seen training with boats within some miles of our area of operations. All those directly involved in raid training and operations would be known as WILFORCE.

When he had finished his briefing, Hugh asked for my reactions and I can remember my enthusiasm. Many of us were tired of watching the enemy retain his initiative at night from the time of our arrival west of the Maas. Now, at last, we were to have the opportunity to develop our own expertise and put the enemy to the test. From our early discussions on the employment of WILFORCE I could not have wished for a more straightforward plan, of which the CO's first paragraph of his *Notes on Proposed Raid over R. MAAS* read:

1. OBJECT

(a) Cross the river at about 782398 in approx strength of 2 officers and 20 other ranks.

(b) To lay an ambush on the AFFERDEN Rd anywhere from SOUTH wood at 795407 to one mile NORTH of this wood. This only to be carried out if it is considered possible as a result of recce.

(c) Bring back a prisoner if opportunity to take one should arise at any time during the operation.

The same directive also provided the dates within which the operation should be carried out, RA support, communications and so on. Because of the snow which, in daylight, would reveal our tracks, it was specified that the reconnaissance and raid must be undertaken on the same night. Our training went well from the start and there was a powerful spirit at work among all ranks. For my second in command I selected Lieutenant Denis Hodgetts, an excellent troop commander on whom I knew I could depend in all circumstances. He, with one trooper accompanying him, would carry out the reconnaissance to establish whether the route was clear or, if not, to try and gauge whether the patrol would be able to deal with any enemy encountered. The main body of the patrol consisted of two sections of eight men, including NCOs, under my command.

We knew from the start of our preparations that the weather was bound to play an important part and were right in assuming that the snow and low temperatures would remain with us. Soon it became clear that, for reasons beyond our control, the operation would have to take place within the period of full moon, and visibility would be a major factor in the choice of night; without some cloud cover at the least, we would be as vulnerable as by day. It was certainly as well that all our training had been carried out in snowsuits and that we had learned the importance of attention to detail with regard to dress, equipment and weapons. Anything that was not wholly white was wrong. The hoods of snowsuits restricted hearing and were discarded in favour of cap comforters bound with white linen. White flour was rubbed over faces and gloves and sprinkled in the hair. Where possible weapons and magazines were bound with bandage-like strips of white linen. We also had to study the choice of background and routes in connection with visibility. All this mattered and paid off on the night, as did the intensive training on river crossings which 'were carried out under all conditions of weather by day and night until it was felt that the crossing of the patrol would be the most straightforward part of the op'.

We had billeted ourselves in a group of farms situated out of the usual range of enemy patrols, where the men could be accommodated in the scrupulously clean unoccupied part of the cow byres. I was accompanied by my driver and wireless operator, Troopers Mitchelmore and Hastings, in one of these farms and they, both of whom were smart and intelligent soldiers with outgoing personalities, were soon invited into the kitchen where, in addition to the middle-aged farmer and his wife, there was an attractive daughter, in her early twenties. I was fully occupied with planning and training matters, but after a few days became aware of laughter, which was little heard among the locals during that winter.

There was no problem in keeping everyone occupied and, in response to a priority request, we received several sets of aerial photographs of the area in which we were interested, taken on a sortie flown as we waited. All members of the patrol then had to memorize the features on either side of our route and throughout the length of the road on which our ambush was planned in case, for any reason, anyone should become detached and have to make his way back independently. By this stage, observation of enemy activity had been stepped up, not overlooking the smallest detail. Several points of interest emerged, including a few minor changes within successive days around an isolated house lying back some distance from the east bank, until then thought to be unoccupied, because no smoke had been seen from its chimneys. Another set of aerial photos was requested, for, although these perceptive observations had no bearing on our impending raid, they might be of use later.

As our agreed window of opportunity for the raid approached, I was able to inform the CO that we were ready to go and it then became a matter of waiting for suitable weather. Three days passed, as we hoped for fog or snow, and then, with only two more days available, we decided to rely on cloud cover on 27 January, the night of the full moon. Everyone who needed to know was informed and we set off to launch the boats. It had originally been planned to float them down the Beek, a small tributary of the river east of Sambeek. Two days earlier, however, the Beek froze and a large wooden sledge had to be made to carry the boats most of the way by track. When tried out, this performed well in principle, but was extremely hard work, so we then harnessed a Jeep to the sledge and this worked admirably in another setting well clear of the river. Now it was put to the real test. All went well and I wished Denis Hodgetts and his companion good luck, before watching them set off with their boat crew. They were lost to sight before reaching the far bank, well downstream because of the strong current, and the boat crew returned in about fifteen minutes with a 'Nan Tare Roger' (Nothing to report).

Less than an hour later, my own patrol of two sections arrived at the river bank and we set off at once, reaching the far bank at the point intended, before following the same route as the recce patrol to the RV about half a mile away, using an old farm track as far as the chosen point. Here we lay down and waited for the recce patrol's return from the Afferden-Heyen road, another half mile beyond us. Before long Denis and the trooper appeared ahead of us walking briskly. They were slightly out of breath, but quite composed, and it only took a few seconds to learn what had happened:

'Sorry, sir, we've lost surprise. We found what looked like a disused trench just short of the road and got into it to watch and listen. Before long a pair of sentries came along heading straight for us. We had no option but to open fire before they spotted us.'

'Did you kill them?'

'Yes, without doubt – we couldn't have missed – they were almost on top of us.'

'Were you aware of any reaction?'

'Not that we could hear – we didn't wait.'

It was obvious they had done the right thing and I told them so. There is little time for thought in such situations, though the level of concentration is very high. I had two reactions: first, there was no future in our original plan and, second, it would be a hell of a shame to pack up altogether and go home. I called the section commanders to bring them up to date, then issued the briefest of orders. Every second we lost could matter; probably the alarm had already been sounded and the enemy would be looking for us. I decided to take No. 1 Section on a reconnaissance upstream and sent Denis, with No. 2 Section, back across the river.

As they left, I had a quick word with the remaining section and explained what I had in mind. We would follow the other party as far as the river, then choose a course parallel with the river, towards Afferden. This would take us past some massive wharves with a prominent building adjacent which, from our bank, showed no signs of occupation. We would move in arrowhead formation, taking our time, every man with his eyes skinned; they had been trained on these lines and knew just what was required of them. The sky was no longer overcast and the moon was illuminating the snow-covered landscape far more than we would have wished, but its angle was in our favour, should we encounter any enemy on the move. I was gambling on the unlikelihood of the enemy committing men to hours of watch in

95

exposed slit trenches in 20°F or more of frost. They would, I guessed, soon become useless in such conditions.

In a state of some expectation we made our way up the river, though not too close to it as to find ourselves at a disadvantage on 'contact', and we were abreast the wharves when, almost as one man, we saw two figures in snowsuits approaching us about 100 yards ahead. We dropped to the ground without signal, or command, and waited. They did not falter and the distance closed. It can be a matter of some importance, in this type of situation, how long to wait before opening fire. If too soon, it will be less accurate than after a few further seconds of delay, whereas by delaying too long an alert enemy will see or sense trouble; then the advantage is lost. The manuals of instruction at the time were still coloured by the 'Thin Red Line' complex, that called for fire orders to be shouted out as stentorian commands, as they were throughout earlier wars. However, by 1945, most of us had learned that, when small groups of well-trained men wish to achieve surprise, every weapon must be in the aim, with a finger on the trigger, waiting for the command to fire. No command is clearer or quicker than a bullet, or burst of fire, from the commander's own weapon, which on patrol was never a pistol. On this particular night, possibly owing to the moonlight, we might have waited another few seconds, although the outcome was advantageous for, instead of two dead Germans with no story to tell, we had one wounded and one unscathed. They were quickly disarmed and taken prisoner and, once again that night, time became critical because we knew that those two would have been part of a larger group, unlikely to be far away.

The wounded man was in considerable pain and quite unable to move. He was also heavily built, but somehow he had to be carried to a boat many hundreds of yards behind us. After covering 200 yards, which took us twenty minutes over very rough ground, the rear protection party warned that an enemy patrol was approaching. Again, either better visibility or superior alertness gave us the all-important initial advantage. This time there were ten of them to eight of us, with the added complication of two prisoners, one *hors de combat* and the other needing watching to prevent him from escaping while our attention was diverted. Between us we had two LMGs (light machine guns) and six Sten sub-machine guns with fixed bayonets. The CO's report written after his debriefing of the patrol the following day concluded thus:

This patrol approx 10 strong was allowed to draw level and was then engaged with two LMGs.

Casualties were inflicted. The enemy closed and a Section battle ensued. This lasted nearly an hour while our boat was brought close up under the bank and the two PW were evacuated. Our own patrol stuck to the river bank and the enemy moved round in the arc of a semi-circle. Three men were killed at short range and others were soon to be killed or wounded.

DF [Defensive fire, in this case from a field regiment RA of 3 Div Artillery] was called for to add to the noise and allow our patrol to disengage. The boat had returned to our bank and was waiting 200 yards down stream. Our patrol disengaged and prepared to cross the river. Smoke was most necessary as visibility down the river was now about 500 yds, and the enemy were using mortar flares in addition to SA [Small Arms]. This was called for [from 'A' Squadron mortars across the river] and as soon as it was effective the party crossed without incident. Our patrol suffered NO casualties.

Two days later a full report of the operation in 3 Div's daily Intelligence Summary contained a warming sentence, which was good for the squadron's morale:

Thus casualties were inflicted, locations discovered and a vital identification was brought home without loss to ourselves – a textbook patrol.

This all gave us much encouragement, for we had already been thinking ahead to the next venture across the river that would involve a recce patrol of three men operating independently, over ground well to the south of Afferden. There were convenient tracks we could use to take the boat to the river bank, the main one of which was screened from the far bank by trees and dead ground. This was used from time to time by our own squadrons when patrolling and, for this reason, was swept for mines at intervals. Accordingly when, on 2 February, I wished to take a boat by day down this route to a convenient hiding place I enquired when it had last been swept and was assured by RHQ this had taken place only two days before. I therefore detailed a small party to load an assault boat on to the back of a 4x4 armoured personnel half-track and half a dozen of us set off from Sambeek to the point where the boat would be offloaded.

We were approaching a track junction east of Groeningen, just short of our destination, when there was an ear-splitting explosion under the vehicle, which appeared to leap into the air before lurching to a stop over a large crater. Inside the vehicle there was a scene of chaos with debris, weapons and bodies scattered everywhere. I had been sitting behind the driver alongside Trooper Edwards, and I realized it was probably he who was on top of me. He made no effort to move and, being one of our larger men, I had some difficulty in extricating myself. Having done so I found he was dead, also that two others were wounded. The rest were, not unnaturally, shaken, but fit for duty. The crew of another vehicle, having heard the explosion, soon appeared and we got things sorted out and the wounded on their way. When I examined the wrecked half-track it was clear that it had encountered a more effective mine than we were used to and a Sapper was requested to give his opinion. He knew at once, when he saw the crater and what was left of the half-track, that the cause had been a 'double R mine', which the Germans laid when they wished to damage a road in addition to destroying a vehicle. A 'single R mine' was designed to immobilize and cause structural damage to a tank; two of them taped together were at least doubly effective. Later that afternoon I bumped into Chips, who at the time was second in command of 'B' Squadron. He was unaware that I had been involved in the incident a few hours earlier and we conversed for a while before I mentioned it, whereupon he offered me a mug of tea! In the circumstances I personally had little to complain of, though my hearing has never been the same since.

That night an enemy patrol entered Groeningen and was effectively seen off, leaving one dead and two POW behind. They, too, came from No. 5 Company, 2nd Battalion, 2 Parachute Regiment. They must have felt their luck was out, getting two black eyes within a few days. The enemy across the river would undoubtedly have heard, and probably pinpointed, the explosion and their patrol that night may well have been tasked to assess the outcome of their handiwork on their way to Groeningen. In any case, it behoved us to find another departure point for our impending recce patrol, which presented no problem. Two nights later Lieutenant Johnny Johnston and Troopers Johnson and Bulmanory crossed the river after last light, north of our intended launching area of two days earlier. Nothing happened for half an hour, and then in the distance we heard the reports of small-arms fire and exploding grenades. We waited for their return in vain and a troop remained until dawn, hoping for sight or sound of them. They failed to show up and some months later we got word that all three had been either killed or died of their wounds that night.

Before this ill-fated recce patrol came to grief, I had discussed with the CO an outline plan for another fighting patrol, for which we already had some excellent data. The proposed target was the small, isolated and slightly elevated farmhouse, of which we had requested aerial photographs earlier. It was far enough away from the river to be clear of the defences we had already encountered and the occupants might be less alert. I had also asked our Dutch liaison officer, who had access to certain clandestine sources, for information about the house and the family who owned it. After a few days, he reported that the family was no longer in occupation and, among other points of interest, the house was believed to have a cellar. This was worth knowing, because the enemy often used cellars for sleeping in. For a while, the lack of smoke from its chimneys, which we had under observation by day, had made us wonder if it was occupied, but photographs taken after a fresh fall of snow showed paths in use round the house, one of which led to a hedge about forty yards away, on the river side. With the help of a photo-interpreter, I concluded that the house was likely to be in use as an enemy OP by day and a listening post by night, and held by not less than six men. The short footpath on the river side was probably only used by night, most likely by a double sentry. There was a good choice of approach routes open to us and I was thinking in terms of a fighting patrol with a strength of twelve to fifteen all ranks, which should be strong enough to enable us to get the better of any enemy patrols we might encounter and provide plenty of fire support at the objective. Two of our most dependable men, physically strong and experienced in night fighting, would move ahead of the remainder, with instructions to use their initiative should the opportunity arise to deal with any sentries in silence; otherwise they would keep the house under close observation. Hugh Merriman accepted this approach and our preparations continued.

From the outset I was determined to avoid, if possible, becoming involved in fighting another rearguard action before re-crossing the river. My aim was to carry out the attack on the farmhouse in silence and not to try and take prisoners for intelligence purposes. On the previous raid they had slowed our progress considerably and almost been our undoing. This intention, however, would in no way affect our duty to take prisoner any enemy who surrendered to us. One of our main problems, therefore, was how to deal with the occupants of the farmhouse, assuming we had been able to dispose of the sentry or sentries in silence. From this stage we had to plan for two eventualities: first, some of them might be awake, in which case we would have no option but to use Sten guns to deal with them and hope the noise would be muffled inside the house or, secondly, they might all be asleep which, with two sentries mounted outside, was quite likely. It was the latter situation that began to dominate our thoughts and plans, and I was soon asked by one NCO what weapons I had in mind. At this stage I favoured bayonets, a scaled down model of which was now issued with the Sten sub-machine gun, which most of our men carried at night. No one demurred, though I sensed one or two took longer than others to come to terms with the possible need to use them on sleeping men. It is so much easier to remain at arms length by throwing grenades and then finishing the task with firearms which was, and no doubt still is, one of the standard procedures for dealing with enemy inside buildings. But this is likely to raise the alarm and all advantage will be lost to the attackers.

So, where does the impulse come from to act silently against men caught unawares? Where ethics are concerned – such as they exist in this context – a notional distinction *may* be possible between, on the one hand, attacking by stealth an armed enemy who is off his guard, with the intention of killing him and, on the other, attacking a sleeping enemy with the same intent; the first should be capable of defending himself, the second will not. The practices of others can be cited; our own Special Forces when operating behind enemy lines would rarely be in a position to make any distinction – the slightest hesitation could jeopardize their own survival. If that is accepted, as it must be, might a fighting patrol on the wrong side of a wide river not find itself in a comparable position? Such preoccupations with 'fair play' and ethics were, in my experience, shared by few of our friends and allies. The Goums from French Morocco, who specialize in silent killing and who were part of the French Expeditionary Corps on the left of the British Eighth Army in Italy, are in a class of their own and often leave one enemy, and one only, to sleep on – a practice not unconnected with their enemy's morale. The Gurkhas certainly use their kukris in silence when opportunities are presented, but we do not share their expertise. The solution remained elusive, yet I felt reluctant to rule out any 'acceptable' option in case it might suddenly appear as the right and natural course of action. When the lives of one's own soldiers have to be weighed against those of the enemy the answer is usually easy. War is war.

As far as WILFORCE was concerned there was a dual, if not triple, intervention that aborted the raid shortly before it was due to be launched. First, the thaw came with unexpected suddenness as the temperature rose, causing the Maas to flood; second, General Montgomery launched an offensive on 8 February to clear the enemy from east of Nijmegen, southwards through the Reichwald Forest, in preparation for the crossing of the Rhine and, third, on the same day 3 Recce received orders to move back into Belgium to prepare for more important things than mounting or countering minor operations across the River Maas.

In retrospect, the reason why the memory of 'the raid that never was' still returns to me more often that I would wish must be obvious. The idea of killing an enemy while he is asleep and defenceless, even were he to be wearing the SS insignia on his tunic, may be one stage beyond the point where the most determined of British soldiers would willingly go. Recently I began to search for the ethical guidance that we lacked at the time, and was not unduly surprised when I failed to find any. A friend who works for the Imperial War Museum told me that he had never been asked about this before. 'Could it be,' he mused, 'that the intention was to keep this subject woolly in order to avoid a complex and probably inconclusive debate?' I think he may be close to the truth and, knowing something of the subject, I believe it may prove beyond the wisdom of man to improve on the status quo.

Looking back now, I can recollect the momentary regret many of us felt, when the raid was cancelled, that we were thwarted in our efforts fully to assert our advantage over an enemy who, until recently, had had too much his own way. Yet now, sixty years later, I must admit that my conscience is almost certainly easier than it might be, had the operation taken place successfully, with its aim achieved in silence among sleeping men.

Chapter Nine

Operation VERITABLE

And my dark conductor broke
Silence at my side and spoke,
Saying, 'You conjecture well:
Yonder is the gate of hell.'

A. E. Housman

The last night of our Maas vigil, 7 February, was marked by the opening of the battle for the Rhineland which, in just over one month, dredged the depths of human suffering among those who bore its brunt. 3 Recce Regiment had its orders to hand over its positions on the Maas, prior to a period of rest, vehicle maintenance and training. In fact, the whole of 3 Div was withdrawn for the same purpose to an area east of Brussels, with the expectation of being out of the line for the remainder of the month. Consistent with this, no whisper had reached our ears of any imminent offensive, nor was any envisaged by us because of the impossible weather conditions, but that night our preparations for the forthcoming move were interrupted, as a continuous stream of aircraft from RAF Bomber Command passed overhead and began to attack the towns of Goch, which lay some five miles to the east of us, and Cleve to the north of it. Even at that distance it was an awesome spectacle. It was a relentless onslaught, which seemed to go on for hours through the middle part of the night, stoking up the fires and adding to the distant explosions and reverberations, as the deluge of bombs continued. At the time we had no idea what was the purpose of two such devastating raids against two small towns; attacks on such a scale were usually reserved for Germany's war production in the Ruhr.

The following morning 3 Recce Regiment handed over its positions on the Maas to 52 Recce Regiment of the Lowland Division, before wending its way back, through Holland, into Belgium. It was a slow journey, over deteriorating roads following winter frosts and exceptionally heavy use as a supply route. Along the way it was the people, once again, who took our attention. There was a noticeable change in the demeanour of the jubilant folk who had waved us through six months earlier. They were still as friendly as before, but the sparkle had gone from their eyes, which now reflected war weariness and the debilitating hardships that were facing the majority of the population after what had become known as the 'Hunger Winter'.

After a few weeks out of the line we became embroiled in Operation VERITABLE, about to enter its third week. On 24 February, 3 Recce Regiment spent the night near Tilburg, from where, according to its history, 'it sent forward the carrier troops of 'A' and 'B' Squadrons, under the command of Major Wilson, to help out 1 East Yorkshire Regt of 8th Infantry Brigade who had taken over rather an extended front from 15th Scottish Division'. Our crossing of the Maas, at Gennep, was made by means of the longest Bailey bridge any of us had ever seen and three miles further along a road, before it bifurcated to Cleve and Goch, we crossed the frontier into Germany, just short of the Reichswald Forest.

Re-entering Germany after nearly seven years was, for me, a profoundly symbolic experience. There was positively nothing anticlimactic about it, as so many of us found about the end of the war little more than two months later; rather it was a threshold, reached at last, from which another whole and utterly different story would begin. And because both sides of the frontier looked alike – the same species of trees, the same smells, the same sky – I tended to concentrate on the people. This is what we really wanted to see – Germans. How would they appear when confronted by their enemies, invading their homeland? Would there be guilt, shame, arrogance or indifference? These and countless more questions had been going through our minds for months, and if we thought the answers would be waiting for us we were wrong. Here there were no Germans, and the first we were likely to meet would be soldiers fully armed, ready and waiting to do their duty. The only sense of change was in the mind.

What *was* going on in our own minds? I believe, by this stage, the feelings of retribution, which had earlier been uppermost, had given way to a sense of relief, that from now on the war was going to be fought to its conclusion mainly on German soil, rather than within friendly countries. It was natural that our thoughts were still close to the Dutch, whose land, stock, homes and even lives we had helped to put at risk during nearly six months. How long the war would continue no one could foresee, but the writing was on the wall and nothing was going to prevent the Allies from overrunning Germany within months.

I had been told that my ad hoc force of seven carrier troops (six carrier-borne assault troops and one of support weapons) would come under command of 2 East Yorks, taking over from two rifle companies of 6 Battalion Royal Scots Fusiliers, and I soon located the area where we were intended to dig-in, between 2 East Yorks and 1 Suffolks. Here, in rather scrubby country with a scattering of trees, I was able to find good defence positions and was soon joined by my troop commanders, three of whom belonged to 'B' Squadron. I had been delighted to find earlier that one of them was Sergeant Harry McCarten, who had been in my platoon in the early days of the war and whom I had not seen for several years. He was now commanding 10 Troop, in an appointment usually held by an officer.

There was no time to be lost, because of the need to be dug in before dark. Already parts of the area were looking war-torn, and it was still attracting enemy artillery and mortar fire at frequent intervals. After I had shown most of the troop commanders their areas and they had gone to fetch their men and vehicles, McCarten and I were standing only a few yards apart, when the area around us suddenly erupted with explosions, as a salvo of *Nebelwerfer* rockets landed without warning. One of them apparently propelled me several yards with its blast, knocking me out briefly in the process. I came to after a few seconds, surrounded by smoking craters, the nearest of which was very close. Almost at once there was a hand on my shoulder and a familiar voice shouted, 'Are ye aal reet, sor?' As I sat up, McCarten concluded I had suffered no serious damage and exclaimed: 'Ye bugger, I thowt we'd lost ye!' There was a short pause before he added, with his characteristic smile, 'It's just like aad times!' Such interludes, however brief, are invaluable in restoring one's equilibrium when under pressure. At the time, I was totally unaware that he himself was wounded in the head, and he managed to conceal it from me until it had been dressed, after which he remained at duty. How we were not both written off I cannot explain, but it strengthened my belief that it is difficult to exaggerate the value on the battlefield of soldiers like Harry McCarten.

After we had returned to the assembly area, I was leading my head-quarters group, including signallers, stretcher-bearers and others, towards the perimeter of our new positions, when I saw a slow-moving snake of 'Jocks' approaching in single file. As we closed on them, everything about hem suggested that they were totally exhausted. They were commanded by a young officer, in so far as he

104

was managing to lead the way, and he passed us in silence, with no sign of recognition, as did the remainder, some of whom were wounded or otherwise in need of support. The last man to pass was *in extremis*, semi-conscious and trailing his rifle by the sling, its muzzle in the mud. There was nothing we could do for them as they passed us and the worst thing at that moment would have been to delay them; several would have slumped to the ground at once. My mind went back to Dunkirk, but the comparison was unfair; these men had given all they had during a succession of exceptionally bloody actions, which had begun more than two weeks earlier, and they deserved admiration as well as sympathy. The sight of men coming out of action too exhausted to recognize their own contribution to the successful outcome of the Reichswald battle was indeed a sad one and has left a haunting memory.

By late evening, we were fully prepared and settled into our defence positions. Earlier, I had heard from a Scottish guide that they had been shelled and mortared liberally in recent days, and had suffered a number of casualties as a result. The prospects for an untroubled night were not good. I ordered all troop commanders to ensure that no one would leave his trench during the hours of darkness, except in emergency. This would permit the presumption that all movement in the open was likely to be hostile, which enabled challenges to be reduced to a minimum before opening fire. Although the moon was full, it was obscured by thick cloud and visibility was restricted.

I guessed that, if a firefight were to open up, our main problem might be more concerned with our own fire control than with the enemy, for we had the firepower to take on a much stronger force than he was likely to have at his disposal. Although we were reasonably dispersed, we had some 200 men on the ground, mostly equipped with a light machine gun or automatic. There was, therefore, a need for everyone to be mindful of his neighbours before opening fire.

Well before midnight, the first of a series of enemy incursions took place within our defended locality and, after each challenge, to all of which there was no response, fire was opened. There appeared to be no cohesion linking these intruders and I concluded they were either probing for information, from which an attack might follow, or they were small parties of stragglers who had been cut off and were attempting to regain their own lines. Before long we knew we had drawn blood when a series of piercing screams, denoting a serious wound, came from a position not far in front of my own HQ trenches. A sporadic firefight ensued, during which the screams of a man in agony continued unabated and the enemy's fire, far from being suppressed, appeared to increase. Not for the first time, I felt there was a callous streak in evidence. There was something in the mental attitude of the most ruthless Germans that made them at times as impervious to the suffering of their own comrades as they were towards their enemies. In this instance, their fire appeared to be directed more towards the area in which the wounded man lay than elsewhere. After a lapse of time, it became clear they had no intention of effecting a rescue, but rather may have been using their unfortunate comrade to lure us into doing it for them. While some Germans would have felt constrained to hold their fire in such circumstances, there were too many others, certainly in the First Parachute Army, who would have deliberately used any such opportunity to even the score. For this reason I had already decided to do nothing, although no one could have been unmoved by the plight of a man remaining in such pain without attention. Had he been one of our own, there would have been no shortage of volunteers, but the Army's slogan with which we had been trained since the early days of the war had made its mark: 'Know your enemy.' In the meantime, every man within earshot had this diversion on his mind, to the detriment of his attention to what the rest of the enemy was up to; at times I could detect muted voices, which were indicative of a loss of concentration.

It was during a pause in the firing, as the screams were now alternating with moans, that a Geordie voice was raised in one of the troops closest to me: 'Hey, Mattie, just shift yor fior to the reet – we're away oot te fetch thon bugger in – mevvies ye can giv wa sum coverin' fior – but not ower cloose, mind.' Then, as a barely audible afterthought: 'The bugger's gettin on wor bloody norves.'

The covering fire was immediately forthcoming, and a short period of tension followed while we waited. In less than a minute the screams were moving in our direction and soon two figures carrying the wounded German arrived at my trench. I led the way to a trench not far behind where our medical orderlies were waiting, with a syringe of morphine. They put him on a stretcher and carried him into the makeshift aid post, which was little more than a hole in the ground without any facilities. Then we waited for the screams to stop, while his wounds were examined and dressed. He was still fully conscious, with multiple bullet wounds, and I have never seen anyone in such agony. We hoped the morphine would soon take effect, but this was over optimistic. I told the medical orderly to administer another shot of morphine, but was informed that it might kill him. I hesitated, while contrary advice persisted from others less qualified: 'Put the bugger oot of 'is misery' came through loud and clear.

It was one of those situations that fitted the old Army dictum: 'Right or wrong, make your mind up.' I took the view that, by this stage, if the enemy in our vicinity were able to report our position they would probably have already done so. But I also felt unable to risk taking the life of a wounded POW. I therefore passed the word round that he would leave us at first light and I wished for no more advice from anyone. His screams and moans, though weaker, continued until we were able to put him, still alive, into the hands of the RAMC an hour or two later. Although our night had been unpleasant, it had not been unsuccessful. We accounted for a number of enemy, one of whom was not far from my own trench. The following day the advance was resumed, with the village of Winnekendonk as the final objective. This time 3 Recce took the lead and had a good run with Typhoon support from the RAF, before the Lincolns went through to attack the village at last light.

It was vital in fast moving battles to ensure that no vehicle commander ever lacked the correct map. These were rapidly provided as we moved forward and, on occasions, captured enemy map paper had been utilized. I still have one such map, of the area north-east of Frankfurt, printed by our own Royal Engineers on the reverse of a German map of the Harrogate area of Yorkshire, produced in 1940 when Hitler was planning the invasion of England. As we progressed the old problem of mines returned, causing the loss of two Daimler heavy armoured cars. On 3 March 'C' Squadron made excellent headway, capturing Kevelaer and Wetten, together with two demolition parties in the act of preparing charges on two bridges over the River Niers. They were later held up by an enemy SP gun and tragically Lieutenant Ferguson, whose troop was prominent throughout, was killed. This spoilt an otherwise splendid day, which included the capture of more than 100 POW.

From this stage in the clearance of the Rhineland, conditions improved and the momentum increased until, at last, the Rhine itself came into sight. For all those who got their first glimpse of the great river, it was a moment of immense relief as they emerged from what Bolo Whistler referred to as the 'a******e of Germany', an appellation which soon caught on among those who had shared the miseries of the previous month. For the next two weeks Germany would have to share the *Die Wacht am Rhein* with others. (*The Watch on the Rhine* was taken from a poem written in 1810 by Schneckenburger and became the title of one of Germany's most popular national songs.)

Following these operations, 3 Recce Regiment was relieved of all duties on 4 March in order to rest and prepare for what was yet to come. An air of optimism was spreading throughout the Allied Armies and within those countries that had suffered most at the hands of the Germans. While the British and Canadians had been closing up to the lower reaches of the Rhine, the Americans had been conforming, and here and there setting the pace, to the south. However, there were still German rearguards holding on grimly within fast-shrinking areas close to the west bank of the Rhine, one of which contained the approaches to Cologne.

A day or two earlier, an intelligence summary issued by 3 Div had observed that 'Cologne is in imminent danger of capture'. After giving this some thought, I had an idea I was soon discussing with Hugh Merriman. I suggested to him that there could be lessons learned in Cologne which might be applicable later to other towns on our future 'centre-line', where we might meet similar situations, albeit on a smaller scale. I then mentioned that I had spent some weeks in Cologne, before the war, and this could be an advantage in finding my way around. He required no further convincing and gave me permission to leave as soon as we heard that the city was in American hands. My timing was right, for the news came over the wireless later that day, 6 March, that the city had fallen. Early the following morning I set off in a jeep, in order to attract less attention among our Allies, accompanied by Hastings and Mitchelmore, on whom I could always depend. The journey of little more than fifty miles was without incident, though it was slow because of all the damage caused to the roads by the German Army, in order to delay the Allied advance.

As we wended our way round endless craters and diversions, I tried to picture what we might find in Cologne after all the bombing. I guessed I would be in for a shock, yet what I visualized bore no resemblance to what we actually found in the stricken city. I certainly had no conception of the damage until I saw it. My first concern was the fate of Cologne's dominant feature, the Dom, Germany's greatest cathedral, to which I had been introduced by the Blasnecks. As we approached the city, I could not conceive any way by which such a vast building, situated at the focal point in the layout of the city, next to one of the largest bridges spanning the Rhine, could escape destruction or, at least, major damage. I was wrong again. While we were still several miles short of the city, the first features to break the skyline were the familiar twin spires of the cathedral, rising to more than 500 feet to proclaim its message as a creation of men to the Glory of God. At that moment I experienced a feeling of profound relief.

Eventually my crew and I arrived in the shadow of the cathedral, to behold what countless Germans have since regarded as a miracle.

There it was, intact, with a few scars, but nothing beyond repair. All around was total destruction, a knocked out German Tiger tank in the foreground, still smoking, bearing witness to the recent fighting. Close by was the Hohenzollern bridge, broken and twisted, like a Meccano creation, come to grief and abandoned by a tired child at bedtime but, in this case, just one of nearly thirty in a similar state, spanning the Rhine throughout its length. Part of the rubble was what had been the world-class Kaiserhof Hotel. There, before the war, a splendid dinner, with turbot, had been rudely interrupted by one of Hitler's brown-shirted storm troopers, with swastika armband, stifling conversation until all diners had contributed to *Partei* funds before we were at liberty to continue with our meal. A faint look of embarrassment had crossed my host's face as I declined to contribute, but nothing was said.

Late in the day, as I had intended from the start, I set course for the residential suburb of Köln-Junkersdorf, with the hope of finding my way back to Auserka and the Blasnecks. I realized that the reunion, if there was to be one, would not be easy, but first I had to find my way across a four kilometre stretch of Cologne and its environs. All of it had suffered from bombing and some of it had been fought over. Many were the diversions and I began to wonder if I would be able to find the house, though I recognized landmarks from time to time. At one point I found a GI in a stationary bulldozer, scratching his head while trying to plot his position on a crumpled copy of an old town plan. Though unsure of his own whereabouts, he was most obliging in helping me on my way and before long I found the name of the road I was seeking, on a directional sign off the main road.

I recognized Auserka more from its situation and its immediate surroundings than from the house itself that, though mostly still standing, was heavily damaged, with half the roof missing. The garden, which had been the Blasneck's pride and joy, was a shambles, with bomb craters in full view beyond. I stood for a while lost in thought; there above me, with part of an outer wall missing, was what remained of the bedroom I had occupied. Stepping round debris and broken glass, I eventually came to the remains of the front door, to which a card had recently been pinned, for it was quite clean and unweathered. Written in a shaky hand, it simply informed visitors that Frau Blasneck had lost her life and the Doktor had been evacuated to another address. Any meeting with him would have been difficult for both of us and I was relieved he was not at home.

I felt sad, not out of any feeling of remorse, for that did not apply, but for other understandable reasons. I had been their guest and they had been hospitable and helpful with my studies. They were also the two Germans whom I had known best. But, like most of their countrymen, they had been duped into accepting National Socialism, if not actively becoming involved in it. I remembered the Doktor's last words to me: 'War? There are no signs of war here.' Sad, indeed, it was.

Chapter Ten

'Over the Rhine, then, let us go'

Over the Rhine, then, let us go. And good hunting to you all on the other side.

From Field Marshal Montgomery's personal message
to 21 Army Group, 24 March 1945

The 'eve of battle' during the Second World War, unlike Agincourt, was apt to be a flexible prelude. Apart from the logistical build up necessary to sustain each offensive, it often needed days, or even weeks, in which to deploy large forces. The crossing of the Rhine was just such a case. Thus, some divisions had longer to wait than others and the question might arise how, within units, to avoid the tedium caused by repetitious preparation, whether in training, care of arms and vehicles, planning or administration.

I found myself wondering how to occupy my squadron and, if possible, stimulate their interest with something out of the ordinary. A letter home, written near Wetten and dated 18 March, described the solution:

Generally speaking life at present is quite pleasant though habitable houses in these parts are few and far between. As we moved into our present surroundings in a rather thickly wooded area of pines, I ordered all the troops to build themselves log huts of the real 'log cabin' type. I gave them 2 days in which to do it and offered prizes in cigarettes for the best. The results have been astounding; a number of really strong and durable huts sprang up and the designs are many and various. Most are very picturesque and all have windows in, the glass being got from garden frames and windows which have not been broken. Some of the huts will be standing for years to come.

As the Allied armies continued to close up to the Rhine, it became increasingly obvious that the seriously weakened Germans could no longer stabilize their remaining salients west of the river. One final offensive by the Allies was necessary, in which the crossing of the Rhine on a broad front would lead to the final checkmate. In the context of the Rhine crossing we saw that classic combination of outstandingly successful commanders and battle experienced troops on top of their form; there were no war-weary troops in evidence during the final stages of this long and bitter struggle. Even so, all the effort and achievement on the ground was fully matched in the air by Allied air forces, whose contribution before and during the land battle was immense. Watching and listening to much of this aerial activity, it was obvious that PLUNDER itself must be close; what we were eagerly awaiting was the massive artillery bombardment that would herald the ground offensive. This came at 2100 hours on the night of 23 March, when 3,500 field, medium and heavy guns opened the greatest artillery barrage of the war, much of it in support of the 51st (Highland) Division, which was the first to cross the river to form a bridgehead in the Rees sector and went on to achieve spectacular success.

There followed two days of intense activity, as routes were cleared through the rubble of Wesel and the bridgehead was expanded to admit the passage of a succession of formations, the leading one of which was to be 6 Guards Armoured Brigade. On the evening of 26 March we were ordered to move from our harbours, some miles west of Wesel, in order to cross the river over an American rubber pontoon bridge that had just been completed, in record time, opposite the ruined town. The approach march during the night was not uneventful, first due to some impressively fast and low flying by a few determined *Luftwaffe* pilots, who attacked our column and, second, from some misdirected light anti-aircraft artillery, thought to be American. They had been sited to protect the bridge and the routes leading to it but, unfortunately, when depressing their guns to engage the highly skilled *Luftwaffe* airmen with cats' eyes, they failed to take account of our vehicles, some of which were directly in their line of sight and, as a result, we had several casualties. The air around our Geordie column remained blue until we reached our bridge.

As we crossed the river, the significance of the occasion made an impact on everyone, and the knowledge that the Prime Minister had already been on the far bank ahead of us added to it. This had been reluctantly permitted by Montgomery (just like Alexander in the Gothic Line), deprecated by Eisenhower, who felt a personal responsi-

112

1. Dare Wilson, Director of Land/Air Warfare 1968 and Army Aviation 1970.

(Author's collection)

2. Sydney Erskine Dare Wilson and Dorothea Grace Wilson, née Burgess.

(Author's collection)

3. Dare in 1923.

(Author's collection)

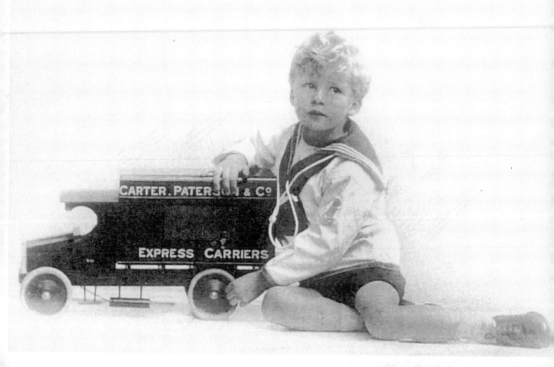

4. Band Sergeant Wilson as cornet soloist in Shrewsbury School Speech Day concert, 1938. *(Author's collection)*

5. Poppy Day in Cambridge, 1938. *(Author's collection)*

6. The family at home, 3 September 1939. *(Author's collection)*

7. 'Ben-Hur' ready for an exercise near Child Okeford. The author with Fusiliers Charlton and Frazer in summer 1941. *(Author's collection)*

8. Bren carriers of the author's platoon training in the Dorset countryside, spring 1941.
(Author's collection)

9. Dutch refugees helping to extricate 3 Reconnaissance Regiment Medical Officer's jeep from the mud, October 1944.
(Courtesy of the Archives of the Royal Northumberland Fusiliers, Alnwick Castle)

10. 'A' Squadron 3 Reconnaissance Regiment having a campfire sing-song on the eve of crossing the Rhine, March 1945.

(Courtesy of the Archives of the Royal Northumberland Fusiliers, Alnwick Castle)

11. Cologne, early March 1945. *(IWM)*

12. *Above:* British troops during an action in Haifa, 1948. *(Photo by author)*

13. *Left:* A chance meeting with Arab irregulars on Mount Tabor, Easter Day 1948.   *(Author's collection)*

14. *Below:* The author *(right)* and Tony Deane-Drummond at an Arab feast in Oman, 1960.

(Author's collection)

15. Two Fusiliers snatching a rest, Korea 1951.
     (Courtesy of the Archives of the Royal Northumberland Fusiliers, Alnwick Castle)

16. Mode of transport for Royal Northumberland Fusiliers' communications equipment, Korea 1951.
     (Courtesy of the Archives of the Royal Northumberland Fusiliers, Alnwick Castle)

17. Final briefing of 22 SAS team before the world record high altitude drop, January 1962. *(Author's collection)*

18. Closing in for a baton pass at 120 mph in free fall from 13,500 feet above ground level – the author in a GB/USA exchange. *(Author's collection)*

19. A Royal Northumberland Fusiliers Land Rover arriving to quell a riot in Aden, 1967. *(Courtesy of the Archives of the Royal Northumberland Fusiliers, Alnwick Castle)*

20. Burial service in Silent Valley Cemetery, Little Aden, 1967. *(Courtesy of the Archives of the Royal Northumberland Fusiliers, Alnwick Castle)*

21. Aden – Reprimand.
(Courtesy of the Archives of the Royal Northumberland Fusiliers, Alnwick Castle)

22. Aden – Reassurance.
*(Courtesy of the Archives of the Royal
Northumberland Fusiliers, Alnwick Castle)*

23. Child courier captured in Vietnamese
War awaiting interrogation, 1969.
(Photo by author)

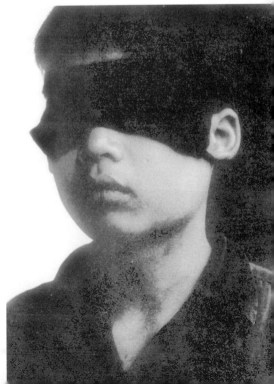

24. St Moritz, early 1958 – surveying the Cresta Run. *(Author's collection)*

25. Braking on a fast bend. *(Author's collection)*

26. Royal Northumberland Fusiliers Depot football team v. Newcastle United, 5 August 1958. Charlie Mitten was Newcastle's manager and Bobby Stokoe the team captain. *(Author's collection)*

27. Returning with Corporal Lock's patrol after a month in the Malayan jungle, 1962. *(Author's collection)*

28. Hanna Reitsch talking to Hans Drebing and the author, 1970. *(Author's collection)*

29. Ready for take-off.

(Author's collection)

30. The oldest and
youngest 'mature
student' under-
graduates at
Cambridge, 1972.
(Author's collection)

31. Summer holiday
in Cornwall, 1983.
(Author's collection)

32. Sarah and the boys with three generations of Labradors, 1992.
(Photo by author)

33. Feeding snowbound sheep.
(Author's collection)

I be the shepherd o' the farm:
An' be so proud a-roven round
Wi' my long crook a-thirt my yarm,
As ef I wer a king a-crown'd.

* From a poem by William Barnes (1801-1886) contained in *Poems of Rural Life,* published in 1884.

34. Reunited with Dirk Kuipers during the Fiftieth Anniversary of the Battle and Liberation of Overloon, October 1994. *(Author's collection)*

35. The author with John Painter in Whitehall prior to marching past the Cenotaph, Remembrance Sunday 2000. *(Author's collection)*

36. Reviewing the Old Comrades of the Royal Northumberland Fusiliers during the final Regimental Reunion in Newcastle upon Tyne, 23 June 2002. *(Author's collection)*

bility for the PM's safety, and thoroughly enjoyed by the old warhorse himself. Altogether seven regiments of the Reconnaissance Corps took part in the crossing of the Rhine. Their firepower, mobility and armour made them ideal for the purpose. A major advantage they had over tanks in such a situation was stealth, which achieves surprise, and surprise tips many scales in war. It was not until much later that we read: 'The Geordies of 3 Recce had been the first to cross the Rhine, doing so on the 26th after an order to do so immediately.'

In the middle of the night, Wesel was a forbidding sight; as far as we could judge, totally destroyed and still smoking from the destructive forces that had been unleashed upon it. Once clear of the town, we made better headway and after about six miles were harboured near the village of Peddenburg by 0330 hours. The scene a few hours later is set in the regimental history:

After much frantic map folding at an 'O' Group, mid-day 27 March, we learnt that our objective now was Münster. 'A' Sqn. was to lead, supported by the Scots Guards who were carrying one of the American Para Bns. The next eight days are so full of incidents, both sad and amusing, that the writer neither knows nor is able to record them all and therefore has considered it better to give the bare bones of this action, making a dry story of a most exciting period, in which the Regt took over 700 prisoners and never was out of contact with the enemy throughout the whole period.

We were fortunate still to have Hugh Merriman in command, with his flair for thinking ahead and exploiting the enemy's weaknesses. At this stage he drove his squadrons hard, though he was never ruthless, preferring to lead by example. Such was the exceptional pace of events across 3 Recce's front, there was little rest for anyone. Day after day and often at night, the fighting continued, but always we were going forward and we knew we were winning, though from time to time we got a bloody nose in the process. Success is a wonderful stimulant, but cumulative fatigue cannot be wholly shrugged off and when it becomes excessive its effects on the battlefield can eventually become serious. One is the progressive failure of the human memory, which in this operation contributed to a dearth of information later about the full extent of the damage and casualties we had inflicted on the enemy. It became apparent that they had been much greater than was reported at the time, due to other preoccupations of an operational nature. When men are fighting, often for their lives, little writing is done and days may pass before the need comes to mind, by which time the tide of war has moved on and tired memories are of little use. As soon as I was able, I began to make retrospective notes and without these original impressions I could not have written much of what follows.

As 'A' Squadron set off in the direction of Münster, which was some fifty miles to the north-east, our immediate task was to make contact with the American parachute battalion ahead of us. I had ordered my leading armoured car troop commander to report when he found our Allies, and before long he was doing so, in terms of finding their vehicles blown up on mines. Then, somewhere ahead, there was gunfire to be heard, which soon swelled into the full cacophony of a fair-sized engagement. The armoured cars closed to within a discreet distance, took up positions of observation and, in the parlance of the day, 'painted the picture' for me, as briefly as they were able. With this completed, the moment had come for me to liaise with the Americans.

It is not easy to link up with a unit of a foreign army in the middle of a battle, even one of a close ally, if one has never met before. It is also out of the question to pass it by in order to join in without a word of introduction. With some care I made my way through the para-troopers' positions, trying to look inconspicuous, and they were all so intent on the battle they appeared not to notice me. I was struck by the obvious determination of every man to get his share of the action, and, if the volume of gunfire was going to count, they had it wrapped up. Eventually I located the company commander, recognizable by a major's badge of rank on his steel helmet, in the thick of the action. It occurred to me what an unpropitious moment it was to introduce myself and observe the formality of reporting our arrival. At that moment, a GI close to me jumped to his feet and, firing from the hip, charged alone in the direction of the enemy. He got no further than twenty yards, before he was shot and lay still. Thereupon, without a pause, another soldier shouted out 'That's my buddy' and followed him, presumably with the intention of bringing him back, only to meet the same fate. At this, the company commander intervened with a 'Hey, you guys, cool it' to those within earshot. He then noticed me, no doubt looking puzzled at a scene that to me resembled more a Hollywood movie than the real thing and, guessing that I had something to tell him, came to join me.

Lying on the ground, we had a short conversation while the firefight continued. I told him who we were and what our task was, before sug-gesting we should try and find a way round on his left flank, to apply pressure on the enemy from that direction. He agreed, but also wanted some assistance to deal with one or two enemy tanks in the wood to his right. Within minutes, before I was able to pass his request over our wireless net, magically a squadron of Scots Guards' tanks appeared on the scene and were soon in action. Before leaving, I asked him to inform his battalion HQ and all his sub-units that we were about to work our way round on the left, with the intention of regaining the main road ahead. At that time the term 'friendly fire' was not in use, but it was still a problem. We were to see more of the 17th US Airborne Division during the next week and their effervescence and initiative were refreshing. In short, they were all enjoying their war and we took to them. They had a high proportion of unseasoned soldiers and they made their mistakes, particularly where mines and booby traps were concerned, but they were quick to learn and no units, however experienced, were immune from the ingenuity and expertise of the Germans in this speciality. All roadside verges had to be 'read' for signs of disturbance, as well as the changes in the texture of road surfaces that often concealed mines. What appealed to us particularly about these 'Yanks' was their lightheartedness, as shown by those who varied their dress with German items they picked up along the way, including top hats, tail coats and umbrellas. Others pushed prams, which were full of ammunition and therefore doing a good job. These eccentricities apart, however, what mattered was their undoubted fighting ability and sky-high morale.

In the meantime we made good progress, albeit at varying speeds according to the resistance we met. Every day there were some casualties and, on 28 March, 'A' Squadron lost two men killed and three wounded (including Trooper Rudler, my batman) when enemy artillery intervened. But the momentum never slackened for long, and the Guards and American Paratroopers, working as closely together as it is possible for infantry and tanks, were virtually unstoppable. Whenever, as part of their recce force, we ran into situations that were beyond our resources, we left small parties to inform those behind us, while we made a detour to right or left according to the suitability of alternative routes. By this means, we almost invariably found a way round the trouble we had left for others to sort out with their heavier guns, and in the process often intercepted parties of enemy withdrawing to their next position. These paid a heavy price, because there was no means of knowing what they intended and our opening bursts from the armoured cars' Besas were deadly. If they were armed they were engaged, and it was the reaction of those who were unscathed that determined what happened next. I was more than once struck by the humanity of our soldiers in these situations. Though the majority of them were battle experienced and could be very tough when the need arose, most of them would far sooner take prisoners than overwhelm their opponents with more force than was necessary. Even so, we were still meeting many German parachutists, who would stand their ground and fight until they realized they had no chance of escaping to fight again later. With these, as with the SS, there was unlikely to be any soft option.

Very early on 29 March, our third day after crossing the Rhine, we reached the large village of Haltern, halfway between Wesel and Münster. A few hours later I received an order to establish whether the road was open to the village of Lavesum, some three miles north of Haltern, and I sent Steve Wallace's carrier troop and an armoured car troop to investigate. Lavesum was a sheltered little village, lying in a hollow of meadowland overlooked by extensive woodlands. Steve's small force paused as the village came into sight and remained in observation for a while, because nothing stirred and, although it was early in the day, in war this can be suspicious. Then they advanced with caution until just short of the village, where they listened. They thought they heard a single tank or SP gun move a short distance in the woods on the other side of the valley, then all was silent again. At this point, Steve asked me on the wireless for further instructions. I told him I first needed to see the ground and set off to join him in my armoured car, with Hastings and Mitchelmore.

As we approached the village I saw the armoured cars ahead of us, with a bank on their right and Steve's troop dismounted under cover in a field to the left. As there was nowhere to halt under cover, we stopped alongside the troop commander's vehicle and I dismounted, intending to join Steve. Before I had moved more than a few paces there was an ear-splitting metallic bang, as a high velocity armour piercing round from a large calibre gun struck my armoured car just behind me and, after a second or two, more rounds followed. In that very brief pause, the smoke canisters on the armoured car exploded, causing an instant cloud that screened the remaining cars. By then my own vehicle was burning fiercely and I saw a gaping hole through the turret. There was no doubt about the instant fate of my crew, nor the origin of the rounds as an enemy tank some 1,000 yards distant, thought to be a Panther, withdrew from its well-camouflaged position. There was no question of extinguishing the fire, which was consuming the car and crew; it took many hours to burn out. Fortunately there were no other casualties, though I noted the faces of the crews of the adjacent armoured cars that had been obscured from the enemy's view. Their expressions I have not forgotten.

All that took seconds rather than minutes, and soon I was with Steve

Wallace, who had seen what had happened from a little further off. Strangely, one does not discuss a fait accompli of this nature at the time, apart from any action required as a result of it. In this instance, I was anxious to get a section of 3 Recce's anti-tank guns into position before we began to clear the village, in case more tanks were lurking. While we were waiting, I joined one of Steve's sections in the garden of a farmhouse overlooking the road that bisected the village. It contained several ex-members of WILFORCE, and they had all seen what happened earlier. Whether it was for my benefit or their own, they soon found a subject to take minds off the incident. On a clothes line stretching across the chicken run directly in front of us was the weekly washing of a large family with, it seemed, a preponderance of female underwear. They were still discussing it when I left to position the anti-tank guns.

By the time we had cleared the village of enemy remnants and established control, evening was drawing on and orders arrived from RHQ to remain in Lavesum for the night and resume the advance at first light. At this stage, troops needed to know their areas so that the nightly routine of replenishment and preparation of defences could begin. It was also a suitable time for a squadron commander to visit his troops after a day's action, to catch up on losses and sort out any other problems. Sometimes a few words of appreciation, encouragement or sympathy were called for. In the British Army, and in many others, loyalty and comradeship are strongest at sub-unit level, moreover this attitude of mind brings out the best in men in terms of selflessness and concern for others. In this way, the crew of a tank or armoured car, who have lived and fought together, frequently develop a relationship and regard for each other unaffected by rank or status that is seldom found elsewhere.

During my rounds in Lavesum that evening this was brought home to me from a new angle. I realized that, on this occasion, our roles were reversed, when NCOs and troopers approached me in their different ways, to convey their feelings in simple and touching terms. They had known Hastings and Mitchelmore as well as or better than I, but they also knew how I would be feeling as the surviving member of the crew. There was also some mention of relief that the outcome had not been worse and, from one or two of the more light-hearted, a reminder that by their reckoning this was my third 'let off' since rejoining the squadron, for some remembered me from more than five years earlier, and they hoped I was not getting careless.

Making my way back to the centre of the village by myself, I realized how exhausted I was, after three days and nights of gruelling activity, much of it in contact with the enemy, and no doubt I was wondering how much longer I could stick the pace, almost without sleep. On the way, I was met by Andy Brough, my second in command, and Squadron Sergeant Major Powell, a wonderful man who in civil life was a policeman. I had seen neither of them all day, but they had been in close touch with events and showed their concern. My armoured car was still burning a short distance away and I mentioned my intention to supervise the removal of the bodies when it had cooled down. The SSM intervened: 'With respect, sir, I think that is my responsibility.' Andy agreed and the subject was changed. In the end, because of the time the red-hot armour took to cool, it was dear George Fox, our padre, with his assistants, who did it for us and conducted the burial and service after we had left early the next morning. Some of his diary makes grim reading, but helps to illustrate the man he was:

This time we left early in the morning, but before going to our location I had to get two men out of an armoured car who had been burned to death. It was another of those unpleasant sights which I had to witness in France; they were so badly charred that the smell was not so unpleasant as I had previously imagined.

After side-stepping the issue I had raised with Andy and the SSM, the former took the initiative by announcing that what I needed was a good night's sleep and that he and the SSM would share my duties. He then took me a short distance to a large house, which he had requisitioned, and into its sumptuously furnished drawing room, where dinner would be brought later. He then suggested I might like to listen to some music, indicating an impressive-looking gramophone; he had even selected a few brand new records. Conscious of the fact that I already knew our musical tastes did not coincide, I felt doubtful, and in any case I was not feeling like listening to music, even of my own choice. However, as he had been so thoughtful, I did not demur. He wound up the gramophone, put the first record on the turntable and left the room.

The record Andy had put on, by sheer chance, was Beethoven's Seventh Symphony, played by the Berlin Philharmonic with Furtwängler conducting. As I listened, all other thoughts were dispelled from my mind and I can only think it was the music alone that enabled me to sleep that night as though I had not a care in the world. However, such was the impact it made on me that when I heard the same recording for the second time, on the radio almost exactly fifty years later, even without an introduction I recognized it within a bar or two, and one of the most profound musical memories of my life was reawakened.

After that welcome night's rest, I rose to find I had missed an incident in the early hours that had left a deep impression on those who had been involved. A pair of our sentries on guard in a trench by the side of the road leading east out of Lavesum heard a faint noise some distance in front of them, that they could not recognize and had difficulty in describing. As it came closer, they could detect a shuffling sound, as of something being dragged along the road, coupled with a sort of moaning. They challenged it and there was no reply, but very slowly it was coming closer. They held their fire and waited until it was near enough to use a torch. 'It' was a British soldier, very seriously wounded and in the last stages of exhaustion, with a leg badly shattered and other multiple injuries. He had crawled more than a mile since the previous afternoon, as the sole survivor from a Royal Artillery vehicle that had apparently lost its way from another road and been blown up on a German anti-tank mine. He was treated by our medical orderlies and recovered sufficiently to give this and further information, before being taken back to the nearest Field Ambulance unit equipped to operate on him. By coincidence he turned out to be a Geordie, and finding himself among friends was thought to have played a critical part in keeping him conscious and his willpower alive. As would be expected, all involved in looking after him were full of admiration and praise for his guts and his determination to pass on information. He was dangerously ill for some days but, so far as we were able to establish later, recovered. When we resumed the advance, soon after first light, we came across the mined vehicle from which the bodies had already been removed, we assumed by the enemy because we were the first of our own side to pass that way. How, we asked ourselves repeatedly, was it possible for a wounded man to have crawled that distance?

The following day, 1 April, was Easter Day, but for most of us its true significance was overshadowed by *bella horrida bella*, and the urge to 'Bash on, Recce'. The day was full of incidents and we narrowly avoided an ugly clash with the SAS, of whose presence across the Rhine there had been no mention. One of my leading troops reported considerable enemy vehicle movement in a large expanse of woodland, more than half a mile ahead. I brought more troops forward in expectation of trouble, moving with care in order not to be seen, and then we waited to see how best to outflank them. Before long a string of vehicles gradually and indistinctly came into view. We were sure they could not belong to us, so it was up to the first troop

119

with a good view of them to open fire. Fortunately, a sense of doubt prevailed and soon the vehicles, stripped for action, were recognized through the optical sights of the armoured cars. The SAS appeared mildly surprised to find us waiting for them and, after we had exchanged information, made their way past us to replenish and rest in security. We then continued our advance and late in the day took many prisoners.

The following morning there was still plenty of activity, with many more prisoners being taken by all squadrons. They varied between those who had clearly had enough, and were relieved to feel their war was over, and those younger reinforcements who showed determination and sometimes fanaticism. The youngest of all those who went into 3 Recce's bag was taken that day, aged eleven. When asked how he had managed to get into the Army he proudly answered that he had given a false age; he had said that he was fourteen. Because of the plethora of events and incidents that week, there is no record of the occasion when 'A' Squadron became engulfed in a tide of POW that exceeded our resources to deal with them. The usual procedure was first to search them for weapons and ammunition, then to segregate the wounded and officers. If time permitted, we were also expected to put members of the SS under special escort. On this occasion we were unable to take any of these measures and, because most of the squadron was operationally committed, I had only one armoured car troop available to control and guard some hundreds of prisoners, who were homing in like bees to a hive. All I could do was request assistance from the rear, and we were aware that for quite a long period we had no means whatever of controlling the prisoners, because the small force on hand was confined to the four armoured cars, in communication with each other but with no means of conveying instructions to the concourse, which continued to increase. Loss of control in any situation is viewed by soldiers with misgiving, but in this situation we were not unduly concerned; those giving themselves up were doing so of their own volition and the formalities we would just have to leave to others. My parting view of the prisoners, as I drove off to attend to other problems, was of an expanse of milling bodies with four armoured car turrets rising above them.

The following day, 3 Recce, which had been given a circuitous route, with a night's staging in Holland, arrived in Lingen, while the environs were still being combed for enemy. A force of unknown strength had been identified three miles to the south, on the east bank of the canal, in the vicinity of what had been two major road and rail bridges, now demolished. It was adjacent to them that a new Bailey bridge was urgently required for use by 51st (Highland) Division which would soon be on its way north to the Bremen area. The next morning, 7 April, at 0930, 3 Recce was ordered to send a squadron to clear this area, where the enemy force previously observed was still in occupation. 'A' Squadron was given the task and we left within half an hour, taking the road that follows the east bank of the canal. Several hundred yards north of the demolished bridges we came under small-arms fire, and before long were involved in the liveliest engagement I recall during my time with the squadron. It was also the only time when all seven troops of the squadron were simultaneously involved in a coordinated action against a cohesive enemy force. By 1405 hours we were able to report that some of the enemy were showing signs of withdrawing, which may have been premature because later I accepted both artillery support and a troop of tanks, but this was from the other side of the river and their view of the enemy was limited. However, our armoured cars and mortars, with all our infantry weapons, were having their effect and within an hour 'A' Squadron was firmly on its objective and two platoons of enemy were pulling back to alternative positions, from which they continued to engage us.

Until then, in view of the resilience of the enemy, I had been reluctant to launch a dismounted assault but, because of the urgency to clear the whole area so that the Sappers could start their bridging operation, I felt it could be delayed no longer. I therefore ordered 4 Troop under Steve Wallace and 6 Troop under Denis Hodgetts to support 5 Troop into the enemy's trenches, while the rest of the squadron provided covering fire. 5 Troop, after fixing bayonets, advanced into the open with determination, and it was not long before they were fighting hand to hand with bayonets and grenades. At this stage Sergeant Thomas Cottrell, in command of a section, was conspicuous for leadership and gallantry, for which he was awarded the DCM. At 1645 hours, HQ 3 Div was informed that there had been no further enemy activity, apart from a few shells that had landed 'indiscriminately' during the previous half hour. Later that evening, 'A' Squadron was relieved by 2 KSLI complete, which we took as a compliment, and they scoured the area, adding to the number of prisoners we had taken. We rejoined the regiment in Lingen shortly before midnight.

It was during the third week of April that, quite by chance, I bumped into my old friend Hubert Dixon, on a road south of Bremen. I had not seen him for a while and at once detected that he was not his usual cheerful self. After learning that he was still commanding 11 FDS I asked him bluntly what was on his mind. He paused, before counter-ing with the question: 'What do you know about concentration camps?'

'Very little,' was my answer, 'except that they reflect one of the evils of Nazism.'

He paused again, before continuing slowly and thoughtfully: 'There's one called Belsen. I've just been there. It's worse than the worst nightmare you could imagine.'

In the interim, we had left Lingen and advanced most of the way to Bremen. Though they are only some seventy-five miles apart, we had travelled much further, for the Germans were still using delaying tactics, including much reliance on anti-tank mines. Even at this late stage there was no thought of letting up or affording the enemy any respite. The advance had been going well and we had made contact and taken POW, when a further action ensued, in which Bill Purkiss's armoured car troop bumped an enemy rearguard. In this Bill was wounded and, having got out of his vehicle, he had been able to sit on the outside of an LRC for the short distance to our medical orderlies. As the driver turned round at a nearby road and track junction, a mine was detonated and Bill was wounded a second time within minutes, this time very seriously. I came on the scene moments afterwards, having heard the explosion. Later that day, George Fox visited Bill in hospital where he learned that both legs had been amputated. The entry in his diary for this visit is followed by an observation that illus-trates how those chaplains whose duties took them into the forward areas shared the general interest in mine survival:

> Great care has to be taken in travelling; because a vehicle has been there before you, it does not mean that all is well, for generally it is only by constant pressure and by vehicles running over the earth that they explode, for the mines have been dug deep into the earth.

In this instance it was my own vehicle that had been previously turned on the same spot, not once but three times, as my driver and others recounted later that day. Bill survived the loss of his legs and multiple wounds, regaining his mobility with artificial legs and remaining the cheerful person we had known.

By this time, halfway through April, it was clear to those in a position to know that the enemy was intent on making a major stand in Bremen and a large area to the north of it. XXX Corps was therefore ordered to plan and carry out a full-scale attack to capture the city and to this end 3 Div was placed under its command on 17 April. From that day the noose round Bremen began to tighten, with all three brigades and 3 Recce closing in from the south and west, while 43 and 52 Divisions prepared to deliver a 'Monty right hook' from the east. In the event it took 3 Div the best part of two weeks to subdue the defences of Bremen west of the Weser. In addition to parachute troops, SS formations and Hitler *Jugend*, both the German Navy and Air Force provided ground troops, many of whom fought with courage and the desperation born of despair. Some fought suicidally, deliberately sacrificing their own lives as gestures of defiance.

The outer defences were located well to the south of the city in the neighbouring small towns and villages, in low-lying land that had been deliberately flooded. During the course of the battle, 3 Recce made further ground to the north, into the gap that was then narrowing between XXX Corps and the Canadians. The latter had been fighting hard and doing great humanitarian work on behalf of the Dutch people, many of whom were still suffering from starvation. Here the regiment not only protected the Division's left flank, but kept up the pressure as best they could against the enemy in open country. Eventually, we were halted to prevent a gap opening behind us and, from a position to the west of Bremen's airfield, 'A' Squadron was able to keep in touch with the Third Division's last battle of the war, then in its final stages. We were also able to harass the enemy to the north, where they were still active. Before long 'A' Squadron found two excellent OPs, from which we were able to direct artillery fire on to a road in full view, about 1,000 yards in front of us.

The enemy were obviously dependent on this road, because traffic continued to use it despite good shooting by our Gunners. However, they were soon making it more difficult for us by spacing out their vehicles and ensuring that they drove only at high speed. Soon our Gunners were out of business. I felt the situation invited the use of a fighting patrol late one night. I did not have to wait long for Hugh Merriman's next visit, when I put my plan to him. I proposed to take a patrol of ex-WILFORCE members and set up an ambush on, or close to, the road to make life as difficult for the enemy as we could. Hugh listened with interest and appeared to be all for it. Then he hesitated and, in the nicest possible way, began to change his mind:

If the war wasn't likely to end in the very near future I would be asking 'What are you waiting for?' But, as things are, I am asking myself, 'What are we going to gain from it?' I know it makes tactical sense and you would almost certainly succeed, and probably kill lots of Germans as well as closing the road. But what if we were to lose even one man? I should hate that to happen at this late stage, and so would you. Do you see what I mean?

I did, only too clearly – he was a move ahead of me. We agreed to take it no further, unless the enemy became stroppy. They chose not to.

That was, I believe, the last day of April; had we had any idea, as we spoke, of what was happening in Berlin the subject we were discussing would probably not have arisen. As it was, although the news of Hitler's suicide was not broadcast until the following night, it came as little surprise, though the full extent of the drama being played out in his bunker under the Chancellery was concealed from the world until all its strands were known and woven together. The principal surviving witness was Hanna Reitsch, Germany's illustrious wartime test pilot. Many years later I met her and was able to form my own impressions of a very remarkable person.

As April gave way to May, all the signs pointed to an early end to hostilities and, though our patrols continued until 4 May, and we were still pulling in POW, we had fired our last shots and the impetus had gone out of our operations. The end came as we were having breakfast on 5 May in a written signal from RHQ: 'Cancel all offensive operations and cease fire.' I have the signal still. But there was no respite; that afternoon we moved seventy-five miles to Osnabrück, to take up our peacetime duties as a mobile reserve within the 3rd Division's area of occupation. Gradually the enormity of what had just happened sunk in and few minds were without some trace of confusion. My own raced forwards, but then flitted backwards. There was thankfulness, without rejoicing, and there was a yearning for sleep as one clutched at random thoughts. One of mine was a reminder that I had just finished the war in the same company, now squadron, as I had joined, nearly six years before. Considering the course I had followed, it seemed the Fates had been on my side.

Chapter Eleven

Triumph and Turmoil

A thousand years will pass and the guilt of Germany will not be erased.
Hans Frank, Nazi Governor General of Poland,
later tried and hanged at Nuremberg

It was a phenomenon of the war, that a high proportion of those who had been closest to the action found the greatest sense of anticlimax in its ending. But what most of us failed to recognize at the time, was the nature and extent of the metamorphosis that the end of hostilities had triggered within an unstable and war-weary continent. Most European countries were swept into a maelstrom, at the centre of which lay Germany, and it was in northern Germany that the British Liberation Army became part of the Allied Occupation Force.

From the moment hostilities ended, we became absorbed in a process of which we had little warning, as the shifting balance of power to which we had contributed dissolved, leaving a partial vacuum and many uncertainties in relationships within Germany and those areas of neighbouring countries where German control had prevailed. At the stroke of a few pens round a camp table on Lüneburg Heath, and later in Reims and Berlin, Germany lost all its remaining power and influence everywhere. Suddenly, where for the Germans there had already been no friends, there were now only enemies. Although most of these were unarmed, they soon assumed a baleful attitude within a simmering cauldron of bitterness and resentment. Thus, millions of men and women who had been prisoners and slaves, woke up in a changed Europe, where Germany no longer constituted any threat. It took only a few days to sink into minds that had become dulled by starvation and repression that the tables had finally been turned and vengeance was theirs for the taking.

It took longer before any of us could marshal our impressions of what had happened to Germany during the latter part of the war, as

125

the entire system by which the country functioned suddenly collapsed. It was not easy for anyone to grasp the implications of what they saw and knew, because virtually everything was in chaos. Germany was prostrate; its towns and cities were destroyed, its communications were mostly at a standstill, its water, gas and electricity services were out of order, food and fuel distribution had ceased, hospitals were overflowing and law and order were in danger of breaking down.

This, then, was the situation that confronted the British Army, as it assumed its occupational duties. Before we became immersed in our new role, however, there was one last event associated with the war against Germany: the concluding Thanksgiving Service. With commendable forethought the Chaplain General had produced an order of service attractively printed, with a multi-coloured cover bearing the insignia of all the Second Army's corps and divisions. This was circulated among all ranks – a pleasing memento of the occasion. It was just the service to which many of us had looked forward, for thanksgiving had been a theme uppermost in many minds since the fighting ceased. There was no fixed date or time for the service, because many padres took it in several locations. George Fox held ours on Sunday, 13 May. It was memorable, with lusty singing and a sense of awareness of its importance. There were many names to recall, associated with the gaps that had appeared in our ranks. Everyone found it moving, because recollections were vivid and memories undimmed. When I thought about it later, I realized there was only one infantry battalion of the ten in the 3rd Division in which I had not lost one or more friends.

Thence the Army dispersed to its multifarious duties, most of which I think it would be fair to describe as unpleasant, although good soldiers always strive to find a humorous side if they can. Even so, sometimes not a trace of a smile crossed a single face all day. I have already alluded to Belsen, a herculean task that the RAMC, assisted by many others, accomplished so humanely under the most awful conditions. The genocide relating to what Hitler had perversely regarded as the cleansing of non-Aryans from Europe was the province of the SS and, contrary to what was widely believed at the time, it later became accepted that little direct blame could be attributed to those outside the Nazi Party, beyond complicity. Most Germans, it would appear, had some knowledge of what went on within the concentration and extermination camps, but had no wish to be better informed, preferring to remain as ignorant of them as possible. Within many German families the subject was forbidden.

126

It was easy, but, as later became apparent, misguided, for those of us in the Army of Occupation to attach more blame than was justified to all Germans. Such was the overt acceptance of National Socialism within Germany that, for a while, we – I guess nearly all of us – were not prepared to make any allowances in favour of any minority holding contrary views. This outlook was strengthened by the non-fraternization code of behaviour that all Allied forces had to observe from the moment they entered Germany. The German civilians, in turn, were also required to follow the same code. After the war, it became a matter of some contention, but while hostilities lasted there was no relaxation of the rules. Over the years I have found myself questioning our policy and must confess to some uneasiness but, at the time, I believe that the 'non-frat' rule was initially accepted by all ranks of the British and Allied Forces in Germany, from field marshal to private soldier because, broadly speaking, not one of us was willing at that stage to make any concessions to Germany or to the German people.

I remember now, not without a twinge of conscience, how easy it was, even when the war ended, to spurn any attempt by Germans to enter into a dialogue – even more so when they gave the impression of regarding us as liberators. It never occurred to us that anyone approaching us in this way could be sincere. The fact that those who did approach us were a small minority we also may have misinterpreted, because most of them had no more wish to converse with us than we had with them. There were, of course, inducements from time to time, including attractive young women who offered to provide laundry and other services. One came to me with the suggestion that I might wish to engage her as my housekeeper. Such approaches often followed an emphatic dissociation with the Nazi Party and everything related to it. These advances, most of us instinctively rejected, in the belief that such views professed by Germans at large were spurious. I now believe that in some cases, although perhaps not many, we were wrong.

It took several months before the non-fraternization code was relaxed, and then only by stages. Eventually it was human nature, rather than men sitting round a table, that provided the necessary enlightenment. British and American soldiers are very fond of children, and children who are hungry or unhappy soon capture their hearts. But it is difficult to be kind to children while ignoring their parents, and when those parents are genuinely appreciative, because their children are benefiting from gifts of things that are otherwise unavailable to families, it is churlish not to respond. The Americans

127

were the first to waive the rule where children were concerned, while British soldiers were still liable to be court-martialled for doing what the US Army by then approved. In these circumstances, our higher authorities recognized that the time had come for them also to relax the rule, but only in regard to children.

It was not long before the high priority tasks became obvious, and soon most units within Second Army were working at full stretch. Eventually many had their own area of responsibility, working within the familiar framework of their higher formations. Third Reconnaissance Regiment, still operating under command of HQ 3 Div, was probably fairly typical. Almost overnight, we had become policemen, security guards, relief workers, medical assistants, escorts and transport agents for vast numbers of displaced persons and former prisoners of war.

After four weeks near Osnabrück, we were sent to take up occupation duties in the Warendorf district, lying between Münster and Gütersloh. There we became responsible for maintaining law and order and guarding vulnerable points, including a distillery and a castle containing art treasures. The main task, however, was the administration of camps containing Russian, Polish, Italian and Yugoslav DPs and PWX. At the same time, 'A' Squadron was detached from the regiment, to manage a transit organization for Russians at Rheda, a town on the main railway line linking the Ruhr with Hanover and eastern Germany. There we would have to supervise the entrainment of 10,000 Russian DPs and PWX within one week. Already by this stage 21 Army Group had sent more than 180,000 Russians on their way eastwards, and nearly 65,000, including British and American PWX, in the opposite direction. We were assisted at Rheda by RAMC parties from 223 British Field Ambulance and a Field Hygiene Section, plus a Russian interpreter. It was forecast that each afternoon 2,000 Russians would start arriving at intervals by road, to pass through our organization. Every Russian had to be disinfested as a precaution against the spread of typhus, to which a number had already succumbed. They all arrived at Rheda having had a recent meal and were marshalled into the goods yard where their trains were waiting. Their journey to Russia would take between two and three days and twenty men shared the limited space of a German railway covered goods wagon.

We eventually became accustomed to the heartless business of running a human conveyor belt of grim-faced, ill-clad and emaciated creatures who, less than three weeks earlier, had been suffering from starvation. From such a condition, recovery is slow and animal instincts for survival were still prevalent among many whom we supervised. The major problem we had was the lack of communication, because none of us spoke the others' language. One of my officers worked ceaselessly with the interpreter, much of the time in trying to prevent the constant arguments between ethnic groups developing into violence, which could include the use of knives. Tempers were apt to reach flashpoint with little warning, though none of the trouble was directed at us. From what we saw that week, it seemed as though few of those passing through our hands were in any way looking forward to their return to Russia. Within this scenario were accusers and accused, in relation to treachery against the motherland; on arrival in Russia they would report, or be reported by, their adversaries. Only one punishment was visualized as the likely outcome in this situation for some, if not all, of them – death. Several were so convinced they were doomed that they committed suicide in the presence of our own troops, one with a razor to his own throat as one of our officers was trying to intervene.

The Russians were given three days' rations and water, but much of the food was eaten before they left. The animal-like behaviour of these men was the outcome of years of deprivation, starvation and violence. Each wagonload was required to nominate a leader, to take the rations and the means of making tea for his companions. No sooner was each leader back with his group, than a brawl broke out to seize what each man could for himself. It might be a loaf of bread, a large tin of potatoes, a tin of meat or the tea ration for the whole party for three days. Each man who was lucky, or strong, enough to secure his 'share' would detach himself from the others, as a dog might with a bone, and eat as much as he could, before stuffing what was left inside the open neck of his smock or coat. The weaker ones, who failed to gain something more substantial, were left with bags of loose tea, which they ate dry by the handful, or tins of butter, which they emptied with fingers and tongues. They had little difficulty in opening tins without tin-openers; although these were provided they were not recognized as such and were soon lost in the general mêlée. One could only pity them, yet most of the time we were powerless to help them, beyond carrying out our orders, all of which were designed to assist them. When we intervened in the cases of violence, it was on behalf of the weaker who were suffering at the hands of the stronger. At the end of the week none of us ever wished to see another Russian again. Yet there was always an undercurrent of compassion, however much it was thwarted by the total lack of communication.

Early in July, RHQ issued fresh instructions to 'A' Squadron, which

129

introduced a new slant into our responsibilities. They began as follows:

Occupation Duties Instruction No. 3.

1. Introduction

(a) During the past week there has been a considerable increase in the number of incidents of looting, murder, and rape in the Regt. area (LK. WARENDORF).

(b) The area WEST of WARENDORF is the worst area.

(c) As a temporary measure it has been agreed with Mil. Govt. that the Regt. will send out a number of patrols in an effort to put down this lawlessness and to catch the criminals. This phase will probably last 7 – 10 days.

Three *Bürgermeister* were authorized to contact troops on the ground to request assistance and this was the beginning of positive cooperation between German local government and the Occupation Forces within our area. The problems stemmed from the number of starving Russian PWX, enslaved workers from all over Europe and roving bands of drunken, frenzied Poles, Russians and Italians on the rampage, intent on vengeance against the Germans. Their passion to loot, rape and kill was inflamed by a craving for alcohol and, when they were unable to steal it, some – particularly the Russians – would distil it from potatoes. Wherever German troops had fought their last engagements before surrendering to the Allies, the countryside was littered with discarded weapons and ammunition. These were there for the taking, and embittered former enemies of the Reich – particularly, it seemed from a wealth of evidence, Poles – developed a lust to kill Germans. Their newly-acquired rifles soon bore notches, one for each German they accounted for. This was not difficult to understand: apart from the rape of Poland in 1939, the Warsaw risings of 1943 and 1944 led to the extermination of nearly 250,000 Poles by the Germans. For a very short while the understanding felt by British troops verged on acceptance, but this soon evaporated when we found ourselves charged with the maintenance of law and order.

It was during this period that some of us were introduced to levels of violence and depravity we had not previously encountered. One such incident has remained engraved on my memory and I recently discovered, among my papers, an account, still in draft form, that I believe I wrote up from notes nearly twenty years after the war, when I was once again serving in Germany. It may lack polish, but, verbatim, I think it conveys my feelings at the time more truly than my

130

current memory could have done:

It became clear that we were dealing with a problem arising largely out of the Eastern Europeans' uncontrollable hatred, having suffered at the hands of the Germans for six years. It seemed that while some of the German farmers had treated their foreign labourers with consideration and occasionally with sympathy, others had driven them to breaking point. The consequence was an uprising in which Polish and Russian marauders indulged in an orgy of pillage, rape and murder.

During this difficult period, those of us who were entrusted with the task of restoring order witnessed scenes none of us will easily forget. I recall being called to the squadron wireless command net about 3 o'clock one morning by one of my troop sergeants, a well-decorated veteran from Dunkirk onwards. He was obviously shaken and asked me to come at once to a farm a few miles away to see for myself what his troop had just discovered. I did so, and on arrival found a scene of indescribable savagery. The German farmer and his wife lay, battered and bayoneted to death, in the hall, the walls and floor of which were covered in blood, while upstairs, incoherent and demented, were their two teenage daughters who had been raped repeatedly by a gang they estimated at about 20 strong. They had first been forced to watch the murder of their parents.

As I stood there with the members of the patrol, I realised that in nearly six years of war I had never before seen such anger on the faces of British soldiers. In battle there are many expressions to be read on soldiers' faces: exhaustion, determination, fear, elation and many others but, curiously enough, very rarely anger. It takes something that offends his sense of decency to make the British soldier really angry, but in a situation such as this, one meets real anger; one may share it, and occasionally may have to steer oneself and then others away from an ill-judged reaction. For this reason, I kept my men away from the displaced persons' camps where recently we had been welcomed.

From that moment on, until we finally got on top of the problem, these troops virtually imposed their own hours of work and rest – except that they took no rest. Only one small consolation emerged: many Germans got an earlier glimpse of the humanity of the British soldier than they would have done otherwise. And since we were to remain there as part of the Allied, later NATO, force entrusted with the defence of Northern Germany, some ultimate good was destined to come out of the evil.

In conclusion I have to mention that, on the occasion I have described, Poles, not Russians, were responsible for the multiple crime.

In July, in response to a request I had made at the suggestion of my former CO, Eric Bols (by then commanding a division in Airborne Forces) I received my posting order from the War Office to join the 6th Airborne Division, now back in England. Trooper Dean, my driver batman who had also volunteered for an airborne transfer, would accompany me. Before we left, 'A' Squadron organized a party that still lives in many memories, one feature of which was an enormous campfire in a secluded rural setting. It took several days to build, until a pyramid some thirty feet high had been completed. As darkness approached on a perfect summer evening, it was thoroughly soaked with petrol and ignited from a safe distance with a Very pistol, causing an explosion which echoed through the countryside and a fire which lit the surrounds for hours to come. There followed a meal of comparable proportions, accompanied by a supply of local barrelled beer generous enough to keep almost the entire squadron out of their beds for the night. It had taken us until then to celebrate the end of the war in the style we had visualized, but for which the spark had been lacking at the time. It also served as my farewell party and after breakfast I was given a memorable send-off.

Within a few hours I was on my way home, travelling by Jeep as far as Ostend. I had also planned to make a diversion to call on the family who had billeted the three of us so hospitably, close to the west bank of the Maas, way back in February. I was aware that a friendship had developed between the farmer, his wife, their attractive daughter and the two handsome soldiers who were always welcome in their kitchen. It was highly unlikely that they would have heard of what had subsequently happened and I felt they would wish to know. We retraced much of our wartime route back to the Rhine and Maas, over roads that were little better than when we had last used them, and eventually drove into the farmyard. As we stopped in front of the house I was totally unprepared for what was to come. I was barely out of the vehicle before the door opened and there was the daughter, looking radiant and welcoming, then puzzled as she noticed two soldiers with me whom she did not recognize. Her smile disappeared as she waited for me to speak. 'I'm sorry,' I said. 'I have some bad news – we have lost both of them.' She turned white and her expression changed to horror as she grasped my meaning, then without a word dashed into the house. Through the open door I could hear her sobbing and then her mother's voice, trying to comfort and question her at the same time. Soon her father joined them and after a few minutes all three of them came out. 'Are they really dead?' the mother asked. I did my best to find the right words, as I feared what had happened. Confirmation of what I suspected came from the girl who, with difficulty, told me that she and my driver, Reg Mitchelmore, had fallen in love and had planned to marry after the war. Suddenly I found myself sharing their grief, as I realized the gravity of the bad tidings I had brought, and we became much closer as I explained what had happened and was able to answer their questions. They must have sensed my embarrassment over failing to perceive what had been developing while I was their guest. I left the family coming to terms with the news; sadly, circumstances had combined to prevent either of us knowing the other half of the story for nearly six months. I reproached myself for having been so absorbed with the problems and fortunes of WILFORCE that I had failed to notice a romance going on under my nose.

Fortunately new challenges lay ahead, before which a spell of home leave would help to put this and other recent experiences into perspective. And of course it did, although, as with most old soldiers, many vivid memories remain, particularly of those friends and others who were less fortunate than oneself:

> ... and their names shall live on, not graven merely in the stone above them but far off, woven into the fabric of other men's lives. (Pericles, c. 490-429 BC)

After an overnight Channel crossing we made our way to an outlying camp near Larkhill, on Salisbury Plain. Here 6 Airborne Armoured Reconnaissance Regiment had been based between its successive operations in the British Liberation Army, which began with the air-landings of D-Day. Now the regiment was in the throes of reorganizing and re-equipping in preparation for a move to the Far East theatre, where planning was in progress for new offensives on a massive scale and arrangements for Operation ZIPPER, the invasion and reoccupation of Malaya, were well advanced.

Back in the shadow of Stonehenge, life in 6th Airborne Armoured Recce continued, sometimes with élan. Here, behind the bustle of operational activity, there was an air of levity, as befitted any airborne unit consisting of seasoned volunteers who had recently acquitted themselves well in battle. My introduction was full of interest. I was welcomed by Major John Cordy-Simpson, the second in command, who told me that I was to take over 'A' Squadron immediately, and then spend five days learning about the regiment, its roles and organization, before going on twenty-eight days embarkation leave. There were many differences between the infantry and airborne recce regiments, the main one being that the latter was equipped with tanks instead of armoured cars. In the airborne landing role, they took in glider-borne Tetrarch or Lotus tanks, but following the link-up with ground forces these were reinforced by Shermans. For the second time I found myself exchanging my Reconnaissance Corps cap badge for that of the Royal Armoured Corps. I was delighted to find myself moving from one 'A' Squadron to another and even more so to find a comparable spirit.

On 26 July, the day of the first general election for almost ten years, I went home. The next four weeks provided just what so many of us needed during the aftermath of the war including, in my case, plenty of fishing and shooting, which blended well with a family reunion. I sensed the thanksgiving of our parents and realized more clearly, though woefully late, what they had been through for close on six years.

Kitty and Betty were both happily married and the first two of many grandchildren were flourishing. Both husbands were fit and well, though still serving with the Army overseas. Peter, now a lieutenant, had just returned home after an eventful war, mostly at sea and as full of activity as a seventeen year old midshipman emerging from Dartmouth in 1940 could have wished. He served in a succession of ships, two of which were heavily damaged in action. The first was the cruiser HMS *Orion* which had the fateful mission to evacuate as many troops from Crete as she could carry. During the voyage to Alexandria there was no air cover and *Orion* received three direct hits, one of which penetrated to the crowded decks below, killing some 600 soldiers, as well as sailors going about their duties. She was disabled, but remained afloat and limped into Alexandria harbour where she settled on the bottom. Later, for Peter, came the 'Tobruk runs', the Malta convoys, offensive operations in the Adriatic and the combined operations of the North African landings, followed by successes against U-Boats in the Atlantic and the protection of the convoys that maintained Britain's lifeline. Even more demanding were the convoys on the Northern Route to Murmansk and Archangel, which operated under the coldest conditions known to sailors.

Priestfield was a perfect place for our homecoming and return to family life. For me, it had provided a refuge for my thoughts when they became burdensome, due to excessive preoccupation with the rougher side of war. The stabilizing influence of a strong family and a happy home can be very powerful in stressful times. More than that, it can give one the strength to assist others, who may be in greater need of reassurance than oneself. That summer of 1945 there was no garden fête at Leazes Hall. The country was drained by war weariness and shortages, which only the celebrations of VE-Day and VJ-Day momentarily surmounted. I never met the gypsy palmist again, but already some of the blurred edges of her pre-war predictions were becoming clearer.

Before my leave had expired, atom bombs were dropped on Hiroshima and Nagasaki; less than a week later Japan surrendered. This was the moment when the prospect of a widespread and lasting peace began to hallucinate impressionable minds. Sadly, such thoughts were barren. Countries in many parts of the world were incapable of regaining the stability that some had known and others had craved. In Britain, the post-war recovery was soon under way, but her Empire was creaking and the Commonwealth was yet to find its feet. There were few prophets around and the wisest of them kept their own counsel. In the meantime, gripping news had reached HQ 6th Airborne Division in the south of England:

For 'Far East' now read 'Middle East'.

That meant Palestine. My travels were about to resume.

135

Chapter Twelve

Strife in the Holy Land

We looked for peace, but no good came; and for a time of health, and behold trouble!

Jeremiah 8 v.15

Three weeks after Japan formally surrendered to the United States the vanguard of 6th Airborne Division arrived in Palestine. However, contrary to widespread suspicion, the apparent haste was in no way linked with any operational requirement there; at that time there was no immediate threat to the relatively peaceful situation which prevailed and any internal security problems arising out of dissidence were still mostly in the hands of the Palestine Police, a strong and experienced British-led force. It had already been made known within the Division that it was moving to the Middle East in order to strengthen the Strategic Reserve in that theatre and that Palestine was the obvious deployment area on account of its modern airfields and excellent training facilities. The need to maintain a high standard of airborne training was considered paramount.

6 Airborne Armoured Reconnaissance Regiment, with several more airborne units, had left Glasgow in HMT *Cameronia* on 12 October 1945. After disembarking at Haifa, we travelled by rail almost the length of Palestine to a desert area south of Gaza where we occupied a large cluster of tented camps and learned some useful lessons. The first and probably most important concerned camp security. Routine guards and 'prowlers' proved ineffective in deterring Arab pilferers, whose expertise at night surpassed anything of this nature previously encountered. They entered tents with stealth, stealing with impunity until effective counter measures were introduced. The most noteworthy occasion concerned a commanding officer who woke one morning to find that his tent and its entire contents had disappeared, with the exception of the camp bed and bedclothes on which he lay.

Palestine under the British Mandate, 1920 - 1948

137

Fortunately, his pistol had been under his pillow.

Although a problem for the guards, these incursions were regarded merely as annoyances and we enjoyed a brief tranquil interlude, with the chance of a daily swim in the Mediterranean. But very soon what we had regarded as an inviting, peaceful prospect erupted into violence. We then became immersed in what would prove to be three years of trouble.

Initially, we had to learn the identities of the Jewish dissidents who were bent on inflicting casualties on the Security Forces. The Stern Gang, otherwise known as *Lehi* (acronym for Fighters for the Freedom of Israel), had up to 500 members and specialized in assassinations, usually by shooting. More significant in terms of potential was the much larger *Irgun Zwai L'eumi* (IZL), commanded by Menachem Begin, with a membership of 3,000 to 4,000. This organization applied itself to larger scale and more ambitious operations in which the resulting deaths and destruction were accepted in order to achieve publicity or some political end. Their 'achievements' included the partial destruction of the King David Hotel in Jerusalem on 22 July 1946 with the loss of ninety-one lives. The largest of the Jewish armed organizations and one of considerable size was the Defence Force, known as the Hagana, with a strength of over 80,000, though in fact not all were armed.

As time passed, the number of ambushes and hit and run attacks against small groups of off-duty troops increased, but so too did the larger scale operations against installations, police stations, clubs and restaurants patronized by members of the Security Forces. Such attacks served to increase the frustration that all units were reporting. Yet morale itself, certainly within 6th Airborne Division, remained consistently high throughout the duration of the campaign. Closely linked to the frustration affecting all ranks of the Army and Palestine Police came the virtue of forbearance which was so prominent and commendable throughout the British forces at times when attacks involving small arms, grenades, bombs and road and rail mines by Jewish extremists were costing many lives. There were admittedly a few, but so very few, cases in which British troops showed their anger and sought opportunities to retaliate in kind and these were recorded. Nevertheless I can add that, to the best of my knowledge, no Jewish life was taken by troops of 6th Airborne Division other than in the course of duty, within the proper chain of command and in response to hostile action. Our relationship with the Arabs was much easier because, until the closing stages of the Mandate, when both Jews and Arabs started to clear their decks for action, the Arabs by their

138

exemplary behaviour caused neither the Government nor the Security Forces the slightest embarrassment.

It would be misleading to leave the impression that we never became closely acquainted with any Jews, because in some of the larger towns we met quite a number when the security situation permitted as we visited shops and restaurants. The attitude of the Jewish community in the north, particularly in Haifa and Galilee, was noticeably more reasonable and the situation more stable than in Tel Aviv and Lydda. During our last year, after the Division had moved into northern Palestine, I met a stamp dealer, one Dr Hoexter, who had a shop in Haifa. At the time I was a keen stamp collector and before long we were on good terms. I found him highly intelligent, cultured and able to discuss the problems of that troubled land with an open mind. I was not surprised to learn later that he was a member of the Hagana but, when I said goodbye to him shortly before leaving Palestine, we parted on the best of terms.

Before we left in April 1948 I was asked if I would write a history of 6th Airborne Division during the Palestine Campaign (*Cordon and Search*). This I did in the period immediately following the end of the British Mandate, after the Division had returned to England. Any soldier attempting to write an account of such a sensitive and complex subject, beset by confused and often discreditable politics, before the dust had time to settle needed to be aware of the importance of sticking to his facts and curbing his opinions. Thus, for a relatively junior serving officer invited to produce a balanced and illuminating account of his Division's part in events, the constraints far outweighed the opportunities to throw light on sensitive aspects, let alone indulge in criticism. Now, looking back nearly sixty years, my memories of Palestine remain so vivid I decided the best way to convey something of the atmosphere prevailing at the time was to quote from a selection of the numerous letters I wrote to my parents:

October 28th 1945   6 Airborne Armoured Recce Regt
We are due for a move before long but in view of the possibility of trouble in the country, once again security is stepping in and I can't give you details.

Nov 4th 1945   HQ 3 Para Bde
Well you can see that I have changed addresses again. Tomorrow I start a new job as Brigade Major of the 3rd Parachute Brigade, which is one of the Bdes in 6 Airborne Div.

Nov 20th 1945

139

This morning the Brigade marched out of Tel Aviv having spent just under a week in trying to force some discipline into the 200,000 inhabitants. It all started a week ago when, after Bevin's [Foreign Secretary] announcement on Palestine, the Jews got together 40-50,000 of them and started to run amok. I dare say the papers kept it fairly quiet at home but we have had quite a 'hot cup of tea' restoring order – £200,000 worth of damage to British property; possibly an indication of the shape of things to come. However, the Brigade came out on top and everything is once more quiet again.

March 11th 1946   HQ 6th Airborne Division
Well, as you can see I am now at Div HQ. In an ordinary way I can expect to be here anyway 6 months, possibly longer. It is all very good experience. ...The Jews are still up to their old tricks. A party of 12 entered my old Bde camp at Sarafand last week dressed in Airborne berets and smocks and with 2 stolen army trucks. In broad daylight they drove up to an ammunition store and started to load up their trucks. Fortunately our chaps smelt a rat and started a battle. We shot them up good and proper and those who weren't killed were eventually captured with the stolen ammunition and trucks. Our only casualty was a poor girl who had just arrived from England with a small party of WVS attached to the Div. She got a stray bullet in the tummy and will be lucky if she lives – still D.I. [This was Mrs Jean Marjoribanks who fortunately made a wonderful recovery. She belonged to a splendid team of volunteers under Mrs Majorie Fildes who ran a canteen service, particularly during parachute dropping, and were known by all as 'the cygnets'.]

March 17th 1946
The new general appears to be just as good in every way as the last one (General Bols). The new one is General Cassels. Very young for a general [Then aged thirty-nine, he concluded his military career as Chief of the General Staff and retired as Field Marshal], but I expect that will always be the case in this Div. ...This afternoon I am motoring up to Haifa for a threesome party with Chips and Ian Battye. We were all at Cambridge together and in addition I was at the Staff College with Ian. And of course we are all 3 Div members or ex-members so we shall have plenty to talk about.

April 9th 1946
...Today we had one of those rare things (fortunately) a parachute that didn't open. The poor fellow (an officer) wouldn't know much about it. It's very nearly a safe game and it's just that odd chance that

makes it what it is!

The Yids continue to make a nuisance of themselves. This week it has been the railway again but we caught 30 of them on their way back. All armed to the teeth but 10 of our chaps set about them and they soon threw in the sponge when a few of them had been hit. They opened fire first.

8 May 1946

We had an airborne exercise in Khartoum on Monday and Tuesday so I have been away since early Sunday morning and arrived back this afternoon. It went with quite a swing and there was no doubt that Khartoum was very impressed. In fact it struck me that it was the biggest thing that Khartoum had seen since its liberation in 1898! The jump was a rough one owing to the wind but those who were not detained in hospital had a grand time last night going round the town well bandaged up and getting free drinks all round! [Exercise 'Gordon', as it was called, turned out to be an event of historic airborne interest. As the Dakotas carrying 108 parachutists approached, in a temperature of 110ºF (43ºC) in the shade, the wind was marginal, but acceptable for jumping. The decision was therefore made for the jump to take place and a green Very light was fired as the aircraft began their run-in. At this stage the wind increased and by the time the parachutists jumped it was gusting to an estimated speed of 25 mph. As they landed a high proportion were unable to collapse their canopies and were dragged across the airfield with no means of releasing their harness, and choking from sand and dust. Fortunately a disaster was prevented by a single strand of barbed wire marking the perimeter of the airfield. This certainly saved many lives, but even so the casualties amounted to one killed, three major injuries and seventy-four minor injuries out of the 108 who jumped. The exercise carried on as planned and ended with the defeat of a dervish force on the site of the Battle of Omdurman, 1898. Despite the abnormally high casualties it was judged by all concerned to have been very successful and I never saw higher morale after an airborne exercise. It even had its lighter side when the parachute company commander, Major Dover, landed in telephone wires from which he was unable to release himself. While in this predicament a fuzzy-wuzzy opportunist relieved him of his boots and made off before help arrived.]

August 5th 1946

Never has firm handling been in greater demand than it is today in Palestine. Since we came out here a year ago not one Jew has been executed – in spite of the fact that dozens of British soldiers have been murdered, to say nothing of the Palestine Police. It is all so disturbing and infuriating to those of us who think things out (and there are many who do). The British Armed Forces are here supporting and representing a Government who pay lip service so frequently that they must have difficulty in making a new choice of words on each occasion – but what happens? Nothing, except to discredit publicly our GOC in C [Lieutenant General Sir Evelyn Barker] who, as a man with the courage of his convictions, puts his thoughts on paper in the form of the truest and straightest statement that has appeared in this country or outside for many years. He has the wholesale backing of all his troops, to a man, but what happens at home – a whole lot of noodle-headed, hypocritical, cranked and useless politicians get up and talk about inopportune and malicious statements calculated to breed anti-Semitism. They should come out and see the realities of the situation for themselves – anti-Semitism isn't being bred like that, it is here of its own accord, produced by the repeated acts of terrorism and fostered by the exasperation of not being allowed to deal with the situation in a manner dictated by common sense.

We are heading for worse, for before long we shall be involved not only with the Jews but the Arabs as well unless we change our policy, but I think it is already too late and one can only wait and see what further acts of insanity, incompetence and ignorance the Govt have in store. There now, I feel better!

November 6th 1946

I find I have plenty to do with the G1 away in UK, particularly at the present time with another wave of terrorism in full swing.

We are all shattered by the latest Government folly. If they honestly think the release of all these Jews will result in the end of terrorism, they have got another think coming. Many of us are rapidly reaching the stage of being thoroughly ashamed of the various steps that are being taken in this country in the name of the British people. It is the most vicious political scandal that has ever come my way. In the last week we have had between 40 and 50 British soldiers killed or wounded and our answer is to let out of detention the Jewish leaders who were proved to be closely associated with the very terrorists who are responsible, and on top of that we raise the curfew. I wonder what will happen next. ....

November 12th 1946

My prophesy of last week was not far wrong. Several lives have been lost and much damage done to property since we raised all the restrictions. …We lose General Cassels next month and Gen Bols returns to take over command again. We liked the latter but have grown to love the former and no one will like seeing him leave.

January 26th 1947

I am sorry I got no letter off last week but it was the most hectic in many ways that we have had so far. First of all we have moved and are now looking after North Palestine and our HQ is in Haifa. I am billeted ½ mile from the place I was in exactly 3 years ago when I first came out here. [Divisional HQ moved on 22 January and was now located in the Carmelite Monastery of Elijah at Stella Maris.] Things are comparatively quiet at present but we are all expecting a recrudescence within the next day or two as a result of this Shonk (local uncomplimentary term for Jew) being condemned to death. Guns are carried loaded and cocked these days! We have to go about in 4s now and fully armed at all times. By night vehicles have to go in pairs and so it goes on. …

February 5th 1947

The country is in what one might call a state of organized confusion. The 'evacuees' are having a very difficult time of it and naturally we are having to see them through all their difficulties. We have had an immense amount of work to do during the past week or so and at night there always seems to be enough work to keep one busy right up to bedtime and often afterwards.

At times it is amusing: for example, here we are with our HQ in a monastery with monks walking about in the courtyard outside and on the flat roof and one will hear extracts of telephone conversations echoing through the building: 'How many pregnant women on the next train?' Army officers have been seen in the shops bargaining for lots of 500 nappies and wondering why the price has gone up since yesterday! Mrs Lichtenstein has three children by a German husband and one by an Irishman; which of them shall be evacuated and should she go with them, she being a Russian by birth? [Note. The 'evacuees' were the British women and children and certain other civilians who, without warning, were informed in a Government of Palestine broadcast at 1400 hrs on 31 January that they were to be evacuated from Palestine '…so that the Government and armed forces will not be hampered in the task of maintaining order'. Thus plans for Operation POLLY had been secretly prepared and 1,500 women and children were evacuated to the UK and Egypt within a week.]

March 2nd 1947

Yesterday was noisy and we had quite a lot of trouble, likewise the day before when they blew up Barclays Bank which houses a number of our chaps and British civilians (being protected!!).

Last night I went to a cocktail party given by 3 Para Bde HQ (my old Brigade) just up the road. In the middle "they" started to blow things up in the town. I was asked by the General to go and have a look-see what damage had been done. After viewing said damage I returned up the hill. Before we had reached the top a jeep below us was blown up halfway down by an electrically detonated mine. Three of the occupants were killed and the fourth blinded. I think they may have let my jeep go past as there was only one other apart from myself in it and by waiting a minute or two they got a full jeep. The unfortunate chaps were four of our Airborne military police. Such is life; you can imagine feeling runs very high after a bit and the sense of frustration caused by the fact that we are in such a helpless position does not improve it.

April 5th 1947

The week has been rather more eventful than most. We have had the largest fire Palestine has ever seen just down the hill [an IZL effort against oil storage tanks near the harbour]. It's been going for about 4 or 5 days now and is still going well, right out of control. By day the sky was darkened to such an extent that we had to have the lights on at one stage in broad daylight and the fire 2 miles away. The pictures of the atomic bomb test had nothing on it! At night the glow is terrific.

Apart from that we have had 2 officers murdered while out riding (ambushed with tommy guns) and one of our Div HQ trucks blown up by a mine just down the hill. I have never seen even during the war a vehicle quite so riddled and battered and the occupants to remain alive, which is the case up to now with the chaps in this vehicle.

Various other acts of sabotage go to make up rather an expensive week.

August 3rd 1947

The country is in a state of turbulence rather above the normal and the hanging of two British sergeants last week has created a wave of anger and disgust among all ranks. [Sergeants Martin and Paice, employed in uniform on Field Security duties, were captured by the IZL and hanged from a tree in retaliation for the execution of 3 IZL gangsters in Acre Gaol. A full account is given in Cordon and Search.]

Unfortunately the Government has been typical and through failing to react immediately has already lost the initiative. We have enough to put up with the Jews but when we are also handicapped by the Government it makes it doubly hard. No wonder under such conditions the troops and police have in one or two instances taken the law into their own hands.

Incidentally the G1 has been ill since I left and there appears to be quite a chance he will have to go home. That will be the third G1 I have outlasted if he goes. ...

October 14th 1947

Life in the Army is getting very difficult and there is little enough time to enjoy oneself even at weekends. We are being cut down so rapidly that each regular soldier has to work twice as hard and however enthusiastic one may be about one's work it begins to pall after a bit. I get into my office every morning of the week bar Sundays between 7.15 and 7.30 and work right through until 8.15 pm and then after dinner at night until after midnight. Sometimes I have had barely 6 hours sleep between the end of one working day and the beginning of another. We wouldn't mind this so much if we knew our efforts were appreciated outside the Army but there are already too many signs that the country has got back into its peace time habits of regarding the Army as an expensive and unnecessary luxury except in time of war.

...Still no G1.

December 2nd 1947

Since the announcement of the decision of UNO to divide Palestine we have had the expected repercussions. The Arabs are taking great umbrage and I don't altogether blame them. It is amusing to note also that there are already signs of the Jews wishing we weren't going after all – they are all quite ready to forget what they have been saying all along about us clearing out as soon as possible (that is all except the dissident groups, who are still 'at war' with us).

Christmas Day 1947

My Christmas started with Midnight Communion held in our Camp Church and attended by a number of officers from our Mess. Matins followed after breakfast this morning at 9.30 and at both services we sang carols and Christmas hymns lustily.

...In the meantime the Holy Land remains uneasy with bloodshed on all three sides taking place daily and feeling and tension rising steadily. There will be a war in this country before very long and it remains to be seen whether we get clear in time.

January 14th 1948

I have been selected to go to Germany on a short visit in the near future with one other officer and will probably be leaving here by air on 26th Jan.

...My second piece of news is a change of job. After being G2 (Operations) for 2 years the General [by now this was Major General Hugh Stockwell, destined eventually to become Deputy SACEUR] has changed me to G2 (Intelligence). This will be a welcome change as far as I am concerned as it is just as interesting and not quite such hard work.

...On the way back from the marsh on Saturday night we were attacked by Arabs armed with a variety of weapons who thought we were Jews I think. We replied with 12 bores as well as more orthodox weapons and definitely came off best. Two days before I was shot at by Jews in Haifa so you can see life is looking up and rarely a dull moment!

February 4th 1948

Palestine continues to go its own way, rapidly down hill most of the time and both sides are now openly preparing for a showdown in a big way as soon as the Mandate ends. There have already been some bloody clashes and the Arabs have shown themselves to be second to none in the atrocity line. You will have read no doubt of one or two massacres, one of which took place in Haifa oil refinery. Over 40 Jews were killed in 30 minutes without a shot being fired.

Today we engaged a Syrian band in a proper little battle in the Huleh area. We came off best and they, or what was left of them, beat a hasty retreat eventually over the Jordan back into their own country.

March 30th 1948

Had a most amusing and exciting weekend. Visited Mount Tabor and were ambushed by Arabs, some 60 of them, but were fortunately differentiated from Jews in time. Had long talks with them and gained some invaluable intelligence and photos which you will no doubt see anon.

April 4th 1948   HQ North Palestine District

I went to Jerusalem during the week and did some useful shopping although most of the shops are shut and the town is almost in a state of siege. As we darted round to one or two places we were accompanied by bursts of machine gun fire in the streets and were eventually glad to get clear. Poor old Jerusalem is in a sorry state with deserted streets and few if any public services operating and a small arms battle in progress almost without stopping in one part of the town or another.

April 12th 1948

Div HQ, less us few remnants, left for UK on Saturday, the majority were very glad to get away. The country gets more and more chaotic every day and I don't suppose either the Press or BBC can really put over a sufficiently accurate account of the real state of affairs. I can't see anything now preventing war in the country. We have all but reached it now.

Today Sally, the Yellow Labrador I have been looking after, was successfully despatched for UK on board a Swedish ship. I have cabled her owner the news.

And so our unproductive spell of nearly three years' service in Palestine came to its bloody end. The situation we left behind was tragic and its outcome, in a national sense, not far short of shameful. Yet the responsibility for the course of events could not, with fairness, be laid at the Army's door. We had seen the Jews and some politicians at their worst, although the former clearly resented what they regarded as our lack of understanding of their problems.

What the Jews overlooked in all their aspirations for their 'promised land', however, and have continued to ignore to the present day, is that to the Arabs Palestine is not a promised land but their homeland, and the only one they have known. In this situation Arabs have resorted in desperation to extreme measures and for this they are criticized. Yet should it not be the so-called civilized world that deserves criticism for its indifference to half a century of Arab suffering? But even this dispassion is surpassed by the refusal of too many Jews in both Israel and the USA to acknowledge that the Arabs have any rights at all in the land of their birth.

What is so pleasing now is that it is the pleasanter memories that linger, rather than those of the more difficult times that so often prevailed. Of those we met who belonged to Palestine, including the more recent arrivals, there is no need for reiteration. Some we found likeable and they remain part of the memories. Others whom we disliked I prefer to forget. But it is the beauty, the charm, the peace and quiet where it existed and the lasting friendships that have kept intruding into my thoughts as I have researched and written this chapter.

My favourite view was looking across the Plain of Esdralon and the Bay of Acre from the top of Mount Carmel but, with the total absence of tourists, there were countless other attractions, often with Biblical associations that added to the interest, sometimes compellingly. If I have a favourite recollection it is that of the wonderful sense of peace that came over me on the quiet evenings when I returned to work late in the Monastery of Elijah on Mount Carmel, where my office was formerly a monk's cell. There all thoughts of the ugly problems that demanded my presence would be temporarily dispelled as I listened to the monks chanting their form of Compline. My office was the last one on our part of a shared passage, separated from their section only by a cardboard partition through which their melodious voices could be heard clearly.

Fifty years later I wrote to the Father Superior telling him of my memories and voicing my suspicions that our activities could hardly have been conducive to their work and worship. His reply reached me through his English-speaking historian who assured me charmingly that the presence of our soldiers had in no way disturbed his community. He ended his delightful and interesting letter with thanks for the insights I had given of our time in his monastery and the promise of the support of his 'poor prayers'.

Chapter Thirteen

Weapon-testing in Georgia

Wherever brave men fight and die for freedom you will find me;
I am the bulwark of our Nation's Defense;
I am always ready, now and forever;
I am The Infantry, Queen of Battle. FOLLOW ME!

US Army Infantry Center, Fort Benning, Georgia

The *Empress of Scotland* berthed at Liverpool on 2 May with close on 1,000 well refreshed troops of 6th Airborne Division, including the 8th/9th Parachute Battalion and Rear Divisional HQ, and soon after I was heading for home on four weeks' leave. Following family celebrations, it included performances of *Tosca* and *Carmen* in Newcastle, fishing on the River Coquet and a joyous reunion with my Black Labrador, Duchess (daughter of pre-war Dinah). Following this leave I reported to the Airborne Forces Depot in Aldershot, taking with me the large laundry basket full of records of 6th Airborne Division's tour of duty in Palestine that I brought back as part of my baggage. This I deposited in the office I was given in which to write *Cordon and Search*.

At much the same time as I arrived in Aldershot General Hughie Stockwell assumed his next appointment a few miles away as Commandant of the Royal Military Academy, Sandhurst. Soon afterwards, at his invitation, I moved to Sandhurst to continue my writing in a quieter setting where he could also keep in touch with my progress and help to find a publisher. Three days before Christmas, with *Cordon and Search* off my hands, I was granted leave before my next posting, which took me to the 1st Battalion of the Parachute Regiment, by then stationed at Brunswick in northern Germany, where I took command of 'C' Company. This, partly on account of some of its personalities, turned out to be memorable. The Battalion was commanded by John Cubbon, who was remarkable in many ways, but none more so than for his prodigious energy and enthusiasm. As far as he was concerned, only the best was good enough at all times, whether at work or play.

Before long I had taken on the training of a rifle team to compete at Bisley, where all acquitted themselves well. I also benefited from the training and then had my best ARA meeting, finishing as runner-up in the Army Championship. At the end of the Bisley meeting I returned home to Priestfield at a sad time after my parents had decided that, with their family grown up and dispersed and my father having retired, the time had come to move south. They would leave behind the rigours of the north, including snowbound winters, and many friends but, after much thought and effort, they had found a house on Exmoor some three miles from Dulverton. Undoubtedly for them it was the right decision and I made every effort to conceal my disappointment. Priestfield was the only home I had known and I loved the countryside and the people of those parts, which I still visit as often as possible.

I returned to Germany in time for the annual season of unit and formation training, the first stage of which, for the infantry and airborne units, consisted of battalion exercises. Inevitably they were searching and rigorous and those planned by John Cubbon were intended to put companies to a comprehensive test.

Our tour in Germany reached its climax at the end of September, when we participated in NATO manoeuvres in the valley of the River Moselle. Before the exercise began the battalion had to complete a long approach march by road of some 400 miles, much of it following the Rhine, via Hanover, Dortmund, Cologne, Bonn and Coblenz. On arrival we joined the French 2nd Infantry Division with which we opposed the US Army 1st Infantry Division, known to its members as 'Big Red One'. It turned out to be a memorable encounter, which became more realistic as it progressed to the climactic battle of Thalfang, east of Luxembourg. Here there was physical contact, which the umpires succeeded in bringing under control in time to prevent the occasion being marred, although it was later regarded by 1 Para as a peacetime battle honour.

By the time we returned to Brunswick from this final exercise the battalion's tour in Germany was at its end. It had not been typical of many, mainly because of the emphasis placed on the importance of commitment and exertion in the achievement of fitness for war and a wide range of activities and sports. It was also a contented unit, which reflects on sound administration, and in this happy state we returned to the UK.

I had not been in Aldershot for more than a few weeks when I heard that I had been selected to take part in an extensive programme of rifle trials due to begin in the United States a few months later. Further details would follow and within days I was ordered to report to the War Office for a briefing. All this came entirely out of the blue. I was to act as the British User Test Officer, assisted by a high-powered team of Small Arms School instructors, during a series of rifle trials likely to last nine months, mostly at Fort Benning, the US Army Infantry Center in Georgia. It was a very exciting prospect and my preparations began early in the New Year. For the next few months I virtually had two jobs, retaining command of my parachute company while learning the background to the project that would occupy me for the rest of 1950. The familiarization with my next job included a week spent at the small-arms factory at Enfield, where two new rifles in .280 inch calibre had been developed and produced. A third model had also been sponsored by the War Office and contracted out for production in Belgium.

At last, on 18 April, I set off on the first leg of my journey to Fort Benning. At that time those crossing the Atlantic, whether for business or pleasure, were only a small fraction of today's massive numbers and most went by sea. By comparison, long distance air travel was still in its infancy and to most of those who chose this option it was quite an experience. In my own case the choice was made for me and at Heathrow I boarded a BOAC Speedbird Boeing Stratocruiser, which cruised at around 210 knots, completing the journey to New York, after refuelling at Prestwick in Scotland and Gander in Newfoundland, in about twenty hours. It was without doubt the best-equipped and most comfortable aircraft I ever travelled in. It was designed as a true double-decker where the upper deck was for sitting and sleeping and the lower for meals. Both were spacious and the meals served by a noteworthy cabin crew would have done justice to any good restaurant. After a leisurely dinner one returned to the upper deck to find a bunk made up ready for use in place of the chair one had vacated earlier.

I was met in New York by a delightful American member of the British diplomatic staff, who gave me an unforgettable tour of the city, the like of which I had never seen. A few hours later I was on my way to Washington, where I was not only briefed in some detail on my task at Fort Benning and other locations I would visit, but also given a valuable insight into the organization I was about to join and guidance on some of the customs and procedures of the US Army. Early the next morning I was taken to the Aberdeen Weapons Proving Ground, not far beyond Baltimore, some fifty miles to the north. By British standards this was a vast and impressive establishment where all new American weapons, and no doubt many others, were proved and tested ballistically. I was shown round its facilities and learned about the technical tests to which our weapons would be subjected. The ammunition would also be evaluated to assess its performance, including related wound ballistics.

From Aberdeen I travelled by train to Fort Benning, passing through Virginia, North and South Carolina and then south-westwards across Georgia almost as far as Alabama, on a journey spanning twenty-four hours. On arrival my first impression was dimensional, because here was one military establishment occupying an area larger than that of most, if not all, of the military camps and barracks of the UK combined. Within this massive post were all the facilities, plus extensive training areas, for a vast garrison including a complete infantry division, the Infantry Center and Parachute School.

At the testing centre I met my opposite number in the US Army, Lieutenant Colonel William Moore, a delightful and highly competent officer who ensured that the trials ran smoothly. We were provided with a sizeable body of selected marksmen, representative of the two countries concerned, with the British interest being represented by the Canadian Army. And so the trials began and continued successfully, with good humour and plenty of opportunities for everyone, including the British, to participate in baseball and other activities. Throughout, Bill Moore exercised his gift for getting the best out of everyone through example, personality and a light touch. He was a relaxed Georgian with a typical drawl who never raised his voice, except when calling the changes in a Southern square dance in which we were all expected to join during periodical social evenings. He was a keen game shot to boot, who rated turkey shooting (of the wild genus) as his most challenging and enjoyable pastime. I was fortunate to find myself working with a cross-section of competent and friendly Americans and do not recall a single disagreement throughout the course of the trials. The Georgians, in particular, not only made our task easier than it might have been but were overwhelming with their hospitality.

It would have been almost impossible as a visiting airborne soldier at Fort Benning not to become involved in parachuting at the 'Jump School'. In my own case it was not long before I was hailed by several of its staff who had noticed my red beret and Parachute Regiment badge. They asked if I would like to see round the school and there followed an invitation to jump with them, which I readily accepted. As this activity began early each morning all I needed to do was book a jump the previous day. In this way I was introduced to their aircraft, parachute designs and techniques and shown the mental preparation of their recruits, all of which were different from our own. Here, too, for the first time I wore a reserve chute. When, later, it was adopted by the British Army the old hands were inclined to regard it as sissy, but that view soon changed after it had saved a few lives.

One day in mid June our range programme was suspended to enable us to watch a demonstration for the benefit of a party of congressmen who were accompanied by no fewer than thirty generals. I searched for an appropriate collective noun for them and came up with a 'bellowing' of generals; at the time I was still a major. As we took our seats and studied the programme my mind went back to a demonstration by the Fifth Fusiliers that I had watched at the School of Infantry at Warminster earlier in the year, at which a rifle company was drawn up with detachments of support weapons as a prelude to the live-firing exercise that followed. Any similarity I might have anticipated disappeared as a fanfare of massed trumpets was followed by a formal greeting and the statement: 'Gentlemen, in front of you we have on display an infantry division complete with its supporting armour and artillery, to be joined later by close support aircraft.' During the next hour they fired more ammunition than I suspect Salisbury Plain would witness in a year. I returned to our task of testing four rifles in thoughtful mood.

Less than two weeks later, on 25 June, North Korea, which was closely linked with China's regime, without warning invaded South Korea, which enjoyed strong American support, including a military relationship. With the USSR in volatile mood the possibility of this limited war developing into the Third World War, with the sinister connotation of a nuclear exchange, was all too apparent. The USA at once mobilized for war and within hours this grim awareness changed to widespread apprehension. Meanwhile the United Kingdom and the Commonwealth, under the United Nations umbrella, became involved in the support of South Korea. As an observer on one of the largest US Army posts I was struck by the state of shock that suddenly affected wives and families as husbands and fathers were whisked away from them. I had never seen it before, partly because I had been a participant rather than an onlooker. Everywhere one noticed worried little groups of mothers and children sharing their feelings and as one passed their married quarters there were anxious faces staring sadly out of the windows. As I thought about it I realized how much easier it is to march off to war than to watch a loved one doing so.

153

Early in August I was asked to visit the 82nd Airborne Division at Fort Bragg in North Carolina, where the airborne unit equivalent to the Infantry Board was located. During my three-day visit, which included much hospitality, two delightful young officers from the 82nd, Hal Moore and Jack Bruckner, acted as joint hosts, together with Hal's charming wife Julie. There I also found Robin Couchman, a young Guards officer whom I knew well, then serving with the Parachute Regiment. He was due to move down later to Benning in order to attend a Pathfinder course and was an ideal choice, having just the qualities to ensure he would derive the full benefit and contribute much with his customary charm. While at Bragg I was also invited to make a couple of jumps with the Division and was introduced to the new Hart and T9 parachutes.

My return journey by car took two days and I chose a route that took me through the Great Smoky Mountains National Park, astride the border between North Carolina and Tennessee. It was not only a breathtaking landscape, but renowned as a botanical refuge with no less than 152 species of tree alone. This was the first of numerous American national parks I visited over many years and it helped to shape my later career. On arrival at Benning I found a letter waiting from Charles Mitchell with news that the Fifth Fusiliers, with which he was serving at the time, was being made up to strength with reservists in preparation for its departure to Korea.

Three weeks after my return from Fort Bragg I had a telephone call from there with the sad news that Robin Couchman had been killed that day through the failure of his parachute to open. The funeral was due to take place two days later with full military honours and I was requested to act as an honorary pallbearer. One of their aircraft would take me there and back. Never was I present at a more impressive funeral service, accompanied by faultless military ceremony. Robin had made such an impact on his hosts that they were genuinely saddened, as well as aware that their equipment failure had led to his death. I spent the weekend with Hal and Jack but thereafter never saw them again, although I still keep in touch with Hal. Fifteen years after we had met at Bragg, Hal was commanding the 1st Battalion of 7th Cavalry Division in the Ia Drang Battle, one of the most decisive of the Vietnam War. Later, after retirement as a Lieutenant General, he co-wrote *We Were Soldiers Once...and Young,* acclaimed in many countries as one of the greatest books of modern war and made into a film.

By now the end of our task at Benning was almost in sight, so far as completion of the range work went. Our recommendation in favour of the Belgian-made FN Rifle, with modest modification, was eventually accepted for the British and other European armies, though never, for whatever reason, by the USA. Our final fortnight was hectic, with a crescendo of parties of all kinds. Behind us already lay an intensive succession of drinks parties, dinner parties, dances, picnics, barbecues, lobster suppers, square dancing and assorted games with liquid refreshment. The latter were headed by baseball, which I must confess I much enjoyed. It boiled down to almost continuous entertainment, which reflected the nature of the warm-hearted folk by whom we were surrounded. We greatly appreciated them all but, coming as most of them did after long days on the range, these parties could be as exhausting as they were enjoyable. Shortly before I left Fort Benning I was asked to 'drop in' at the Parachute School where, most unexpectedly, I was presented with the United States Army Parachute Wings, which I subsequently wore on appropriate occasions, and an illuminated certificate describing me as an honorary graduate of the Fort Benning Infantry School Airborne Course. It would have been better still had I qualified for their rate of Airborne 'risk pay', which at that time was ten times more for officers and five times more for other ranks than the British Army's rates!

And so, after one last party, I finished my packing at 0330 on my day of departure and a few hours later set off on my final assignment in North America. This had been initiated by the Canadians, with War Office approval, and involved a 2,000 mile journey by air and rail to visit the Canadian Airborne Centre at Rivers, nor far from Winnipeg, Manitoba. They were reviewing their Airborne tactics and techniques and wished to discuss some of the issues. My visit had been planned to last five days, but we finished the programme with two days to spare, during which my hosts took me duck-hunting. There, for the first and last time, I used a pump-action semi-automatic twelve bore shotgun. The occasion was a wonderful experience and it was thrilling to watch a major migration of duck on a scale I had never seen.

From Rivers I returned to the British Army Staff in Washington DC, who had been so helpful throughout my stay in North America. There I received instructions to report to the War Office on my arrival in London and incidentally got confirmation that the Fifth Fusiliers were due to leave soon for Korea. In fact they left Southampton on that very day, 11 October 1950. Three days later I flew home.

Chapter Fourteen

Reluctant Whitehall Warrior

And so the great ones go off to their dinner but the secretary stays, getting thinner and thinner, doing his best to record and report what he thinks they will think they ought to have thought.

Anon, Cabinet Offices

On arrival in London I reported as requested to the Deputy Military Secretary in the War Office to learn of my next appointment. When I met him he already knew of my wish to join my regiment in Korea, but explained that this was not to be because I had been selected for an appointment in the embryonic Ministry of Defence in London, which at the time was so small that many of those in the War Office were still unaware of it. In fact the Ministry of Defence then consisted of little more than those committees and sub-committees responsible to the Chiefs of Staff. One of these was the Joint Intelligence Committee (JIC), which worked in the Cabinet Offices, and here I would be employed as one of three secretaries. The Deputy Military Secretary then gave me a brief outline of what my work would involve. In discussion I raised a hypothetical question concerning any chance of being posted to my regiment, if in due course it should need me in Korea. This idea was not well received. I was filling an Army appointment and the only way I could be relieved prematurely would be by a suitable civil servant from within the same department.

After a few weeks' leave I reported for duty in the Cabinet Offices, where I was welcomed by John Gardiner, the senior secretary to the JIC. He had joined the Royal Marines before the Second World War after leaving Shrewsbury, where we had overlapped but had not known each other, he being several years my senior. Following my introduction to the modus operandi of the JIC, I was taken to meetings as a secretary under instruction and for a day or two my notes, when expanded into minutes, were regarded as an exercise. When John was happy with them I took on my share of the work. The principal meetings were those of the JIC Directors who met weekly. The Deputy Directors and the Security Committee met less frequently and the various specialized sub-committees when required. It was a matter of pride within the secretariat that the minutes of Directors' meetings were written, reproduced and circulated the same day, which often involved late evenings in the office with the supporting staff given time off later. In addition to the Directors, copies also went to the Chiefs of Staff, the Joint Planning Staff and, when appropriate, to the Prime Minister and Minister of Defence. All JIC minutes were invariably graded 'Top Secret' and those of other committees as appropriate.

The military strength of the Soviet Union and, in due course, China, almost as a matter of course took precedence over all other matters in relation to studies concerned with the balance of power, which was constantly being reviewed. The Directors' meetings of January 1951 were typical in this respect:

3 Jan	1. Indications of Russian Preparedness for War.
4 Jan	1. Review of the Situation round the Soviet and Satellite Perimeter.
10 Jan	1. Soviet long-term Preparations for War. Review of major developments during 1950.

Following these principal items, which also served as a useful barometer of the threat of war, came a selection of disparate subjects of sufficient importance to merit discussion at Director level, of which the following are examples from the early months of 1951:

Preparation of widespread civil defence measures in China, particularly in the Canton area.
Handling of Soviet and Satellite Deserters.
Evacuation of Intelligence Agencies from Germany in an Emergency.

By this stage the Cold War had risen in temperature to one of the hot spots that characterized it from time to time. The Korean War had not only torn apart the fabric of that ill-fated peninsula, but involved the world's principal powers in such a manner that none was able or willing to pull back. From that point the spectre of nuclear or thermonuclear war was feared in many parts of the world and most of all in Russia and the USA, where it was best understood and so reason ultimately prevailed. But in the meantime the Korean War intensified and the fear persisted. Although it had been initiated by North Korea against its southern neighbour, by the end of 1950 their armies, which had suffered heavily, were far outnumbered by their infinitely more powerful allies. Nevertheless, it came as an unpleasant surprise to the Joint Planning Staff and probably to the Chiefs of Staff when, early in the New Year, the JIC published a wide-ranging report on the Chinese Communist threat in the Far East and South-East Asia, which mentioned Chinese 'special measures'. These included the introduction of a new form of conscription to increase the strength of their armed forces, an increase in the number of Soviet industrial and technical advisers, Russian technicians advising on coastal and AA defences and the arrival of 300 Russian aviation technicians at a new airfield near Tientsin.

The same report also provided startling information from 'most reliable secret sources' concerning a reorganization of the North Korean army, where indications showed it was being built up and trained by the Chinese. It was estimated that an additional 150,000 North Korean troops could be put into the field within two months (i.e. by March), a further 200,000 by May and yet another 250,000 by July. 'As a result, the North Koreans will be capable of putting into the field an army of 500-700,000 within the next six months.' The report observed that this would enable the Chinese to withdraw enough troops from their two armies in that theatre for use against 'another Imperial power in South China'. This, the JIC pointed out, could indicate hostile intentions against either Indo-China or Hong Kong, or possibly Formosa.

In the course of all appraisals connected with the balance of power, the current state of nuclear weaponry and estimates of future build-up and capabilities were essential requirements for all intelligence and planning staffs, to enable them to analyse and present this information to those who bore the ultimate responsibility for decision making. Little more than two years earlier, in July 1948, the JIC had expressed the view that the Russians might possibly produce their first atomic bomb by January 1951 and within two years might have a small stockpile. American intelligence appeared to be broadly in line. These views, naturally, were not generally known, but by then there were many sources well enough informed to satisfy media interest. As conjecture spread there was no means of relieving the gloom which settled over the American and British public.

One of the impressions I have retained is that of the JIC with its feet on the ground at times when there were conflicting sources or noticeable gaps in our knowledge. There were occasions when it might have been tempting to make deductions based on likelihood, but these were resisted or qualified. In such circumstances it is sounder to admit a deficiency than circumvent it. The main cracks were fully known only to those entrusted with access to signals intelligence (SIGINT), which played such a vital role in the Second World War and retained its Top Secret ULTRA grading during the Cold War. Unfortunately after the war, like so many other features of our defence capability, intelligence was deprived of adequate resources without regard to Britannia's Shield. This was despite a recommendation by the Chiefs of Staff that the high level of our wartime intelligence should on no account be lowered.

For this reason, perhaps more than any other, we failed to detect either the planning or preparations leading to the outbreak of the Korean War. Unfortunately, a coolness had crept into American relations with the United Kingdom, due to our readiness to maintain a dialogue with China. As a result the United States withheld vital information from the British Government and, sadly, the same thing was happening internally between USA government departments. Moreover, it emerged during the course of later inquiries that the Americans had failed to give due weight to evidence in their hands concerning Chinese intentions, as a result of which it may be presumed that many Allied lives were lost unnecessarily.

There were few informal engagements linked with the JIC and I doubt if members met socially other than by chance. The same was broadly the case within the Secretariat, although one occasion I do recall as both memorable and enjoyable. This was when General Eisenhower came to London on a three-day visit in January 1951, just after he had been appointed the first Supreme Allied Commander Europe. Among his engagements was an evening party at Claridges, where he was staying, to meet a small cross-section of staff officers from the Ministry of Defence, representative of the three services. To my surprise I was included and found myself to be the most junior guest. The General had requested that the occasion should be informal and took the opportunity of saying a few words about the task ahead and his hopes of building up an organization within the Western Alliance which would play its part in deterring the Soviet Powers from further aggression. He then circulated among the guests, who were introduced in no particular order. When my turn came I was struck, as so many others must have been, by his warmth and friendliness. 'Hello Wilson, nice to see you again! What's your job in the Ministry?' The fact that we had never met before in no way detracted from the positive impression it left. Already he had seen the Prime Minister, Clement Attlee, the Defence Minister, Emanuel

Shinwell, and the Chiefs of Staff.

The following day I became responsible for two new duties assigned to the Secretariat. The first was the writing of a daily report on the current situation in the Korean War, using information from various sources and with news, when available, from the 29th British Independent Infantry Brigade Group. This comprised: 1st Battalion Royal Northumberland Fusiliers, 1st Battalion Gloucestershire Regiment, 1st Battalion Royal Ulster Rifles, 8 King's Royal Irish Hussars, 45 Field Regiment Royal Artillery, plus sub-units of supporting Arms and Services. Copies of this report were dispatched to the King, the Prime Minister, the Minister of Defence and the Chiefs of Staff.

My second new daily task was to update the Korean War situation maps, which had just been set up on easels in the Cabinet Room of Number 10 and the office of the Minister of Defence. The intention was to do this, whenever possible, before Mr Attlee visited the room to glance at the map and likewise before Mr Shinwell arrived in his office. Unfortunately, as so often happens, the complications emerged later. Such was the number of stages through which the information of the events in the war zone was collated, and the time taken in assessing casualties, that it was sometimes late in arriving in Whitehall. I was then apt to be found at work on maps in the offices of those I was trying to avoid and questions about current operations might ensue. Clement Attlee had a trained eye for battle maps, while Manny Shinwell was in closer touch with the situation through his daily involvement. Although his constituency lay in the heartland of the Durham Light Infantry it was so close to the recruiting area of the Royal Northumberland Fusiliers that when updating his map I used to take the liberty of including a symbol marked '1 RNF' among those relating to Allied and enemy formations and this he appreciated.

As time passed and I saw more of the committee I became fascinated by some of its members. While they appeared to share little background and few characteristics, their intellect and sense of commitment were, as one would expect, of a very high order. The chairman was Patrick Reilly, who had passed out top in the Foreign Office examination of the year following his Oxford graduation and was elected an Honorary Fellow of All Souls. In due course he was knighted and became British Ambassador in both Moscow and Paris. He was a quietly spoken, rather gentle man, whose grasp of the subject under discussion, whatever it might be, always appeared complete. As a chairman he stood out above all others with whom I can recall being associated. The committee included Sir Percy Sillitoe, the

Director General of the Security Service (MI5), Sir Stewart Menzies, the Chief of the Secret Intelligence Service (SIS, known as MI6), Sir Kenneth Strong, the Director of the Joint Intelligence Bureau and the Directors of Naval, Military, Air and Scientific Intelligence. Other specialists were co-opted as the need arose and together they comprised an exceptionally able, experienced and interesting team. (It is of note today that, looking back on my service with the JIC, I cannot recollect being aware of any female presence in the hierachy.)

Sadly, both Percy Sillitoe and Stewart Menzies, when they retired from their respective services, each having achieved much, were subjected to a measure of criticism in the light of the disastrous succession of British KGB agents, moles and defectors which, over more than a decade, included Blake, Burgess, Fuchs, Maclean and Philby. Such was the effect of these serious failures attributable to shortcomings within the British security system, including parts of the Foreign Office, that it produced a loss of confidence in Britain that endured for many years within American security circles. So far as the JIC was concerned the examination of these security failures, some of which had pre-war roots, lay outside its remit, but squarely with the Prime Ministers who made the appointments in question.

I referred earlier to the debilitating effect on morale in Western Europe, and farther afield, by threats of war and particularly the cataclysm of Korea with its potential for widening the conflict. However, no fear was stronger than that of the Soviet threat to Western Europe, particularly within those countries that lay in its predictable path. The peace of mind of our own people might have suffered a further jolt had they been privy to the first item on the agenda of the JIC's meeting of 12 April 1951 headed INVASION OF THE UNITED KINGDOM. The subject was introduced by Brigadier Johnston, deputizing for the Director of Military Intelligence, who said that he was under considerable pressure in the War Office to provide the conclusions which the committee hoped to reach in the report then in preparation entitled *Invasion of the United Kingdom, 1951-1952*. Its conclusions were required for planning purposes in connection with the 'formation and organization of the Home Guard'. As the Home Guard of the Second World War had only been stood down six years earlier it is perhaps surprising that the War Office was not thinking more in terms of its revival. However, Mr Reilly explained that the Joint Intelligence Staff could not make headway until the Joint Planning Staff had completed their part of the paper. In the meantime he expressed the view that the possibility of an invasion later in 1951 was extremely remote.

The last reorganization of duties to affect me in the Secretariat involved taking over as secretary of the Security Committee which functioned under the auspices of the JIC, meeting monthly. The chairman at the time was Roger Hollis, who later came in for much publicity. The routine, which I inherited from my predecessor, was to visit Hollis in his office as and when required to discuss the committee's business. My impression of him was of a highly intelligent and conscientious man who was very much on top of his job, but with a quiet and cheerful temperament that was in marked contrast to that of his forceful and outspoken director. Sadly this was put to considerable tests in the years ahead.

It was as much due to the limited KGB penetration of the British security system, from which the Foreign Office was not entirely immune, as to the uncanny way in which unrelated rotting apples became associated, that matters came to a head during Hollis's tenure of nine years as Director General of the Security Service. During that time he had to defend his service and himself during three major enquiries initiated by the Government which, as quoted in the *Dictionary of National Biography*, 'both he and the service survived with considerable credit'. This was very much in line with the views of Lord Denning, which appeared in his memoirs. These reflected the confidence he felt in Hollis during the enquiry for which he was responsible.

Much of the debate since has centred on assertions made by the journalist Chapman Pincher in his book *Their Trade is Treachery*, published in 1981, followed, in 1987, with *Traitors, The Labyrinths of Treason*, where he attempted to prove that Hollis was a traitor. Such allegations were refuted by Margaret Thatcher, when Prime Minister, in the House of Commons and by Lord Denning in the introduction to the reprinted edition of his widely acclaimed report relating to the Profumo Affair.

It was a while before I read either of Pincher's books, but then was increasingly troubled as I wondered incredulously whether I could possibly have worked for a traitor in such a position at the heart of Britain's security. It was a very unpleasant thought and prompted me to write to Lord Denning in January 1995 about my concern and requesting information relating to his own findings. In reply I received a charming and reassuring letter containing the following passages:

I am only too pleased to help you in any way I can. I am most interested to know that you were secretary of the Security Committee and your own views of Sir Roger Hollis are of the greatest value. He has been assailed in some quarters as if he was a traitor and I feel that your book should be of the greatest value in repudiating that charge against him. I am particularly glad of this because I feel that his loyalty should no longer be assailed. He came to see me quite freely when I was conducting the Profumo Inquiry and I was quite satisfied with his loyalty and integrity and indeed I accepted his evidence completely and entirely in holding as I did that the Security Service had done their work properly and well.

I am afraid I cannot give you any further information except to repeat, after these many years, my complete confidence in Hollis. I have just seen that in the Profumo Report which has recently been re-printed by Hutchinsons I wrote an introduction in which I refer to Mr Chapman Pincher's criticism of me and his condemnation of Sir Roger Hollis and as you will see in that introduction I repudiated Mr Pincher's comments.

Since then I have come upon an article by Sheila Kerr entitled *British Cold War defectors: the versatile, durable toys of propagandists*:

The witch-hunt for Sir Roger Hollis and the related Peter Wright fiasco were both generated by British officials. Wright's conviction that Hollis was the spy in MI5 was due in part to his near-religious faith in the testimony of Soviet defector Anatoli Golitsyn, and his certainty that another defector, Yuri Nosenko, was a plant. It seems likely that both defectors were genuine, but Golitsyn began to fabricate information and was the victim of his own conspiratorial nightmares. The suspicions which worried British Intelligence and paralysed the CIA were largely of their own making, though the KGB may also bear some of the responsibility. When the Hollis controversy became public the KGB were confused because they knew he was innocent and deduced that this was a dastardly British plot. ...

...The pursuit of Hollis is an English variant of McCarthyism: it utilised McCarthy's favourite techniques – guilt by association, guilt by geographic proximity, and guilt if you cannot prove your innocence.

I have included these extracts in the belief that there may yet be some doubters who may feel as I did and need reassurance about Hollis. He was a good man and served his country well.

Meanwhile in Korea, UN troops, in modest strength when compared with the Chinese, were deployed across the peninsula awaiting the enemy's next offensive. Among them was the British 29th Brigade Group, under command of the 3rd US Infantry Division in which I also had a number of friends from the time when we had overlapped in Fort Benning. There were no firm indications of an enemy build up despite our efforts to detect them by means of air reconnaissance, listening posts and patrols. Throughout the war the Chinese demonstrated repeatedly their ability to concentrate massive forces unobtrusively in the rear of their screen of forward positions, before launching them in such strength and disregard for casualties that they would overrun all but the strongest defences. This is precisely what they sought to achieve across the River Imjin on St George's Day 1951 and partially succeeded.

Those of us on the other side of the world receiving news of the battle were stirred as we followed its course as best we could from early cryptic accounts, which included a forewarning of high casualties. These passed through my hands in the course of my duties and I visualized the Fusiliers in action wearing red and white roses (albeit not real) on St George's Day in honour of their Patron Saint, as they always did in peace or war. Indeed, it is recorded that most of the battalion who had not become casualties were still wearing them on the following morning and many roses survived until the evening of 25 April when they came out of the line. (Jack McManners, in later life Regius Professor of Ecclesiastical History at Oxford, remembers how, when in the desert in 1943, the padre was wounded and his truck carrying the red and white paper roses for St George's Day was destroyed, a signal went back to HQ even amid the chaos of battle, commissioning the urgent manufacture of more roses.)

It was not long before casualty reports were circulating in Whitehall and soon the picture became clear. 29 Brigade had suffered more than 1,000 casualties when, as subsequently emerged, they were attacked 'by the entire Chinese 63rd Army, all of whose three divisions were across the Imjin and at the throat of the British brigade'. The Glosters virtually ceased to exist after three days of fighting, having been cut off and then overrun by wave after wave of maniacal Chinese surging forward regardless of their own vast losses. These it was impossible to assess, but one estimate mentions '10,000 killed and wounded out of 60,000 Chinese who attacked the Imjin line'. Following the battle the remainder of the British brigade regrouped and took up fresh positions as part of the plan to stabilize the UN line. Their gallantry and determination blunted the Chinese offensive and thwarted efforts to capture Seoul.

In England I was one of many awaiting details of our casualties. The

Fusiliers had a total of 164 killed and wounded, including the death of their commanding officer, Lieutenant Colonel Kingsley Foster, who was killed in the final stages of the battle. Twelve more officers were killed, wounded or missing, including two company commanders. In an earlier battle another company commander had been killed. The effect of this news on me, as no doubt on others, was decisive. When regiments suffered battle casualties of this order they hoped to replace officers initially from among those of their own members who might be available from duties elsewhere. I regarded myself as being in this category, so sought and received confirmation of the regiment's need of company commanders. My next step was to discuss with John Gardiner my wish to return to my regiment. Whilst he would have preferred me to stay he agreed not to stand in my way. Fortunately, a trained replacement was available so my conscience was not troubled that I was causing any inconvenience. I had to submit my request in writing and John forwarded my letter to Lieutenant General McLean, Chief Staff Officer to the Minister of Defence who, in a sense, was my commanding officer. Ten days later I was summoned to see him. It was not, at least initially, an easy occasion for either of us. He was at pains to verify the reason behind my request and a succession of penetrating questions ensued. I suspected he did not see it my way and I had much difficulty in persuading him that I was not wishing to leave for some other reason, such as to escape any financial embarrassment or romantic entrapment. Eventually, with more emphasis than appropriate when addressing a lieutenant general, I assured him once more that there was only one reason behind my request and that was my duty, as I saw it, to my regiment. At this point, instead of reprimanding me as I deserved for my excessive forthrightness, his whole attitude suddenly changed. 'I am so sorry, Wilson, but I had to satisfy myself that what you have told me is all there is to it. In my view, in the circumstances, you have done quite the right thing and I shall do my best to support you.' I thanked him with much relief.

General McLean, whose previous appointment had been Military Secretary, then spoke to the War Office and achieved my posting order to 1 RNF in Korea in record time. The rest of the arrangements followed the time-honoured procedure of those pen-pushing days. What remained for me to do was to explain my actions and reasons to my parents, which came to them as a surprise, if not a shock, when they thought I had grown out of seeking excitement. As always they accepted my decision and made the best of it. My foreshortened tour of duty with the JIC Secretariat ended soon after. On 28 June, at the close of the last meeting I attended, I was taken quite by surprise when, possibly for the first time, I unexpectedly became aware of its human face. This was reflected in the valedictory minute I was later given by John Gardiner. As an additional item on the agenda:

> Mr Reilly said that the Committee would be sorry to learn that Major Wilson would be shortly leaving the Secretariat to serve with his regiment in Korea. On behalf of the Committee, he wished him the best of luck and expressed appreciation of his good work on the Secretariat.
> The Committee: Warmly endorsed the above.

The following week I was given a farewell party by the Secretariat and on 2 July 1951 I left the Ministry. In many ways, despite my original aversion to the idea of a Whitehall appointment, I was sorry to leave what I still look back on as by far the most interesting desk job I ever had.

Chapter Fifteen

Korean Contrast

Korea: The Wrong War, at the wrong place, at the wrong time and with the wrong enemy.

General of the Army Omar N. Bradley, Chairman of the US JCS, in his testimony to Congress, 15 May 1951

Part of my embarkation leave was spent at our Regimental Depot in Newcastle, drawing equipment, being briefed, receiving immunization against tropical diseases and other formalities. There, too, I learned that I would take charge of about 100 reinforcements, mostly Geordies, destined for 1 RNF. As we would be seeing a great deal of each other during our six weeks' journey by sea to Japan on our way to Korea I got to know them as well as I could in the time available. They were brimming with expectation, as young soldiers are when they set off on active service, and I foresaw no problems other than minimizing boredom and keeping them as fit as possible, neither of which would be easy. In the meantime, physical training had to be kept at a high level and maintained by every means possible during our time at sea. In Korea, because of the hilly nature of the country and the poor road system, the infantry, in particular, were constantly climbing up and down features covered by scrub-oak, fully equipped and often carrying extra loads.

Towards the end of July we travelled to Liverpool to embark in HMT *Devonshire*, a slow, old, but not uncomfortable ship as transports go. In addition to my own draft of Fusiliers there were others from the Gloucestershire Regiment, the King's Own Scottish Borderers and the Royal Ulster Rifles. They all settled down well and as soon as they found their sea-legs the training began, which included almost every game that can be played on board ship, though from the Red Sea onwards, through the Gulf of Aden and across the Arabian Sea, we had to let up somewhat on account of the humidity. At Colombo we

167

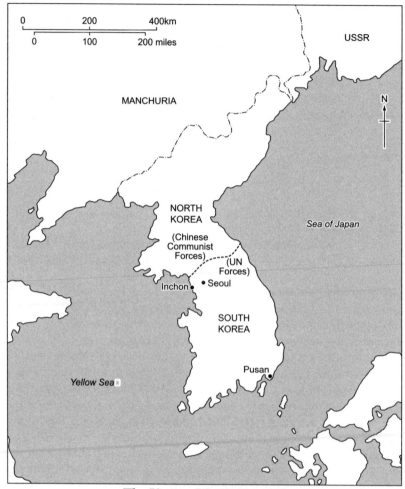

The Korean War 1950 - 1953

were given a brief spell of shore leave and then set off on a brisk training march round the town, with a police guide leading the way. A week later this was repeated at Singapore with a six-mile march and after a further week came another at Hong Kong where we were joined by the band of the South Staffordshire Regiment, which led us through Kowloon. Later the same day we began the last stage of our journey to Kure in south-west Japan. This I found the most attractive part of the voyage, due to the beauty of the sunsets as we passed through the Formosa Strait and the East China Sea. Standing on deck, time seemed to stand still as the sun moved imperceptibly in a blaze of colour, to sink slowly out of sight. What was it, I wondered, that elevated one's thoughts and left one in a state of profound contemplation? It made so little sense in such a setting to be making one's way to join in a squalid and bloody war.

The *Devonshire* arrived at Kure on 9 September and we were taken to 'J' Reinforcement Base Depot (JRBD) some eight miles out of town. There the officers' mess was more like a Japanese hotel, spotlessly clean, full of flowers and very inviting. There was no sign of a Mess sergeant or anyone in uniform, but the Japanese receptionist introduced herself, addressing me by name. She told me that my luggage was already in my room where my batman was waiting. I was then shown to my large and comfortable room where I was surprised to be greeted by another attractive Japanese girl who greeted me with a smile. 'My name is Ayako and I am your batman.' My face must have been a study. She had already unpacked my kit and extracted everything which needed washing or ironing. 'These will be finished by tonight,' she chirped. Then with another smile came the question: 'And when would you like me in the morning?'

'What time is breakfast?' I replied.

She was at a loss to understand my slowness and it was not until the following day, when I was asked if I would like to choose a different 'batman', that I suspected what had lain behind the original question.

All reinforcements passing through the Base Depot had to spend at least a week there getting fit for the rigours which lay ahead, but there was time available for sightseeing and a few of us decided to visit Hiroshima where, six years earlier, the first atom bomb had been dropped. The stark facts were already known: 60,000 inhabitants killed, 100,000 injured and most of their city destroyed or damaged by shock waves and fire. We found our way to a suitable viewpoint from which it was apparent that already parts had been rebuilt, but there was still enough devastation before us, stretching over a vast area. Until then I had not been able to visualize the meaning and magnitude of what had laid waste some five square miles. We stood and stared in silence; there was little to say, but much to think about. Only after much reflection did I reach the conclusion that in the circumstances it had been justified and necessary.

Within the JRBD, bits of a jigsaw puzzle, of which I had been only vaguely aware, were falling into place. It had seemed since my arrival almost as though I was being given special treatment and certainly I had been impressed. After a few days I was told that the CO wished to see me and with minimum preamble he told me that he would like me to take over as OC of his training company, which prepared drafts for Korea. He was informing the War Office to this effect, having been authorized to fill his vacancies from those passing through the base. I declined his invitation, explaining the circumstances of my case. These did not impress him and we had an argument, which he ended by reminding me that at that stage I was under his command. I was then dismissed. I knew that while we had been at sea the 1st Commonwealth Division had been formed under the command of General Jim Cassels, whom I already knew well. I took a few minutes to think through the situation before returning to the adjutant's office where I requested a message pad. On this I wrote:

'From JRBD to I Comwel Div. For General Cassels from Dare Wilson. Stuck here en route to 1 RNF. Please facilitate my release.'

The adjutant was horrified. 'I can't possibly send that,' he exclaimed.

'You better had,' I told him, 'or I'll just get someone in the next draft to deliver it for me.'

He saw the point and agreed under protest.

The next morning the adjutant sent for me to tell me that he had received an order from the Division to send me over on the next ship. No, the CO did not wish to see me. Soon I was on my way to Pusan, Korea, arriving on 18 September and, following a tedious journey by rail, I reached 1 RNF two days later. I was given a warm welcome by Miles Speer, who had taken command when Kingsley Foster was killed, and given 'Z' Company, taking over from John Winn who, like others, had greatly distinguished himself during the earlier battles. A week later, by which time I had found my feet, I brought my parents up to date, writing from 'North of the 38th Parallel':

We are in the line and fairly actively employed. Yesterday I saw my first Chinaman, albeit at a distance, and in common with many others was shot at very ineffectively by same. In fact I feel that my transformation from peace to war is almost complete, having taken to the open air – spent a night on top of a hill – got wet through and experienced various of the other matters of routine to which one becomes accustomed as an infantryman at war.

Getting wet through became a habit and a subsequent letter gave a more vivid picture:

You would be interested if you could see us here and the conditions under which we are living, which resemble far more, I would say, those of the 1914-18 war than of the last one. My Company holds a hill which on its forward slope is surrounded by a continuous trench, into the side of which are a series of dugouts like my own roofed with bivouac shelters. ...The floor is under water as it has rained since dawn and never stopped all day. The water has therefore seeped in and the limited floor space (6ft by 4) is deep in mud. The same candle as earlier this week does duty. My wet clothes are on top of my sleeping bag where I hope they will become less wet during the night. But they are the outer layer as we have to sleep fully dressed.

In the background, planning at a higher level had been in progress involving an advance by three divisions of US I Corps, including our own. The aim was to straighten its line and secure important high ground from which the enemy was overlooking Allied positions and routes leading to them. The Commonwealth Division, which was holding a frontage of some 11,000 yards, would be required to gain about 7,000 yards of very rough and hilly ground in an operation codenamed COMMANDO. Following a programme of 'softening up' by Allied artillery over several days, the principal role was given to the 28 Commonwealth Infantry Brigade under command of Brigadier George Taylor. He, as a battalion commander during the Second World War, had gained a reputation for fearlessness and determination. It was also decided that for this particular operation a further battalion would be necessary and, because they were about to be relieved at the end of their tour, the Fifth Fusiliers were called on to make a last contribution. It was to prove a testing finale.

Operation COMMANDO began early on the morning of 3 October while the Fifth Fusiliers were preparing to take three objectives on a frontage of nearly a mile, including a commanding feature, Hill 217, which overlooked an extensive area of lower ground already in our possession. Very little was known about the enemy's dispositions although, according to a prisoner of war, some three battalions were deployed on the high ground in the area which contained our objectives. The CO's 'O Group' of company commanders had assembled on 1 October to hear the outline plan for the attack and again, in more detail, three days later, after which I was able to carry out a recce and observe Hill 217, which was to be 'Z' Company's objective, and our approach to it from an observation post. I took with me Lieutenant Bill Sheppard (10 Platoon), Lieutenant Humphrey Walker (11 Platoon) and Lieutenant Paddy Baxter (12 Platoon). It soon became clear that there were only two courses open to secure our objective. One was to attack from the south, following the gradual gradient up the spine of the lozenge-shaped feature, which would be exposed to enemy fire, although our artillery might suppress some of it. The other was to

171

attempt to achieve surprise, without supporting fire, by scaling the steep 500 foot eastern escarpment which, for part of its length, appeared semi-precipitous. While neither of these courses was attractive I felt the second would offer the better chance of success.

Even at this late stage, on the eve of the operation, the planning was not over and at 1745 hours the company commanders were called back for the last session. My notebook records three more pages relating to the plans for the next day, including the time of H hour, which would be 0630 hours. Eventually only the choice of code words for our three objectives and the junction point on the ground with the Australians remained and Miles asked for suggestions. I came up with 'Newcastle', 'United', 'Football' and 'Club'. These were accepted and of the four it was the first which later earned a place of prominence in the regimental history.

When we dispersed at about 1830 hours darkness was descending, and I felt critical that the discussion had been so drawn out there was little daylight left for me to rejoin my company and issue orders for the following day. By then 'Z' Company had completed its approach march of several thousand yards and was laagered for the night out of sight, within one and a half miles of our objective. By the time I set off to rejoin it, accompanied by my batman, Fusilier Mann, and a wireless operator from the signal platoon, it was almost fully dark and it would be necessary to make our way cross-country for about a mile on a compass bearing.

We made our way forward counting our steps and stopping frequently to check the bearing. When I calculated that we had covered the distance we stopped and listened. It was a still night with not a sound to be heard apart from distant gunfire. We attempted to walk round in a circle in search of the company – a hard thing to do on a dark night – listening intently as we did so. To attempt further movement would only complicate my presumed navigational error so unwillingly I broke wireless silence to request a Very pistol flare to be fired, if possible minimizing its illumination. After a short interval a report and masked illumination came, not from hundreds of yards away but from very close to where we stood. It was a big relief and I was duly impressed by the standard of training and discipline shown by the company whose primary interest was to avoid detection. I held a quick 'O Group' of platoon commanders to bring them up to date and then all except the sentries slept as best they could without blankets. I myself was under no illusions concerning the problems likely to confront us within a few hours.

We awoke to find ourselves surrounded by a thick mist, which imposed a delay on the progress of all companies. However, as we might later turn it to our advantage, I obtained permission to make such progress as was possible towards the base of Hill 217, which we reached as the mist was thinning. There we waited until we could set course for our objective. My plan was for 10 Platoon to establish itself on a minor feature on the near side of the main spur where it would form a firm base and be available as an immediate reserve should the need arise. Close behind came the rest of the company, with 11 Platoon to my right and 12 Platoon to the left. Notwithstanding their level of physical fitness their rate of climb would be determined primarily by the gradient of the hill, which increased progressively, and the weight of the loads carried by all ranks. The last instruction I gave was to emphasize the importance of silence during our movement, with the object of surprising the enemy if possible.

In the course of my takeover from John Winn he had stressed the importance of the hand grenade in defence and the need to maintain plenty in reserve close by, the reason being the rapidity with which the lightly equipped Chinese infantry had closed on our positions during all their engagements hitherto. After discussion with my senior ranks, therefore, I ordered that all those taking part, other than Bren gunners, their No 2s who carried most of their ammunition and the wireless operators, would on this occasion carry not less than eight hand grenades. I learned later that some had opted for ten, in addition to their personal weapon and ammunition. So far as the scale of hand grenades carried in the attack was concerned, nothing like it had ever been heard of at the School of Infantry, Warminster.

Under these conditions it would have been pointless to attempt any rate of advance beyond that which would take assaulting troops to their objective in a condition to fight. Accordingly we set off at a steady pace, which we were able to maintain until we were confronted by such a steep gradient that hands, knees and toes all had to assist in the process of heaving bodies, weapons and ammunition up the last hundred feet or so. Indeed, the nearer we got to the top the harder it became to gain hand and footholds owing to the destruction of trees and bushes by artillery fire during the previous week.

When we reached the top, fully prepared to find the enemy in possession, our expectation was dramatically confirmed by a considerable number who, in a moment of indecision, permitted 12 Platoon to round up ten of them to be hustled away as POW, before the much larger number that remained sprang into action. Although we had achieved surprise, which is always a bonus, those now confronting us were very soon reacting with light automatics, rifles and particularly

173

grenades, of which, as we were about to discover, they seemed to have an inexhaustible supply. From that moment the tempo of the engagement never slackened and because my route in the final stages of the climb had taken me in the direction of 12 Platoon I was at once aware when Paddy Baxter, its stalwart commander, was severely wounded early in the battle. Until then he had been the epitome of leadership and example and appeared reluctant to accept the immediate need to leave his responsibilities to others. Lance Corporal Hulme deftly administered morphine before rejoining his section while Paddy, shunning all further offers of help, slowly made his way rearwards, holding a shell dressing over a large chest wound from which, as he recounted later, he was able to watch his cigarette smoke escaping. In the meantime Sergeant Smith had assumed command of 12 Platoon until, before long, he too was seriously wounded, as a result of which he died the following day.

By now grenades were flying to and fro during an intense exchange in which I had joined, along with Fusilier Mann and my wireless operator. Already several enemy grenades had gone off in our vicinity and then came another, very close between Mann and me as we lay side by side. I turned my head away as it landed and when I looked back, after a deafening bang, Mann's face looked like a chunk of raw meat. Much of it was soon covered by a shell dressing and remarkably he was still able to see, so after I had pointed him in the right direction with others in need of urgent attention he joined the trail to the Regimental Aid Post at least a mile rearwards. I then had an opportunity to call for supporting fire, although by normal standards we were, at the time, too close to the enemy. However, by attempting to isolate them from those supporting them from beyond, it might ease the pressure. Our own position, which was so vital to get through accurately to supporting arms, was as clear as could be: 'We are at Point 217 with enemy active immediately North and West.' Gerry Strickland, our artillery forward observation officer, who was an experienced and capable old friend, did the rest. Soon salvo after salvo from a considerable number of field guns were landing mostly where they were needed, although the odd round went astray resulting, at the least, in much bad language on our part and occasionally in a tragedy. Next we called on our own support company for mortar and machine-gun fire and before long the heavier 4.2 inch mortars joined in, but despite this the enemy were being reinforced.

By now, having earlier lost Paddy Baxter and Sergeant Smith, both Humphrey Walker and his sergeant from 11 Platoon had also been wounded and evacuated and I was dependent on junior NCOs to deal with problems, one of which was the awareness that our remaining ammunition was steadily shrinking. I gave orders to ensure that all casualties should be relieved of every round they were still carrying before they were evacuated. At this stage I brought RHQ up to date and requested close air support, stressing that the closer it could be delivered to our tight position on Point 217 the more effective it was likely to be. This was not the sort of request to be made lightly, because of its disregard for safety margins. Thereafter we fought on and waited, though not for long. The acknowledgment of my request came not by wireless but from four piston engine P-51 US Air Force Mustang fighter-bombers bearing South African Air Force markings and the distinctive Flying Cheetah emblem of their famous 2 Squadron. (After distinguished service during the Second World War 2 Squadron SAAF had been disbanded, but six years later was reformed for service with the UN Force in Korea, with battle-experienced pilots of exceptional calibre.). They came in very low and fast from behind us and when I turned round as the leading pair was approaching I saw large bombs of napalm drop away, heading in our direction. For a second or two it looked as though they would land among us, but they passed low over our heads to land exactly where required. Throughout the bombers' approach their guns were also blazing, which added to the impressive blast and inferno as the petrol jelly incendiary bombs exploded just beyond us.

This awe-inspiring performance was repeated by the second pair of Mustangs, to be followed by a further pass by each pair using guns and rockets. It was the most heartening and impressive display of close air support I ever witnessed and provided much encouragement for our dwindling force. Their remarkably quick response to my request for support was made possible by their practice during such periods of intense activity of having a 'cab rank' of four aircraft airborne and waiting to respond to such calls. The effect of this intervention on our behalf, so far as the enemy was concerned, must have been considerable in terms of casualties yet, as was so often the case with the Chinese army, it failed to break their resolve. Reinforcements always seemed to be readily available and after minutes rather than hours they were reorganizing and resuming their efforts to dispose of us. We had been in possession of Point 217 for nearly an hour and a half and already both platoons were much depleted in strength. It would have been to our advantage had I been able to call on 10 Platoon, holding the firm base behind and below us, but they were heavily involved in looking after and evacuating the wounded without the use of transport because of the absence of tracks, or even stretchers. Casevac by helicopter was already working to capacity elsewhere.

Of greater importance was the increasing threat of running out of ammunition. I delayed my decision to pull out until we had thrown our last grenade and each Bren gun was down to its last magazine; most of the remaining riflemen had, at best, half a dozen rounds left after gleaning all they could from casualties. This I explained briefly to RHQ over the wireless, before adding that we were about to leave and more supporting fire to cover our withdrawal would be welcome. The remaining ammunition was fired as about fifteen of us withdrew out of the sixty who had assaulted less than two hours earlier. Thirty had become casualties and the remainder had been engaged in the task of carrying or assisting them off the hill.

Many reasons were later advanced for the failure of our assault. Anthony Farrar-Hockley, the Official Historian for the Korean War, states:

> The basic difficulty was that the only covered approach confined the advance to a single company. During a series of intense fire fights as the leading platoons, sometimes in rushes, more often by crawling, closed on the enemy bunkers, 'Z' lost thirty among the leading platoons including both platoon commanders and platoon sergeants. Their situation was not improved when, by rare error between forward observation post and guns, a number of shells from the divisional artillery straddled 'Z' Company.

There can be no disagreement of which I am aware with any part of that statement, but an alternative explanation might couple shortage of men on the ground with problems connected with ammunition supply. As events turned out we followed a well trodden path:

'A soldier with a musket can not fight without ammunition; in two hours he can expend all he can carry.'

The Duke of Wellington.

Our withdrawal was not the end of the story. Brigadier George Taylor was not a man to be thwarted. That evening he again ordered 1 RNF to take Point 217 the following day. 'It has to be said that this was not a good idea,' observed the official historian later. When the second attempt was made, by 'W' and 'X' Companies using the gradual approach from the south-west, together with the steep climb where 'Z' Company had achieved surprise, they found the enemy ready and waiting. Throughout the day the two companies made repeated efforts, but were repelled with heavy losses at the hands of an enemy determined to hold his ground. Had the brigade commander taken advantage of the Australians' noteworthy success in taking Maryang-San to our right by switching 1 RNF to that flank there would, in the view of many, have been a far better prospect of taking Point 217 economically, but this course he appears either to have overlooked or rejected. However, the enemy must have anticipated further efforts on our part, possibly with heavier artillery and air support, for two days later a strong patrol of 1 RNF found 'Newcastle' (Point 217) undefended and took possession of it.

In the meantime I had taken an early opportunity to visit those of 'Z' Company who had been evacuated to the Norwegian Mobile Army Surgical Hospital, known as NORMASH. All but the most seriously wounded were so cheerful that I came away wondering which of us had raised spirits the most. Fusilier Mann's face was swathed in bandages and over the following two years he had a series of reconstructive operations, during which time I kept in touch with him. Fifty-one years later he heard that I would be at the final Reunion and Thanksgiving Service of Old Comrades in Newcastle upon Tyne and travelled up from Yorkshire to be on parade, looking as cheerful as ever.

In the course of the battle both sides had suffered proportionately heavy losses, with those of the Fifth Fusiliers amounting to twenty killed and eighty-seven wounded, while the enemy lost many times more. We were withdrawn a short distance into a reserve position and it was at this stage that a marked change became noticeable in the enemy's artillery strength and capability, as concentrations of heavy fire by day and night arrived without warning. One such salvo wiped out a section from 'Z' Company, of which four members were killed and four wounded. This sharpened up awareness and caused trenches to be dug where hitherto they had not always been necessary. During the redeployment following Operation COMMANDO, the feature allocated to 'Z' Company had earlier been occupied by the Chinese who, perforce, were accomplished diggers and did not ease up until they had established themselves underground with room to sleep and store all their requirements, including a generous supply of rations. In occupying the feature we took advantage of all our predecessors' hard work and set about removing as much as we could of their rubbish before we could feel their shelters were fit for our use. Mine eventually passed muster and as darkness approached the guard was mounted and double sentries given their beats. For the remainder any lingering doubts over whether to sleep underground with shelter and protection despite the smell, or above in the open, were dispelled by some nearby enemy harassing gunfire. Commonsense and experience prevailed as we opted for protection.

I was awoken in the middle of the night by something moving across my body and there were sounds within my shelter that I mistrusted. On striking a match I came face to face with a large rat, while others scampered out of sight. Without hesitation I decamped into the open with enemy artillery no longer in the reckoning. There I was soon asleep again, this time with the moon for company. What woke me the second time was immediately apparent; silhouetted against the moon, directly above me, was the bent figure of a man with a large cudgel raised, about to strike. In the millisecond that such an experience takes the brain to react I had only one thought: 'How have they got through without the alarm being raised?' It was an unnerving moment, but reassurance was swift: 'It's aal reet sor – there was a rat by your heed but the bugger's went.'

Thereafter life, in the regiment of which we were all so proud, took on a different guise. Throughout that memorable week, during which the battalion's casualties in Korea rose to a total of 417, which was over forty per cent of the total strength, a troopship had been waiting at Pusan to take all those who survived the last battle to Hong Kong and eventually home. It was a test of character passed with flying colours. We handed over to 1st Battalion Royal Leicestershire Regiment on 18 October and the following day General Cassels visited the battalion to bid farewell and thank all ranks for their outstanding service. The Korean War is now referred to by some as 'The Forgotten War'. Others remember it as it was; a cruel conflict, costly in lives, economically ruinous and politically sterile. For those who bore arms it lacked any redeeming feature save that of having done their duty and felt again the close bonds of comradeship.

By contrast our last fortnight had much to commend it. I was as happy as could be making use of the shotgun Charles Mitchell had advised me to bring out, shooting a mixed bag of pheasants, quail and pigeons. After I had used it during the previous week, while we were in our reserve positions, I had called in at Divisional Headquarters and left a brace of pheasants for the General. In a letter dated 15 October he wrote:

My dear Dare,

Thank you very much for the pheasants which are most welcome. It was very kind of you to send them. (Were they some of the ones you got when you failed to meet the Brig!??!!!) [The 'Brig' was no longer George Taylor, who had already left rather suddenly, but his successor who visited us at short notice after I had gone game shooting.] Just after your present arrived I saw an old cock land by the CRA's caravan. I leapt to a gun, flushed him and dropped him by the mess kitchen alongside yours! – all very tidy.

Your slight moan that you had come all the way to Korea and were going without a battle has now, I think you will agree, been properly adjusted! It must have been a very sticky little party and I congratulate you on it. I was more than relieved to know that you had not been hurt and you have certainly had the experience you wanted. Well done.

Again with many thanks and all good wishes,

Yrs ever

Jim C.

On what happier note could I leave Korea? We embarked on HMT *Empire Pride* on 28 October and sailed for Hong Kong.

Chapter Sixteen

Outposts in a shrinking Empire

Mau Mau is a Kikuyu word, meaning you want to do something very much and very quickly.

A native witness in the Naivasha Court

Such was the pressure on His Majesty's transport fleet during those twilight years of the British Empire, with unforeseen commitments across the world, that resort had to be made to the use of stepping-stones, as British regiments moved between theatres and stations at peace or war. Thus, the licking of wounds sustained in Korea was undertaken not at home but much closer to the scene of action, in Hong Kong. There, at the furthest extremity of the New Territories, the Fifth Fusiliers spent the next nine months at Norwegian Farm Camp, overlooking paddy fields of rice, with the Chinese border less than two miles beyond. To the south a slow, winding road led twenty-six miles to the island of Hong Kong, with its bright lights and every manner of attraction. By contrast we had the uninviting prospect of the camp, with limited facilities and unlimited hardships, of which an abundance of mosquitoes was but one.

The location of this unattractive camp was linked to the defence of Hong Kong, which was being strengthened in the light of our worsening relations with China. There was, therefore, a juxtaposition between Norwegian Farm Camp and Snowdon, an imposing hill of over 1,000 feet, which towered above the camp near sea level. The two lay astride a likely enemy axis across the New Territories in the event of a Chinese offensive, and responsibility for its defence now lay with us. In terms of sheer physical effort it probably exceeded anything supervised by many penal institutions around the world.

As we settled down in our new surroundings it became increasingly clear that life in Norwegian Farm Camp was going to become very boring unless much thought and effort was put into sport and entertainment. With limited transport, Hong Kong was too far for even weekly visits and there was only intermittent reception of Hong Kong Radio, while television was almost unknown. However, all manner of activities sprang into life to augment games and sports. High on the list came St George's Minstrels, a broadly based concert party which came into existence late in the nineteenth century and prospered within the regiment in all overseas stations. Soon props were being assembled and costumes were arriving. My own, that of a pitman in his dark suit, complete with cap, clay pipe and watch-chain, on his way to St James' Park, had done its duty in many previous stations and put me in the right mood to sing *Blaydon Races* (all six verses with fortissimo support in the choruses from all present).

In May 1952 I applied for, and received, permission to take twenty-eight days' local leave, as opposed to home leave. For my purpose the Pacific Ocean came within the term 'local' and I was grateful for my transport largely to the Royal Australian Air Force, in which my Australian cousin George Burgess was serving as a doctor. My aim was to hitch a lift to Australia where I had two married uncles who had emigrated before the First World War. My plans worked out well, although it developed into something of an endurance test, covering some 15,000 miles at an average airspeed of 150 knots in unpressurized and very noisy aircraft. Leaving Hong Kong on 13 May my route took me to Manila – Labuan – Singapore – Java – Australia (Darwin, Brisbane, Sydney, Wentworth Falls and Townsville) and then, on the return journey, Manus Island, north of New Guinea, where our aircraft became unserviceable. Because the island had only a landing strip for refuelling we were delayed there for a few days pending the arrival of spare parts. We were shown round a camp containing Japanese convicted war criminals, many of whom were 'lifers', but otherwise it was a real Robinson Crusoe island, with extensive sandy beaches, coral reefs and perfect swimming. I began to wonder if I was about to become the first company commander in the regiment to go AWOL, but after four paradisiacal days I was able to resume my island-hopping to Guam and then Iwo Jima, where we remained long enough for me to take a penetrating look at the battlefield which this tiny island had become a few years earlier.

From Iwo Jima we continued our journey to Japan, landing at Iwakuni where our flight terminated. Having lost several days en route I was in danger of running out of time and, having sadly missed the last RAF plane to Hong Kong that week, I had to resort to National China Airways, which ran a service via Formosa (now Taiwan). I was one of a handful of passengers escorted to a very tired-looking Dakota aircraft with a crew of two, the American pilot and a Chinese air hostess. We took off and completed the first leg to Formosa without incident. However, after we had passed the halfway point on the final leg the pilot was warned of a hurricane fast approaching Hong Kong. Kai Tak airport was about to close down and he was instructed to return to Formosa. Unfortunately, he had insufficient fuel to achieve this and informed Kai Tak that his only option was to proceed. Air Traffic Control understood but were gloomy; the wind was already above their limit for landings. All this was relayed to us by the hostess at intervals as she busied herself following the pilot's instructions and securing the baggage.

The approach to Kai Tak was renowned as one that called for a high degree of competence from pilots. Looking out of the windows as we came in to land it appeared that the city of Hong Kong had come to a standstill and we could already see an abundance of flying debris. We finally touched down and as the aircraft settled very unsteadily on to the runway the ground staff vehicles were in close attendance. Using a procedure I had never seen, the aircraft was secured to the runway before the engines were shut down and we were assisted down ladders instead of the usual gangway. Before leaving the aircraft I opened the door leading on to the flight deck to thank the pilot and congratulate him on his airmanship. He was ashen-faced, sitting motionless in his seat looking straight ahead. I asked him if he was all right and he then looked at me. After a pause he said, 'Jesus, never again'. I then had to find some means of returning to Norwegian Farm Camp, which I eventually achieved just as my leave expired.

As time passed, the conditions, including the daily routine of climbing Snowdon with loads of barbed wire and long iron pickets in the sticky heat and humidity, began to tell on the health of the battalion, although up to a point it was accepted with a modicum of cheerfulness. There were, of course, occasional highlights and none greater than listening during the small hours of 3 May 1952 to the Cup Final, which was won by Newcastle United. No better boost to morale for the whole battalion could have been devised. By then, in any case, spirits were rising fast as the day of our departure for home approached and on 25 July we embarked on the *Empire Pride* for the last time. The voyage home took exactly a month and provided all ranks with an opportunity to recover from the extended period of hard labour in an oppressive climate.

The *Empire Pride* berthed at Liverpool at 0315 hours on 25 August, several hours earlier than we had anticipated. It was all the more surprising, therefore, to be woken at that hour by the strains of *The British*

Grenadiers and *Blaydon Races*, played by our regimental band on the quayside, immediately alongside the ship. So began probably the most memorable homecoming any of us on board ever experienced. After disembarking at noon we transferred to a nearby train and seven and a half hours later drew into a siding not far from Brancepeth, five miles south-west of Durham, to be greeted for the second time that day by the band, who had made the journey by road. It was almost dark as we began a march of about a mile to our camp and quite dark by the time we arrived, but on all sides of the parade ground were lines of cars, each with its lights shining inwards, while more than 1,000 people, wives, children, mothers, fathers, brothers and sisters were there to greet their loved ones. Everything had been organized by the regimental depot commander and his staff from Newcastle, but the outstanding personality of the occasion, waiting to welcome the battalion, was Alderman Mrs Violet Grantham, Lord Mayor of Newcastle. When the battalion was drawn up on the brightly illuminated parade ground she mounted a dais and gave a short address, not officially but from her heart, as from a close family friend, with sincerity and affection. Such was the impression she made in two minutes that the battalion responded with a spontaneous burst of cheering and applause, and so began a warm relationship that lasted long after her year of office ended.

Six weeks later all ranks were invited to an official luncheon as her guests on behalf of the City Council. This was preceded by a march through the city with band and drums playing, bayonets fixed and Colours flying. From a saluting base next to the City Hall the Lord Mayor took the salute in front of a great gathering of City and County dignitaries, before the battalion marched to their civic luncheon. Following the luncheon they were the guests of Newcastle United Football Club at St James' Park for their Saturday match. The next day everyone attended a memorial service in the Cathedral Church of St Nicholas for the ninety-three members of the battalion who had lost their lives in Korea and intercession for those who were prisoners, missing or disabled.

Shortly before Christmas we moved from Brancepeth to Barnard Castle, a march of twenty-five miles that began before dawn, headed and tailed by fusiliers carrying hurricane lamps. For the first stage we were accompanied by the band of the Durham Light Infantry and from Bishop Auckland by our own.

The following year heralded an active period, with the Queen's Coronation and widespread celebrations throughout the country. In London the regiment was represented by a Colour Party in

Westminster Abbey and in Newcastle and elsewhere in Northumberland by the 1st Battalion with Band and Drums.

Thereafter there was a pause before the receipt of a warning order for a renewal of overseas service, destination unknown, pending a Cabinet decision late in August. Most of the Battalion went on fourteen days' embarkation leave on 24 August not knowing where they were bound or even if they would, in fact, have to go. However, before leave was over it emerged that we were shortly to fly to Kenya to assist in dealing with a Mau Mau uprising about which, at the time, we knew relatively little. This move was the regiment's first by air, following three centuries of trooping by sea.

The battalion concentrated some 120 miles north of Nairobi at a small settlement called Ol Joro Orok, near Thompson's Falls. There, acclimatization to the high altitude and to the extremes of temperature had to be coupled with training and familiarization with the local conditions, which included a wide variation of bush and forest. The days were scorching hot under the tropical sun, but immediately after sunset the temperature dropped almost to freezing point. For a time, at our initial altitude of some 8,000 feet, we were frequently out of breath and none noticed this more than buglers, whose calls tended to falter and die before completion. Here, too, we had our first opportunity to study in depth the background to the emergency that had prompted our arrival in Kenya. By then the colony, formerly a British protectorate between 1895 and 1920, had attracted some 30,000 Europeans to settle within its 225,000 square miles, in addition to the population of more than half a million Africans and 90,000 Indians. However, the immigrants had not been absorbed without friction, which arose from the inevitable widespread changes in modus vivendi and land ownership. The indigenous people primarily affected were the Kikuyu who, at a later stage, became disenchanted, notwithstanding the economic benefits they derived from the settlers. The situation deteriorated to the point when, quite suddenly, it erupted into violence. Unfortunately, the European settlers were not entirely blameless in the escalation of the problem, showing a profound reluctance to recognize that the Kikuyu were capable of playing a more influential part in determining their own way of life and putting their undoubted abilities to better use.

The Governor, Sir Evelyn Baring, declared a state of emergency and, after he called for military assistance to reinforce the King's African Rifles, for a while the situation worsened. Towards the end of 1952 the Mau Mau stepped up their offensive, killing large numbers of loyal Africans in the process. At this stage the Fusiliers, among others, arrived to step up the restoration of law and order, with orders to search for and destroy the bands of Mau Mau still at large. First of all, however, there was much to learn about jungle-craft, including tracking. Native trackers were engaged and full use was made of the experience that had been gained within those battalions that had already completed their training. Prominent among these was 1st Battalion the Devonshire Regiment, which had earned a reputation for proficiency in the jungle. Courses were also organized in Swahili, the common language in much of East Africa. During the time that we were dependent on native trackers the main problem was communication, which extended much further than speech. Whilst most Africans had an innate respect for 'the White Man' this could be harnessed or destroyed according to how they were treated. Familiarity, sarcasm or swearing were all counter-productive, while encouragement and humour proved more profitable. It was remarkable how so many Geordie soldiers had this knack and used it naturally.

Countrymen, many of whom proved to be natural trackers, and others who were quick to learn, soon realized that in order to move silently over long distances it was necessary to follow existing trails wherever possible, even if, at times, they veered away from the desired direction. Many of them were made and used by big game and because they instinctively avoid slippery slopes their trails were easier to follow. As our patrols were to discover, the Mau Mau also used them, which increased the importance of alertness on the move. Soldiers also relearned the need to 'know your enemy' and the Mau Mau campaign emphasized it constantly. The theory was included in the initial training, while the practical side became part of the tracking skills that all our successful patrol commanders learned and further developed with experience. Eventually everyone recognized the importance of jungle-craft, by observing the effect of rain on tracks in assessing when they had been made, the state and attitude of trodden vegetation, the age and condition of game droppings, impressions in mud, splits in bent grass, displaced leaves, superimposition of game tracks reflecting night movement and countless more aids which all contributed to assessment of enemy activity. This was elementary to the Mau Mau who, as with all Kikuyu, learned much of it in childhood.

As soon as the initial phase of preparation was behind us, companies assumed responsibility in their respective areas, estimated in all at 1,400 square miles, living under canvas and supplementing our rations by shooting local game. Then the main task of rooting out the Mau

Mau began and it was not long before contacts were made. It was, in fact, the sort of soldiering that carries appeal among all ranks, where imagination, initiative and effort were rewarded with success. Among the attractions associated with many patrols were the frequent sightings of big game. Many were the encounters, some too close for comfort, when surprise was mutual between Geordies and buffaloes or rhinos, both of which not infrequently posed threats. Our soldiers soon developed a healthy respect for both of them, and others. On one occasion a platoon was forced to spend the better part of a night high in the branches of cedar trees while a herd of 150 elephants played havoc with their blankets below.

When, after a while, I had the opportunity to take a few days' break, it was to the north that I was drawn. I had learned that some of the best game shooting to be had in East Africa was to be found less than a full day's travel by Jeep from our camp which, by then, was in the neighbourhood of Nanyuki, almost on the Equator on the west side of Mount Kenya. My assistant adjutant, Dick Holmes, and I selected six fusiliers from the large number who volunteered to accompany us, collected the stores and rations we would require, less meat which we would procure ourselves, and set off early on 23 November, heading for Isiolo. After calling on the District Commissioner we headed for 'Champagne Camp', so known ever since a film crew working on *King Solomon's Mines* had used it.

Before pitching our tents we continued our journey to Buffalo Springs where a plentiful supply of running water produced a spectacular deep, rocky pool, perfect for swimming. The following day I shot a Grant's gazelle, which put our minds at rest before we had another swim. That evening we all shared an instructive lesson that I recall only too clearly. Late in the afternoon I decided to go out in search of a few guinea fowl to add to the larder and, as usual, several fusiliers joined me as beaters, and retrievers in the absence of dogs. I was soon able to shoot half a dozen or more birds, which fell all around us. The hunt to find them began at once, but darkness was approaching and before long it became clear to me that we should be heading for camp. My retrievers, however, in typical Labrador fashion, were reluctant to comply without 'just half a minute, sir, and we'll have the lot'. The 'half minute', slightly stretched, was just long enough to mean that we were not yet within sight of our camp before darkness overtook us. At this stage I realized that I had left my compass behind and with neither moon nor stars visible we were stranded. We tried to get a fix by climbing trees from which we could see the lights of the camp, lit by our rear party, within little more than half a mile, but from the next tree to be climbed the camp appeared in a different direction. I soon realized, and had to explain to the others, that we were stuck until the moon rose. I was able to forecast how long we would have to wait and two and a half hours later we returned to camp with the moon's assistance. Thereafter I made sure of never being without my compass and my retrievers became conscious of the need to be back in camp ahead of sunset.

Notwithstanding this minor hitch we continued to enjoy our safari in perfect weather, with a choice of menu to suit all tastes, and returned to Nanyuki on schedule all the better for a rewarding break. It was then 27 November and my time in Kenya was about to run out. I had known since the previous March that my next appointment was to be that of an instructor at the Camberley Staff College and I was due there early in December. I must have mentioned my feelings about leaving Kenya in a Christmas card to General Jim Cassels, by then commanding 1st British Corps in Germany, and I still have his reply:

...I can imagine very well how infuriated you are at leaving all the shooting and fishing, and the regiment in Kenya. However, quite apart from doing you good, I think you will find that you will enjoy the Staff College, particularly as you are at Minley which always, for some reason, has the most mutinous and pleasant students!

As usual, he was right about my time at the Staff College, but it took a while before I got Kenya out of my system. It was the most beautiful country I ever knew and as a soldier one could not have wished for a more attractive station.

Chapter Seventeen

From Staff Officers to Recruits

The fine qualities of the British Soldier derive from the national character. The soldier is influenced by his home and his upbringing and his historical tradition. He is British, with this difference – military training has imposed a certain fixed pattern of behaviour upon him and he has become disciplined.

Field Marshal Viscount Montgomery

I arrived at the Staff College to join the Directing Staff (DS) for three years just as the 1953 course was drawing to its close and I sensed a feeling of relief among students and DS alike, which was reflected in the end of course pantomime organized entirely by the students. The Staff College had been established at Camberley in 1862 and was divided into three divisions, one of which was located in Minley Manor, an attractive, albeit ornate, country house some three miles from Camberley. At Minley I became a member of the DS of whom many went on to greater things, as in the case of Peter Hunt, a Cameron Highlander, who finished his career as Chief of the General Staff. Another was Tony Deane-Drummond, from whom I took over the role of Airborne DS having already swapped jobs with him in Palestine. Before long I became the Army member of a Joint Service team under the direction of Brigadier John Hunt, the assistant commandant and leader of the successful Everest expedition. The team was set up to write an exercise in which all the Service Staff Colleges would participate. After a long search we chose Phuket Island off the west coast of Thailand and not far from Malaya, as the setting for a major sea and air assault by considerable forces, reflecting those available to the United Kingdom at the time. Indeed, such was the scale and nature of the exercise that Selwyn Lloyd, Minister of Defence, was invited to Camberley to launch it with an address to the three colleges, Camberley, Greenwich and Bracknell. The scenario was set against the background of prevailing international relations in that theatre and I took the precaution of obtaining War Office security clearance before we became committed to it. By that stage of the course all foreign students attending the colleges would have left and no objections were raised in view of the high security clearance of the students who remained.

Exercise TRICORN began with some 200 participants at Camberley to attend the opening address and at this point there arose a minor complication. The Minister had risen early and used the journey from London to acquaint himself with the exercise. He noted the setting and formed the opinion that it was much closer than he would wish to current contingency thinking. In the mistaken belief that foreign students from the Far East would be present, and that copies of the exercise would already be in the hands of their governments, he worked himself into a quite unnecessary fit of temper. On arrival at Camberley he made his displeasure known to the Commandant, who had played no part in the evolution of TRICORN, and I was sent for as the resident planner. When I entered the Commandant's office the Minister's anger was all too evident as he expressed the view that the exercise amounted to a serious breach of security at a high level, implying that I had been irresponsible. His fear was that a paper exercise set in such a sensitive area among independent states conscious of extensive British interests in that theatre, with dispropor-tionate armed forces at their disposal, might appear to them to be threatening. Belatedly he then asked me what, if any, guidelines I had sought. I explained that at the outset I had requested and received clearance of the narrative from the War Office, because there was no danger of leakage. He took the point, but ungraciously and without apology for his initial reaction. I was then dismissed and left with a distasteful memory. By happy contrast, following the end of the exercise, the three of us who had written and produced it received a warm letter of thanks signed jointly by the three College Commandants:

Exercise 'Tricorn' has just finished and you will be pleased to hear that it has been a marked success, the joint planning object having been most satisfactorily achieved. We feel that this success was very largely due to the excellent way in which the exercise was prepared. We wish to thank you ....

Upon completing my three-year stint at the Staff College I felt it had been a very worthwhile experience. However, my thoughts were now

189

set on my next job, which would provide the widest of contrasts and the greater challenge. From the instruction of staff officers I was to switch to the training and welfare of recruits at my regiment's depot at Fenham Barracks in Newcastle, which I was about to command. In the meantime I was due three weeks' leave and decided to spend it in Switzerland at St Moritz, on the Cresta Run and skiing.

By then I had become addicted to the Cresta and had acquired my own toboggan, which lived from season to season in St Moritz. The run was first created in 1884 by a group of enterprising English and Swiss enthusiasts and is rebuilt every winter with fresh, tightly packed snow which soon freezes solid on precisely the same course as before, over three-quarters of a mile long with a total descent of more than 500 feet between St Moritz and the village of Celerina. There are twenty named features, including magnificent bends and spectacular drops, on the last of which – Cresta Leap – speeds approaching eighty miles an hour are achieved by the fastest riders. All this is made possible by the use of a heavy and highly specialized toboggan, the St Moritz skeleton, constructed of steel with a sliding seat, on which the rider lies head first. When negotiating the tighter bends, braking and turns are achieved by raking the ice with serrated metal toecaps on Cresta boots. Beginners make full use of these to slow down, while the most experienced learn to limit their use to those bends where they are essential to avoid careering out of the run at high speed.

It is difficult, if not impossible, to convey the thrills that a committed Cresta rider experiences, but for me the sensation of travelling downhill as the twists and turns of the run rush towards one at over seventy miles an hour, with one's face only four inches from the ice, and with the accompaniment of loud thrumming from the toboggan's runners, has no rival, let alone equal, in the whole field of sport. Sadly, however, the relatively short Cresta season tended to clash with another addiction – that of wildfowling in remote places where the magnetic attraction of estuarial settings under moonlight in the company of wild geese pulled even more strongly than the call of a Cresta skeleton. After one further season another thirty-nine years were to elapse before I returned to the magic of the Cresta, but even then, at the age of seventy-six, the thrill was undiminished.

On arrival at Fenham Barracks in Newcastle early in 1957 I found the dreary old buildings very much as I had known them briefly in 1939 at the outbreak of war. Their Crimean character and antiquated facilities must have been daunting to conscripts and young regulars alike, despite the assurances of many fathers and old soldiers that what they were about to experience would make men of them. More to the point, the end of National Service was on the horizon and the Army would once again be dependent on regular recruits, who could not be counted on to join in sufficient numbers unless the Army improved its image and demonstrated genuine advantages that would attract the right type of man.

As the incoming Depot Commander I was fortunate in several ways at a time when all regiments were about to become responsible for finding their own recruits. Primarily, there was a strong military tradition in the area. During the First World War the Northumberland Fusiliers raised fifty-two battalions, which was many more than any other regiment. But, behind the regiment, the county itself, which had its roots in times stretching back to the bloody battles between England and Scotland and later the fighting among Border reivers, provided an enormous amount of support. All this background had left many impressions that were passed on from one generation to another, and having been born and brought up locally I was conscious of bonds that should not be overlooked.

The training of our recruits covered a wide range of requirements. Many of the old practices for which the Army had become known were dropped and in their place a new outlook soon flourished, aimed at encouragement, explanation and winning confidence rather than relying on coercion. After recruits had settled into their respective platoons, known as Badajos, Lucknow, Mons and Tobruk, selected from among the regiment's thirty principal battle honours, I took personal responsibility for introducing them to the historical connections and the part the regiment had played in these events. The Regimental Museum was an important aid in helping to stimulate interest in such a way as to instil a sense of pride, which is the bedrock of loyalty. Even so, one had to accept that although most recruits listened willingly for a limited period to anything that interested them, after that their attention would lapse. The duration of this concentration span on most subjects in the lecture room I found to be about fifteen minutes, before eyes began to glaze or turn towards the windows. At that stage it would have taken the firing of one of the old cannons on the parade ground outside to recover their attention.

When, however, I introduced initiative tests that would take them far from the barracks, requiring individual effort in the open air, their response was immediate and wholehearted. These tests took place in the last week of training. Each recruit was given a mission and provided with a 'covering letter' containing the rules, which were that the task should be accomplished within a day without breaking any laws, spending any money or using public transport. On returning

191

from their missions the recruits were required to give an account of the day's events before the remainder of their intake, representatives of the local press and me. Many amusing and a few noteworthy exploits emerged, which illustrated more than their general initiative and ability as hitch-hikers. Fusilier Halkier brought back a live lobster from Bamburgh, Fusilier Middlemiss had to obtain at least five signatures from Newcastle United players from their last match and played safe by returning with them all, but first prize was won by Fusilier Brotherton, who went to Chillingham, to learn what he could about the wild White Cattle that roam the extensive park, having first been warned on no account to approach them unaccompanied. The enthusiasm of our recruits themselves and the friendly publicity given by the local press were the best form of recruiting we could have devised, with some recruits themselves persuading their mates to come and join them. Sadly, all these recruiting links, as well as much more, which used to exist between counties and their regiments have disappeared.

The following New Year I returned to St Moritz to accept the Cresta's challenge again and had one of my best seasons. Prince Philip had recently presented a new Inter-Services Trophy that bore his name. The Army won this in its inaugural year and I managed to win the Auty Speed Cup for the fastest run made during the two-day event. That summer I took the regimental rifle team to Bisley, which proved to be successful, and I was also able to captain the English Regiments Team in the Methuen Cup, which we won against a field of thirty teams drawn from the three services.

However, in the meantime, the eyes of Fusilier Geordie were focused more keenly on a new relationship with Newcastle United Football Club, whose ground, St James' Park, was only a few hundred yards from the barracks. This connection developed after I called on the manager of that time, Charlie Mitten, to explore the possibility of obtaining assistance in the training of our depot team, which that year was very promising. When he returned the call, arriving at our ground to watch our team playing a local match, he was so impressed that he asked me if we would like to play against the Newcastle team just before their season opened. Our players could hardly believe the news until, on 5 August, a team dressed in black and white striped shirts, all with familiar faces and captained by Bobby Stokoe, arrived at our depot ground. We were assured that they were under instructions to make no allowances, to play without let-up and to score as many goals as they could in ninety minutes. The next issue of *St George's Gazette* reported:

The result of 10-0 defeat was accepted by all as very satisfactory to both teams, since Newcastle, true to their word, played a hard game from start to finish. Twice the Depot came near to scoring, and we know that the memories of beating their man against the 'Magpies' will remain, possibly for ever, in the minds of several Fusiliers.

One memory I cherish is of the recruits' passing out parades, by which stage all those who had shared responsibility for their training and welfare knew them personally and, in many cases, something of their interests. This revealed a lesser-known side of the Army, which made a favourable impression, not only on the recruits but also on their families, whom we made a point of welcoming on such occasions. I never met a parent who was not filled with pride when invited to join us and often they would queue up to tell me how it had taken the Army to make 'a proper man' of their Geordie, Jimmy or Harry. No such relationship could have developed without first-class permanent staff, fully committed to achieving results with humanity and a sense of humour. The sergeant major of Recruit Company was Tom Connolly, one of identical twins whose brother, George, was serving in the 1st Battalion. They were promoted simultaneously at each stage from fusilier to lance corporal onwards and went up rank by rank until both retired as majors with more than seventy years service between them. The existence of two indistinguishable sergeant majors, each with a wicked sense of humour, was withheld from recruits for as long as possible. Thus, as each successive draft left Newcastle Central Station to join the battalion, at that time in Northern Ireland, they were ordered by Tom to arrive as smart as they were on departure and warned that he would be there ahead of them, expecting to find them 'turned out ready for inspection for guard-mounting'. At the other end George was waiting to assume Tom's role and as soon as the draft had departed Tom would get on the telephone to give his brother an updated report. When I reminisced with George more than forty years later he still remembered particular anecdotes, as when Tom told him to greet one ginger-haired lad with the words, 'and don't you get up to the same mischief as last night'. It took some time before the penny dropped.

In November 1958, towards the end of my second year at the depot, I was promoted to lieutenant colonel and early in 1959 was posted to Headquarters 3rd Division, which had recently returned home from Cyprus to Bulford on Salisbury Plain. Major General 'Geordie' Gordon Lennox had commanded the Division for nearly two years and I was to become the senior administrative officer on his staff. However, after little more than a year I received a letter from the Chief of the Imperial General Staff, General (soon to become Field Marshal) Sir Francis Festing, informing me that I was shortly to take command of 22 Special Air Service Regiment. They had recently arrived in Malvern after some eight years of service in Malaya during the emergency of the 1950s and later in northern Oman. I was naturally elated at the prospect of serving with such an elite and interesting unit.

By happy coincidence, before I left Divisional Headquarters a routine instruction came from the War Office requesting our recommendation, being administratively responsible for 22 SAS, for the location of the regiment's long term home from which the squadrons could operate overseas, while leaving their base, including the accommodation of their wives and families, secure. A list of options between the Welsh coast and East Anglia was provided, which I showed to General 'Geordie', who said, 'Well, it's your problem so you had better make your choice'. Time was short, but my administrative appointment at the time had fortuitously given me a knowledge of most of the camps and barracks on the War Office list. None of these appeared to be entirely suitable, although Malvern, following a scheduled upgrading, might have been a possibility. However, I felt it was liable to attract too many visitors, including those from overseas who, at that time, were numerous. Hereford had not been a listed option but, as it was further from the beaten track, I decided to go and see its barracks. At the time these were occupied by a Medium Regiment, Royal Artillery, which, I thought, could benefit from a move to Salisbury Plain. I found that Hereford had much potential, not least on account of its proximity to extensive areas in the Brecon Beacons suitable for training. Following my return to Headquarters the General saw no reason to disagree with my suggestion that Hereford should be recommended to the War Office as the long-term home of 22 Special Air Service Regiment. This recommendation was duly accepted in late 1959.

Chapter Eighteen

'Who Dares Wins'

I have always had a liking for unorthodox soldiers and a leaning towards the unorthodox in war.

Field Marshal Earl Wavell

Before 1 March 1960, when I was due to assume command of 22 Special Air Service Regiment, my predecessor, Tony Deane-Drummond, and I agreed that we should spend about ten days on my takeover. We decided it would be sensible to do this in the Middle East, where the regiment was most likely to be employed and already had 'A' Squadron ostensibly training in Oman. At the same time, 'D' Squadron was training in Bavaria while the remainder, the Headquarters elements, was still at Malvern. It was also arranged that I should make a few static-line parachute jumps with the RAF for refresher training.

On 21 February, therefore, Tony and I left by air for Bahrain via Frankfurt, Damascus and Kuwait, involving fourteen hours actual travelling time. In Bahrain I was briefed on those aspects of the Middle East situation that were relevant to our possible future employment and the following day flew on to Sharjah, close to Dubai, for another briefing. We then changed to a light aircraft and travelled on to Ibri, a small, isolated Omani town on the eastern side of the Arabian peninsula, about 150 miles inland from Muscat with 1,000 miles of desert separating it from the Red Sea to the west. Here we found 'A' Squadron, under the command of Major John Spruell, and two troops were further dispersed in yet more isolated conditions, all quietly maintaining a presence at the invitation of the Sultan of Muscat and Oman. One of these troops we visited by light aircraft, 100 miles farther west in the desert, and found them enjoying their independence, as is usually the case with troops on detachment.

From Ibri we extended our travels to what were then known as the

Trucial States, visiting a variety of towns and villages where the SAS had friends and contacts. By the time we returned to Ibri we were more than halfway through our itinerary and departed for Aden, the site of theatre headquarters and base. There we met many of those who were involved with aspects of SAS training and operations, before returning home after a round trip of 10,000 miles in ten days. By then I had technically taken command of the regiment, although as an infantryman coming into such a specialized unit I was conscious of how much there was to learn before I could be fully effective. I was fascinated by the prospects.

In the meantime, preparations were under way for the regiment's move to Hereford: this took place over a three-week period between 21 March and 14 April and was a highly significant event. I had already been summoned to the War Office for a briefing on the outcome of recent studies and plans which required the regiment to be trained for operations in desert, mountain, jungle and snow environments, in addition to the variations to be found in Europe. Fortunately, in the War Office there was a small cell of experts available to assist with the considerable volume of planning and, within a month, I was able to introduce an outline annual training programme for 'A' and 'D' Squadrons, although there was one early diversion that had long-term implications. In mid-May a team of free fall parachutists belonging to the US 10th Special Forces Group stationed in Germany arrived in Hereford to compete in a friendly contest against a team from our own recently formed free fall parachute club. The Americans had given a silver cup that I was invited to present to the winning team. As expected, the donors won it, but a surprise lay in store. No sooner had I handed over the cup than a US Master Sergeant appeared with a parachute, which he offered to me with the words: 'Colonel, we thought you might like to take a jump with us.' This had not been in the script and, moreover, I had no personal experience of free fall parachuting, which is quite different from the more usual technique, where the canopy is deployed automatically by use of a static line. I thanked the Master Sergeant and explained that I was unqualified to accept his offer, but he appeared reluctant to accept this reason and I noted his sideways glance at my team, who were watching with interest. It was indeed a put-up job, but to avoid letting the side down I then agreed. Little did my men realize what they were initiating by introducing their Commanding Officer to the spell of falling free from an aircraft. This jump with the Americans from a mere 2,800 feet became the first entry in my free fall parachuting logbooks.

Parachuting was just one activity in two and a half unforgettable years, during which I found almost everything worthwhile and refreshing, with good humour one of the main ingredients. Nothing was more stimulating than the men themselves. Soon after I arrived there was an all ranks dance at which quite a number of junior ranks came up and introduced themselves, mainly, I suspected, to form their own impression of the new CO. After I had put several questions to one trooper he asked, very politely, 'And what are you hoping to bring to the regiment, sir?' The young officers were a splendid bunch, including two I only got to know well later because I sent them off on attachment, Peter de la Billière to 21 SAS (TA) and Tony Jeapes to Special Forces in the USA. (Both subsequently in turn became CO of 22 SAS.)

At one of my early meetings with the RSM I had raised the subject of the Annual Administration Inspection that, by coincidence, was due within a week or two and was to be taken by General Harington, who had been my CO when he took over from John Cubbon.

'What about the parade part of it? How many rehearsals?' I asked the RSM.

'I think a couple should do, sir', was his reply. 'One in working dress when the Adjutant and I can run through it with them and the second looking their best with you inspecting them.'

My surprise must have been obvious as I thought of all the preparations made in other regiments. My thoughts were read and I was reassured: 'I don't think they'll let you down, sir.' That closed the subject. On the day they were immaculate, steady as graven images, and then drilled as though they did little else. I was as impressed as was General Harington, but it was not until the next social occasion that I got the explanation from one of the sergeants who had a deep knowledge of the regiment and its ways. It was very simple: 'They dislike drill so much they know the importance of doing it well; that way practice is minimal and everyone is happy.'

Because of its varied roles and specialist training the regiment was subjected to frequent visits by senior officers, including foreigners. These visits became known as the 'circus' and eventually I had to represent their frequency to higher authority because they took so much time. Thereafter, intending visitors had to apply for permission from District Headquarters before they could call on us. In the meantime the men devised a way of relieving the tedium by role-swapping when answering questions from the VIP. On one occasion soon after my arrival I jotted down a note of what had transpired. The four-man crew of a Land Rover, consisting of driver, machine gunner, wireless operator and medical orderly, for the duration of the visit switched specialities, thereby risking disaster through failure to play the adopted part convincingly. Thus the visitor addressed the machine gunner:

VIP: 'What is your job?'

Trooper: 'Medical Orderly, sir.'

VIP: 'And how long have you done that?'

Trooper: 'Nine years, sir.'

VIP: 'You must be very good by now.'

Trooper: 'Haven't killed too many yet, sir.'

VIP: 'What happens when you require a doctor's skills, say in the jungle?'

Trooper: 'I then become the doctor, sir.'

VIP: 'But would you know how to remove an appendix?'

Trooper: 'Certainly, sir, and there are many trickier than that.'

As I looked at the other three faces not a muscle twitched and soon, in the same vein, the so-called driver recalled changing crankshafts in the desert and so on, with each in turn impressing the visitor. I found an early opportunity to warn them that should they ever be rumbled I would show no mercy and they took my point. A sequel to this, however, is noteworthy; within a few years the knowledge and skills of the SAS medics was such, following extensive training, that they were indeed operating successfully on a wide range of casualties, often being of assistance to indigenous populations.

Our training programme for the year included periods in Oman (twice), Bavaria, Kenya (twice), Denmark (twice), Norway, France and Germany. Many of the remoter parts of the United Kingdom also featured. The Norwegians and Danes were invariably helpful in providing opportunities and training areas and, from time to time, made use of our incursions by land, sea and air to exercise their home defence forces, who enlisted the help of farmers in less populated areas. The farmers' children and dogs also assisted in the search for our men, who moved only by night and laid up by day. Those who were captured were subjected to interrogations which, although they stopped short of the real thing, nevertheless provided a strong deterrent from being caught. At that time the threat from the Soviet Union pervaded much of our outlook and effective training needed to be as realistic as possible. There was, of course, a much lighter side to many of our overseas exercises, particularly in Denmark and Norway where there was an abundance of goodwill dating back to the war, which was still fresh in many memories. The grim background had receded, but the widespread gratitude was never far below the surface and our hosts always insisted on providing recreation or entertainment at some stage of each visit.

Three days after my return from Norway I set off to join 'D' Squadron in the Northern Frontier District of Kenya where its commander, Major John Slim, had made some useful contacts. I found that little had changed since my visit with the Fifth Fusiliers years earlier, though on the later occasion we went much farther north. John provided me with a Land Rover driven by Corporal – later Lieutenant Colonel – Mundell and during the next month I got to know the squadron as well as I could have wished. Northern Kenya was still largely without roads and was spacious enough to call for navigation by sextant as well as sun compass. This was no problem to a troop commanded by Captain Mike Gooley, later of 'Trailfinders' fame. I joined them at Nanyuki for a return trip of some 500 miles to Lake Rudolf, close to the Ethiopian border, across the Chalbi Desert where the intense heat towards midday caused all our 'desert modified' four wheel drive vehicles to expire. This they conveniently did almost simultaneously, which removed any choice of action. It was therefore in a rather undignified huddle, in the middle of the desert with a 360° featureless horizon, that we raised awnings and waited in groups of four for the anticipated fall in temperature. Although we had no thermometer we were very conscious of the need to conserve energy and to avoid touching anything metal. Silence reigned.

Our reverie was disturbed by an apparition that took shape slowly through the shimmering heat that limited our vision. The figure of a tall, thin native, naked apart from his loincloth, approached us with spear on shoulder, almost as if in a trance. When less than twenty yards away he stopped and stood quite still on one leg, the other bent with its foot against the opposite knee. In that position he surveyed us quite motionless as we watched him in silence. After a while, without any form of recognition, or change in expression, he resumed his walk, passing us like a shadow within a few yards. The silence was eventually broken by a laconic comment: 'Well, fancy that.' But thereafter I sensed an ongoing interest as questions remained unanswered in the minds of a small group of the most experienced soldiers in the British Army. First and foremost was almost certainly, 'How does he navigate in the middle of the desert with the sun directly overhead?' Other equally practical issues were, 'How long can these natives continue without water?' and 'What physiological differences are there between us that establish their superiority in this regard?' More than forty years later some of the same men were still wondering and discussing as thinking soldiers do: 'There was this fellow striding across the desert as if he owned it ...' Some time later I was able to ask Wilfred

Thesiger if he had any theories about this phenomenon and he confessed that he had not. He did, however, observe that these nomadic tribesmen are in many ways such remarkable people he was not in the least surprised to hear my account.

Back in Hereford the first serious thoughts had taken shape on the subject of High Altitude Low Opening (HALO) parachuting as a means of inserting small numbers of Special Forces in situations requiring clandestine entry. While no operational requirement had been advanced, I took the view that a small experimental project might help to keep us 'ahead of the game'. At the 1961 Farnborough Air Show I was particularly attracted by the relatively new Handley Page Dart-Herald twin-engined passenger aircraft which could operate either pressurized or unpressurized at high altitude and I was able to discuss its characteristics and capabilities with the company's representatives. They were most receptive to my interest and before long this relationship blossomed into a project to assess the aircraft's potential for high altitude parachuting and to establish the problems and limitations facing parachutists. By this stage I had selected my team from among the most experienced 'free fallers' in the regiment for intensive training, which included courses with the French Army, at that time ahead of us in some respects. We had the wholehearted support of British Army Aviation and much of our training and our demonstrations, including the Farnborough Air Show, were carried out using Army aircraft. For the record, I should mention that the RAF played no part in our advanced parachute training. Their own expertise during the early 1960s was still largely limited to static line parachutes and they never took us above 6,000 feet (usually 5,000) during their free fall courses. In consequence we had to make use of the Americans and French for training in preparation for the World Championships in the USA and Germany, and the communist-organized Adriatic Cup in Yugoslavia.

As our knowledge and involvement in this experimental field advanced, and we learned that the Dart-Herald was likely to prove capable of taking a team of eight parachutists to 30,000 feet or more, I discussed with my team members their outlook on how high they thought we should set our sights. Their unanimous view was, 'To the limit of the aircraft's capability'. This would set a new team free fall parachute jumping record and provide the Army with scientific data, as well as being good publicity for both the Army and Handley Page. It then became necessary to take specialist advice concerning technical preparations and training for ourselves. For example, we needed guidance to understand and avoid the effects of both frostbite in an anticipated temperature as low as -50°C and hypoxia, a disturbance of bodily function resulting from a deficiency of oxygen. In this regard we were highly fortunate in having the services of the Institute of Aviation Medicine at the Royal Aircraft Establishment at Farnborough, which provided us with the necessary background knowledge and practical training, including the use of a decompression chamber.

During an early stage of our joint preparations it emerged that the only period open to both Handley Page and ourselves in which to fit our trials was the second half of January 1962. This limitation had the effect of superimposing a meteorological aspect on a project that was already complex enough. At all events, most of my team and I were due thereafter for a period in Malaya, where enough communist terrorists were still at large in North Perak to provide some realistic jungle training. This knowledge had the effect of concentrating our minds on solving any remaining problems for what was about to become known as 'The High One'. The last of these concerned clothing capable of withstanding ultra low temperatures during several minutes in free fall, when any exposure of unprotected flesh would result in instant frostbite. In the event, as appears in the Handley Page report;

...each man was equipped with a R.A.F. type Crash Helmet, Flying Helmet and H type Oxygen Mask and 55 litre Emergency bale-out Oxygen Bottle. Jumping overalls were worn which completely covered arms, legs and body. Hands and feet were covered by normal paratroopers gloves and boots. Normal back type main and chest type reserve parachutes were worn.

Before we could make our first preliminary jump from the Dart-Herald it was necessary to strip the aircraft of all unnecessary equipment to reduce weight and to make a few minor modifications, to which Handley Page readily agreed. The aircraft then had to be cleared for parachuting by the Air Registration Board. The provision of an oxygen supply within the aircraft was arranged by Handley Page, in addition to which each parachutist had his individual bottle fitted into a special pocket attached to the underside of his reserve parachute. A drill was arranged for the changeover of supply when I gave the signal, which would follow an instruction from the pilot to me over the intercom that we were approaching the exit point. To assist the pilot in following a course precisely over the drop zone (DZ) Farnborough radar would report the vector and distance, together with a wind estimate, as we approached the target. This would be indicated by a powerful flare to be lit by our ground party. Pre-arranged signals on the aircraft cabin notice lights were also given so that the whole team could be aware of our position.

We were fortunate in having as our pilot the Chief Test Pilot of Handley Page, Squadron Leader H. G. Hazelden. He went to great lengths to help us in every possible way and gave us two training sorties for familiarization with the aircraft and its oxygen system. Once everyone involved was fully confident of the procedure all we needed was good visibility, plus acceptable ground wind conditions. These coincided on 30 January. The original plan was that we would make two jumps, the first from 25,000 feet and the second from the maximum attainable altitude. However, as we approached the DZ a report was received that the cloud cover was too thick and the Dart-Herald returned to Boscombe Down. The Met. Office there was consulted and the situation carefully reviewed. After discussion within the team it was agreed that one jump was possible before dusk. We took off again at approximately 1350 hours and climbed to reach the maximum altitude of which the aircraft was capable in the pre-vailing conditions. The steady drop in air temperature was impressive as the climb continued. Between 20,000 feet and 32,000 feet the temperature dropped from -30°C to -45°C, at which point it passed the low limit of the aircraft's temperature gauge. The climb continued with Farnborough radar leading the aircraft and it reached the DZ about thirty minutes after take off but, as the altitude was then only 31,500 feet and the rate of climb was still over 200 feet per minute, the pilot requested a further run to allow another ten to fifteen minutes climb. However, by then the wind from the north had increased to between 80 and 90 knots (approaching 100 mph) and at that altitude it was another twenty minutes before the aircraft approached the DZ again. Five miles from the jumping point the Dart-Herald had reached 33,700 feet, with an outside air temperature, according to the pilot of another aircraft in the vicinity, of -55°C. I was later glad we were not informed of this at the time; it would not have changed the plans, but we had enough on our minds already. In the meantime our pilot was experi-encing difficulties in aileron control and in coping with ice forming both inside and outside the windscreens.

We, too, had our problems. I was given successive reductions of our distance from the DZ as we closed the gap, which included an additional two miles to allow for the strong head wind. With two minutes to go we switched over from the aircraft oxygen system by pulling the release cable of our emergency 'bale out' oxygen bottles and then disconnecting our oxygen tubes from the main supply. Almost at once

202

Lance Corporal Beaumont slumped unconscious and we immediately reconnected him to the main supply. By this time we had reached our exit point and I had to make an instant decision whether or not to abort the jump. This would have involved the unrehearsed procedure of reconnecting the whole team to the aircraft oxygen system, the possibility of which had not been taken into account. With Beaumont's recovery to consciousness virtually assured I took the view that there was no need for the rest of us to remain. By then I had no direct link with the pilot so was unaware that thirty seconds after the signal to jump was given he had reported 'Negative Drop'. I gave a 'thumbs-up' signal to the team and exited the aircraft at 34,350 feet, followed in order by Staff Sergeant D. Hughes, Corporal B. Sanders, Corporal R. K. Norry, Corporal R. Reid, Lance Corporal T. Roberts and Sergeant P. Sherman.

From that moment everyone was conscious only of his own problems, the principal one of which was the need to keep the brain alert to activate the parachute approximately three minutes later, following a drop in free fall of close on six miles. The chief problem for us all, however, was with our goggles, which became iced up due to moisture from the eyes being transferred to the lenses. Somehow we managed to glimpse our altimeters enough to provide a coherent impression of progress during the drop. Gradually, for all except one, the problems eased and I sensed a feeling of relief as we landed loosely grouped within 300 yards of the flare. Later, for the benefit of others, I tried to recall my sensations and thoughts while falling for more than six miles at terminal velocity (over 230mph at 34,000 feet slowing to 120 mph at the moment of parachute deployment), but failed to find a way of conveying them. It was as though such an experience was too intense or complex to put into words.

There was a premature impression of unqualified success in setting a new team world record, but then, as we counted our number, we realized there were only six without Beaumont and there should have been seven. Keith Norry was missing and before long a farm worker hurried towards us with the news that he had seen one of us drop to the ground without the use of a parachute. We found Norry dead with both his parachutes intact and realized what a price had been paid for an otherwise noteworthy achievement. The subsequent Board of Enquiry was unable to find any underlying cause of his death, nor were any of us able to conjecture it.

Not long after the six of us had gathered together, a baker's van drove up, out of which Pete Beaumont stepped, with his deployed parachute bundled under his arm. He looked as he always did, composed and cheerful, but he had some difficulty in piecing together his actions since he had lost consciousness in the aircraft. Later Hazelden provided the missing, remarkable information. He and his co-pilot had watched Beaumont's recovery after being reconnected to the aircraft oxygen supply and had been unable to intervene as he struggled to his feet. The co-pilot was about to go to his assistance when Hazelden rightly ordered him to remain in his seat, pointing out that separated from his own oxygen supply he would not even have reached him. In his hypoxic state Beaumont, compelled by sufficient awareness of what he had been expected to do, lurched through the doorway, once again depriving himself of oxygen as he severed his supply line in the process. Loss of consciousness for the second time within a minute or so was inevitable and how long this lasted in free fall could not be assessed, but he recovered when the level of natural oxygen in the air was sufficient. This recovery, followed by the restoration of his faculties enabling him to pull his ripcord, was consistent with his character and physical condition as an accomplished long distance runner. The delay in his exit from the aircraft meant that he had landed some way from the rest of us and had hitched a lift to join us at the DZ. Despite the fatality the media were enthusiastic, reflecting widespread interest in the technical aspects of the achievement as well as awareness of the price paid for it. Keith Norry's funeral took place the following week at Tidworth Military Cemetery and is still remembered for the exceptional number of wreaths that came from all quarters.

The next day I had to fly to northern Malaya where 'A' and 'D' Squadrons had just arrived east of Grik, in the jungle of Upper Perak, for two months' re-acclimatization. By then the Malayan jungle was regarded by some as the regiment's second home, after many years' service during the Malayan Emergency of the 1950s. Certainly the sense of familiarity with the jungle and its ways was very noticeable and I was resolved to find out what lay behind this affinity. I appeared to have two options. The orthodox course for a visiting CO was to set up his headquarters on the periphery, from which he would control operations by radio and visit his sub-units from time to time, usually by air. On this occasion, largely for my own edification, I chose to leave my second in command with the base organization, where he could deal with any emergencies, while I got the feel of what was happening in the jungle. Having joined the patrol led by the redoubtable Corporal 'Joe' Lock, I was able to describe something of the life in a letter to be posted later to my parents:

204

...We normally move on each morning and the amount of progress made depends on the going and whether one strikes a track. The only other inhabitants apart from the animals are the occasional families of Aborigines and the last remaining CTs (Chinese Communist Terrorists) whom we hope to meet, but it is rather like looking for a needle in a haystack. ...So far, very oddly, it hasn't rained, which it normally does every day. It buckets down and the game is to keep as much of one's kit as dry as possible while one gets soaked to the skin in what one is wearing. Anything wet never dries out unless one finds a clearing where the sun can penetrate when it is fine.

It is now 10 o'clock and the camp is quiet. Some have gone to sleep, others are reading. Each man sleeps under a large ground-sheet raised off the ground on a pole slung between two trees. Beneath these he lies in his hammock or on a rough wooden bed which he has made with his 'parang'.

One of the things about living in the jungle which attracts good soldiers is the peacefulness of it. Another is its challenge and the individual's reliance on those he is with. It builds up a wonderful comradeship in which all men are equal. Rank plays little part except when orders have to be given – class, background, means, education count for nothing. A man is stripped of everything except his qualities and on these alone he is judged by his fellows.

What I might also have mentioned was the need for periodic halts in the jungle for the systematic removal of leeches, which gathered around one's midriff, but movement was primarily determined by the density of tall bamboo that required much parang effort to penetrate. Within a month I had completed this patrol, spent a few days out and the re-entered the jungle with another patrol. Prominent among the characters I recall from that time is Paul Wilson, who had recently completed a tour of duty as an outstanding adjutant. He was an excellent all-rounder, ever cheerful but, like the rest of us, much preferred the jungle to the office.

We returned home from Malaya in time to enter our free fall parachute team in the British National Parachute Championships, due to be held at Goodwood in April. There we managed to secure the top six places, which resulted in the regiment representing Great Britain in the Sixth World Parachute Championships held in Massachusetts in August. On most occasions an equally important member of our team was our parachute rigger, the indefatigable 'Stevie' Stephenson.

From time to time during my tenure of command, I invited various speakers to address the regiment on some subject of importance or interest. One such person was Leonard Wilson, the Bishop of Birmingham. I had been deeply impressed by his moving account of life as a prisoner of the Japanese when Bishop of Singapore during the war. There, in Changi Gaol, he and other Christians were subjected to barbaric treatment which sought to break them in body and spirit. I asked him if he would be prepared to visit us in Hereford and address the regiment on the subject of 'Faith in Captivity'. He accepted my invitation and it was arranged for 12 May, when the whole regiment would be present. As the day approached I increasingly wondered if the regiment's religious predisposition, of which I had not been over conscious, would rise to the occasion, remembering previous times elsewhere best forgotten. My concern, however, was groundless; the Bishop's personality and his strong and resonant voice, with substance to match, commanded their attention from the outset and left a message among a hall full of thoughtful men.

Late the following month, I learned that I had been selected as the British Army representative to attend the next annual course at the Canadian National Defence College at Kingston, Ontario, due to begin at the end of August. By happy chance Kingston is only about 250 miles from Orange in Massachusetts where I was competing with my parachute team between 11 August and 3 September and I went straight from one to the other. Our final jump after the end of the Championships was a team jump into The Inn at Orange, which was permitted only on special occasions. The drop zone was a small paddock littered with farm implements at the back of the Inn where we often foregathered at the end of the day. Here many of the safety rules of parachuting were broken knowingly and deliberately, but only with the permission of those who ran the Parachute Center, who disclaimed all responsibility. Inside the Inn were wooden panels on which every jump was recorded. Each entry was indicated by a symbol showing its outcome, one of which was a crutch. The management was very selective in its approvals; we were fortunate to be included and even more fortunate to land without mishap.

I already knew Jacques Istel, a remarkable American personality of French extraction, well known within the international Sport Parachuting world. Before I left Orange he mentioned an event due to take place in Vermont some months later, which he referred to as the Second World Para-Ski Race. He asked if I would care to enter and I was very non-committal as it sounded an extremely hare-brained affair. We dispersed in a haze of international goodwill – even the Russians had begun to thaw – and I headed for Kingston resolved to

206

put parachuting behind me for the foreseeable future.

It was at the beginning of August, therefore, that I handed over command of 22 SAS to John Woodhouse, who earlier had been my second in command. He had become a personal friend and was certainly one of the most popular and respected members of the regiment within the post-war generation. One of the projects that I left in his care was the erection of a regimental memorial. The idea originated when Handley Page, who had been so impressed by the team's commitment to the high level jump, offered to give something in memory of Keith Norry. After general discussion it was decided to extend the memorial to all those who lost their lives while serving in the regiment since the end of the Second World War. Every member of the regiment at the time agreed to contribute the equivalent of one day's pay and this, together with other donations and a generous contribution from Handley Page, provided sufficient funds for a clock tower to be erected in a prominent position in the barracks. The plan having been given the green light, John Woodhouse in due course made all the arrangements.

When the time came for my departure, I looked back on the previous two and a half years as one of the most rewarding and enjoyable periods of my career, and so it has remained in my memory ever since. 22 SAS is a unique regiment and to command it is an honour. This is also reflected in the attitude of the men to their successive COs. To them, one will always be their Colonel and may often be addressed as such in later years. Any further promotion one may achieve is, to them, apt to be irrelevant. After I had contemplated what the regiment had come to mean to me, I wrote a letter to John suggesting that a verse contained in James Elroy Flecker's *Hassan* might be coupled with the Memorial Clock and this, too, was accepted:

We are the Pilgrims, master; we shall go
Always a little further: it may be
Beyond that last blue mountain barred with snow
Across that angry or that glimmering sea.

Chapter Nineteen

Brittle Peace

We have the power to make this the best generation of mankind in the history of the world – or to make it the last.

John F. Kennedy in a speech to the United Nations,
20 September 1963

I arrived at the National Defence College at Fort Frontenac in Kingston, Eastern Ontario during the early Fall of 1962, as the ubiquitous maple trees were at the height of their dazzling splendour in seemingly endless sunshine. The members of Course No. 16 were getting to know each other and already the omens were favourable; by the end of the course many lasting friendships had been made.

Canada's status within the United Nations was at its zenith and the NDC was well placed to organize a succession of visits and tours throughout the course. The first of these was a three-day visit in November to the UN in New York, where several well-known statesmen addressed us, barely a month after the Cuban missile crisis had shaken the world. This was followed by an extensive study embracing all principal aspects of nuclear war. By Christmas we were due for a break and this enabled me to spend it at home, with the prospect of returning to Canada on Boxing Day. It was then that the memorable blizzard of the 1962-63 winter arrived in England and I only just reached Heathrow airport in time to take off before the country virtually closed down.

In mid-January, we left Kingston on a three-week tour of North America designed to gain knowledge of the military potential and strength of Canada and the United States and also 'to obtain an appreciation of the problems of living and working in the Arctic'. I was particularly impressed by the latter subject, because of its novelty. At Churchill, on the west side of Hudson Bay, we visited an army camp specializing in arctic warfare and, in a sense, were lucky enough to coincide with extremely cold conditions. A letter I wrote home later contained some impressions after the two Canadian Infantry members of the course, the American Army officer and I had answered the call for volunteers to spend the night under canvas:

Some of us slept out for a night on the 'Barrens' some miles from camp where it was so cold I couldn't describe the conditions to you. [I have heard such temperatures described as 'beyond the comprehension of urban man'.] It happened to be the coldest night of the winter up there which made it more interesting. They measure cold by temperature and wind combined, making a graph of both (in degrees and miles per hour – or metres per second). The 'Wind-Chill Factor' of 1200 is described as 'Bitterly Cold'. At 1400 the description is 'Exposed flesh freezes. Travel and life in temporary shelters becomes disagreeable'. At 2000 'Exposed areas of face freeze within 1 minute. Travel and life in temporary shelters becomes dangerous'. The night we were out the wind chill factor was 2350.

Even inside a tent faces would become frostbitten if left exposed, so we pulled the hoods of our sleeping bags over our heads, leaving just a tunnel to breathe through. In the night this gradually froze into a block of ice, with a narrow channel kept open by our breathing. By contrast, the most southerly point on our tour was the US Naval base at San Diego, close to the Mexican border. When we returned to Ontario we had completed a 10,000 mile circuit.

I had earlier been reminded by Jacques Istel of the World Para Ski Race, arranged for 16 March at the aptly named resort of Mad River Glen in Vermont. The race was open to teams of two and it was suggested that I should be paired with 'Skip' Doolittle, a young American on the staff of the Orange Parachute Center. From the aircraft we could see the landscape below us thick with trees and the orange cross showing our target set near the top of the mountain in a clearing not much bigger than a tennis court. There our skis were waiting for us close to the side of the run that snaked its way down to the resort below. I had the good fortune to land close to the target, while 'Skip' disappeared into a small ravine about 100 yards away. He was, however, a very accomplished skier and, having clambered back to retrieve his skis, reached the finishing line just ahead of me. The other competitors also had their problems and we found ourselves the winners. A small silver bowl, suitably inscribed, acts as a reminder of a madcap exploit.

Back at the NDC the programme followed its course with due emphasis on the use of its exceptionally fine library to assist our independent studies. I chose as my theme the effects of modern warfare on the fragility of our environment, to which at the time the war in Vietnam was very relevant. In mid-April we left on a ten-week tour, visiting ten countries in Asia and Europe. After Rome our next destination was Israel and I mentioned in a letter: 'I must remember not to call it Palestine and try to be civil to our hosts.'

I was put to the test even earlier than I had expected. We landed at Lod airport, which we had known as Lydda, and were met by an Israeli colonel who escorted us through immigration and customs to a waiting bus that would take us to Tel Aviv. Before long he strolled down the aisle and sat in the seat opposite mine. 'Well, Colonel Wilson, how does it feel to be back in what you knew as Palestine?' This was precisely on the lines I had anticipated and I had my reply ready. My lack of surprise at his question was not what he had hoped for. The visit was, of course, of the greatest interest to me, coming almost exactly fifteen years after the end of the British Mandate. A highlight was the hour we spent listening to David Ben-Gurion, then Prime Minister, and asking him unlimited questions, but at no point during our six-day stay was there an opportunity to converse with any Arab.

From Israel we headed for India where there was a fascinating programme that included an audience lasting an hour with the Prime Minister, Jawaharlal Nehru. He spoke freely about India's problems and gave us his views on China, Russia and Pakistan, before answering our questions. We had gained the impression that he was worshipped almost as a god by the peasants, but he struck us as being tired and showing his age. In this regard he was the complete opposite of his charming sister, Mrs Pandit, with whom we spoke later. In the course of our journey home we spent a week in Pakistan and saw the case there, as in India, concerning Kashmir. Partly in this connection we had a long and intensely interesting audience with Field Marshal Ayub Khan, the President, and were impressed by his ability, honesty and inspiration. He had quite a different personality from Nehru and won our sympathy more easily.

In Thailand we were extremely well looked after and perhaps the most memorable part was a splendid dinner followed by an exceptional exhibition of Thai classical dancing by girls from the National Academy specializing in the art. To any of us who, by that stage of our tour, were beginning to feel a bit jaded this was just what was needed and some of us agreed that Somerset Maugham had a point when he described the Siamese women as the most attractive in the world.

Our tour continued smoothly to Pakistan and then through Teheran for three days in Istanbul before flying on to Ankara, which promised to be rather boring and full of tiresome parties of which we had already had our fill. This was indeed the pattern of the first day, but then miraculously a revolution intervened and we were temporarily spared a continuation of the alcoholic routine. We had gone to bed very tired after a long day of engagements and later became semi-conscious of a disturbance which increased and eventually fully woke me around 0300 hours with a crescendo of small-arms fire approaching the hotel. I reached the balcony of my first floor room in time to watch the revolutionaries, who turned out to be troops from the War College, advance noisily, firing as they came, soon to be followed by 'Government Forces'. The fighting intensified and before long aircraft entered the fray, flying remarkably low in the half-light and adding to the confusion. As we learned later, casualties from this abortive revolution were believed to be well in excess of the official report of seven killed and twenty-seven wounded.

Our subsequent visits to London and Paris, though relatively high profile, were something of an anti-climax, but this was unavoidable. After ten weeks of travel and intense activity, with almost continuous briefings, it was a relief to return to the NDC in sleepy old Kingston and collect our thoughts. We had travelled more than 10,000 miles and it took a week or more to digest and discuss the tour. Thereafter only one major topic remained, a study embracing Canada's priorities and place in world affairs. Realizing that my involvement would be almost irrelevant, I readily obtained permission from the Commandant, Major General Cammie Ware, to absent myself and used the time to visit British Columbia, which I knew to be his own, much extolled, province. I travelled from coast to coast by train, on a journey taking five days, spending one day at the famous Calgary Stampede in the company of an old friend from 6th Airborne Division days, Roy Farran, who had emigrated to Canada.

I arrived back at Kingston as the final major study drew to its close. It had been a fascinating and instructive year, far exceeding my expectations, but soon I was looking forward to my next appointment, which was to be in Germany, as Colonel, General Staff, with responsibility for operations and intelligence under the Chief of Staff to the Commander of the 1st British Corps, Lieutenant General Sir Kenneth Darling.

I returned from Montreal to Liverpool by sea in the Cunard ship *Carinthia*, which was the perfect way to recover from the progression of social events that characterized the final week of the course. Thereafter I was due for leave and spent part of it with my old SAS free-fallers, captaining the British Parachute Team in the third biennial Adriatic Cup contest at Portoroz in Yugoslavia, where we jumped out of Russian aircraft. It was on such occasions that both sides, making a joint effort, managed to achieve a welcome, albeit local, thaw in the otherwise pervasive cold war. Nevertheless it was not long before I had an interesting, almost theatrical, reminder.

The scene was set on a winter's night in a respectable neighbourhood on the outskirts of Bielefeld, a large town lying south-west of Hanover in what was known as West Germany when Russia occupied East Germany. Here was situated the headquarters of the 1st British Corps. I occupied a flat on the first floor of a building adjacent to the Officers' Mess, overlooking a quiet road. I had been reading in bed and turned my light out just as the town clocks struck midnight. About a minute later there was a knock at the door leading into the hallway of my flat. This happened not infrequently when the duty clerk was dispatched to deliver an urgent message, so I got out of bed, put on a dressing gown and made my way from the bedroom, through the sitting room and opened the door, expecting to find an apologetic clerk. Instead I found myself face to face with a stunningly beautiful woman, who smiled and introduced herself in English with an indeterminate accent.

'Are you Colonel Wilson? I have just arrived from Paris and have something of the greatest importance to tell you,' she said. 'May I come in?'

'One moment,' I replied. 'Please wait while I dress.'

I then closed the door and made my way quickly back to my bedroom where I picked up the telephone connected to the duty officer. 'Don't put this on the log,' I instructed him, 'but make a note of the time and what I have to say. There is a strange girl at the door of my flat who says she has something to tell me. I am now going to speak to her and will report to you later.' Too late I saw that she had let herself in and had obviously overheard my conversation. I glimpsed her disappearing in haste out of my flat and down the stairs. I then watched out of the window and saw her get into a car, which was immediately driven off at high speed.

It had been a crude attempt, almost certainly by the KGB, to compromise and then, probably, to blackmail me. Perhaps it was as well that, being myself in an intelligence-oriented job, I had no doubts from the outset what was afoot. The only part of the episode that was not crude was the choice of the girl herself – she was, indeed, extremely

212

attractive!

I had left home for Bielefeld on 20 September, the same day that President Kennedy addressed the United Nations. That the Cuban Missile Crisis of October 1962 had brought the British Army of the Rhine to a high state of alert and operational efficiency was immediately apparent to me. Bielefeld was a hive of activity, although the situation was in no way permitted to interfere with polo, dinner parties (black tie obligatory) and sports on six afternoons a week except, of course, when one of the innumerable exercises took priority. During the winter months skiing was often to be had within relatively easy reach and it was a popular family station.

I personally, and I suspect quite a few others, found much of it boring and strangely removed from the atmosphere which accompanies what many of us regard as 'proper soldiering'. However, in company with a growing number of all ranks, I was fortunate in having the Rhine Army Sport Parachute Centre at Lippspringe, not far from Bielefeld. At the end of July 1964 West Germany hosted the 7th World Sport Parachute Championships and, having maintained my form, I remained as leader of the British team. The demonstration event in these championships marked the end of my competitive parachuting, but I continued to manage the team for some years and served the British Parachute Association as its chairman until 1966. When, later, I had made my last jump of all, I had had the interest and pleasure of parachuting from twenty-eight different types and marks of aircraft in many parts of the world.

I had plenty of warning concerning my next appointment when, in May 1965, I learned that in September I should be taking command of 149 Infantry Brigade of the Territorial Army (TA) and I was delighted at the prospect. The brigade, with its HQ in Newcastle, comprised four outstanding territorial battalions (the 4th/5th, 6th and 7th Battalions of RNF and the 4th Battalion of the King's Own Royal Border Regiment), which between them stretched from coast to coast across the counties of Northumberland, Cumberland and Westmorland, covering 4,300 square miles on both sides of Hadrian's Wall.

The culmination of training each season was the annual brigade camp, which lasted for two weeks and was normally held in the summer at one of the major training areas in the United Kingdom. All members were expected to attend and most made every effort to do so. In 1966, however, there was an ominous difference in atmosphere from that of previous camps; the threat of disbandment then facing the TA had cast a very dark shadow. I discussed with my COs ways of preventing it from leaving a gloom over the camp and we resolved to keep everything in perspective through hard and imaginative training in conjunction with lots of sport. This would require the wholehearted assistance of all officers and reliance on the example of the senior ranks, many of whom were on attachment from our Regular Army battalions. Our confidence in them was rewarded and the camp, held that year near Otterburn in Northumberland, exceeded our expectations in terms of enjoyment as well as in its main purpose of improving our readiness for war.

For me the most memorable part of the week was the sight of the best part of 2,000 men marching the several miles back to camp at the end of the final exercise. Awaiting the brigade, in order to take the salute at a prominent viewpoint some distance short of Otterburn, was General Sir Geoffrey Musson, the Army Commander from Northern Command, with several more generals in attendance. From where we stood there were stunning views of rolling heather-clad hills on all sides and, as we waited on a sunny morning, chatting amiably, with grouse calling in the background, snatches of distant martial music reached us from the regimental bands and corps of drums within the column, augmented by the alluring tones of the Northumbrian pipes belonging to our 7th Battalion, recruited from the north of the county. Before long we had our first glimpse of the approaching column of troops as its head appeared briefly on the skyline in the distance, only to disappear from view into lower ground. As it snaked in and out of sight across the intervening landscape, conversation among those observing dwindled into silence as all eyes focussed on the brigade. The leading troops were still more than a mile away and there was time for those with a sense of history to reflect on earlier occasions when this very ground had been the scene of stirring events.

Thus BORDER FORAY reached its climax as each battalion marched past the Army Commander, headed by its band playing its regimental march. And so, as recorded in *St George's Gazette*, '149 Infantry Brigade, Territorial Army, marched into history'. As the column approached to march past the saluting base there was no trace of the weariness that might be expected at the end of a demanding exercise, nor would it have been in keeping because every man knew the significance of the occasion. So, too, did those watching and many were caught unawares by the unexpected blend of romance and poignancy. I noticed that some of those present who had spent their entire service in the brigade made no effort to hide their emotion when Geoffrey Musson, having taken the salute, eventually turned to face us and said very simply: 'Gentlemen, we shall never see the like of it again.'

Chapter Twenty

Farewell to South Arabia

The Arab's leave-taking is wonderfully ungracious to the European sense,
and austere. The Arab, until now so gentle a companion, will turn his
back with stony strange countenance and leave thee for ever.
            Travels in Arabia Deserta by Charles M. Doughty, 1888

Early in January 1967 I flew to Aden to join Headquarters Middle East
Command as 'Chief Administrative Officer Land Forces' under the
command of Major General John Willoughby. On arrival I found
myself one of a foursome of brigadiers who, of necessity, worked very
closely together and, fortunately, got on extremely well. The senior
member was Roly Gibbs (later Field Marshal), chief of staff to the
Commander-in-Chief Middle East Command, Admiral Sir Michael Le
Fanu; the others were Charles Dunbar, Brigadier General Staff, and
Jack Dye, who commanded the British-led South Arabian Army
(SAA).

Prior to 1967, which turned out to be a critical year by virtue of
Britain's withdrawal from Aden, there had been two years of trouble
within South Arabia following the British Government's announcement that political independence would be granted by 1968.
Nevertheless, it remained HM Government's intention to retain
military independence and to maintain the all-important Aden base,
through which a considerable volume of world trade continued to
pass. However, soon a national plan was prepared, based on the need
to acknowledge that Britain's influence abroad had declined to a point
where she could no longer maintain overseas bases in countries
against their wishes. By then South Arabia had already been assured
of its independence and, in the absence of their support, the Aden base
would have to be relinquished, although the British presence in the
Persian Gulf, some thousand miles to the north-east, would be maintained. In anticipation of our withdrawal from Aden, President

Nasser of Egypt, who had already intervened in the Yemen, encouraged Arab nationalists in their search for independence and before long they were all intent on strengthening their support from wherever they could, at the expense of the occupying power. Thus began, and often flourished, a variety of causes and groups which sought to gain the support of fringe elements by arming and encouraging them in basic opportunism by sniping and grenade-throwing from alleyways and concealed positions, against British troops engaged in their all too familiar role of maintaining law and order.

This, then, became the background to the Internal Security operations that kept our own troops fully occupied and constantly on the alert as they went about their duties in and around Aden, often in squalid conditions and in temperatures which regularly rose above 90°F, with high humidity. My new appointment embraced virtually all administrative aspects of our withdrawal from Aden. When there was a general strike the army also had to take over much of the civil administration and I found myself Chairman of the Essential Services Committee, covering all public utilities for the whole of Aden, which meant that any problem to do with electric power, water supply, sewage, hospitals, mortuaries, homeless, fuel, food, roads, port, airport etc. became my concern. On the military side, in planning for our withdrawal, a balance had to be struck between maintaining the garrison while simultaneously whittling its numbers and running down the stores and equipment. It was described as involving 'a sea evacuation of a size unseen since Suez and an airlift bigger than anything since the Berlin Airlift'.

Initially I was struck by the degree of normality of life in Aden, with comfortable quarters close to the sea and ideal bathing conditions. There were Sunday curry lunches, visiting concert parties, band concerts and a security situation reasonably under control, although the annual total of security incidents during the previous year had risen to over 500. In short, we had time to relax within the periods set aside for it and bathing for all ranks was the daily recreation. However, by the time I wrote a progress report in June to General Sir Alan Jolly, the Quartermaster General, the situation had deteriorated to such an extent that we were beginning to wonder whether we were still justified in counting on an orderly and economic withdrawal. I had to inform him that Aden Port had been strike-bound at intervals since the New Year, shipping was further disrupted because of the closure of the Suez Canal, the Arab/Israeli war had caused oil supplies to cease from BP and Shell because of an embargo by the Arab oil-producing states, food supplies for both the local community and the

Security Forces were running low because shipping lines were avoiding calling in at Aden Port and labour relations could hardly have been worse because of intimidation, where any official or worker failing to observe a call to strike was inviting assassination. Fortunately, when I wrote again four months later I was able to be more reassuring, reporting that the entire position had changed and that most of our logistic problems appeared to be behind us.

All this time Roly Gibbs and I were sharing an attractive quarter within a large secure area, looking directly on to the sea, although bathing there was not possible because of sharks. In my capacity as senior administrator it came to my attention that an outstanding Yemeni cook, who had been employed by a series of British families over many years, was seeking a position and I had no hesitation in engaging him to cook for Roly and me. Ali was a gem and in no time had won our complete confidence, not only with respect to his cooking; just as important were his honesty and reliability. Soon after he joined us he was due his annual holiday and he wrote me a letter in beautiful, clear script, explaining that he had a wife and children in the Yemen and wished to spend his holiday with them. The letter concluded:

When I come back and I am active for working I will work with you until the last second and I will ask God to please you with a long and happy life. Thank you.

Your faitfully,   Ali Cook

Several days of Ali's time away were spent travelling to and from his home, riding on a donkey along rough tracks through the mountains. He was a devout Muslim and prayed inconspicuously five times a day outside the back door. When we had got to know each other well enough, he would chide me if he felt I was taking too much for granted. Thus, every time I mentioned I was going away to attend meetings in London or within the Gulf States and would return in a few days he would smile and interrupt me reprovingly with 'Yes, sir, but only Ensh' Allah'.

One of the bonuses I found in Aden was the presence of the 1st Battalion Royal Northumberland Fusiliers, who had arrived from the United Kingdom some months before me. Although on arrival they had assumed their internal security role in Crater, which was the crowded heart of Aden town, they found conditions no worse than they had anticipated. Nevertheless, enough was happening to keep everyone on his toes and provide the younger soldiers with much to

217

learn. The number of incidents involving the use of firearms and grenades was on the increase and during 1966 five British soldiers were killed and 218 wounded. All the Security Forces showed commendable restraint in their peacekeeping role and even when the occasional boot was put in most of the international press, of whom at one time there were more than seventy, recognized that strong action was required in a riot situation. Reports such as that headed 'Better boots than bullets' offset the few allegations that unnecessary harshness was sometimes shown. The Fifth Fusiliers received particularly good publicity at the beginning of April when they had to disperse 1,200 rival FLOSY and NLF demonstrators, with reports of the help they gave and kindness they showed, especially to women and children caught up in the riots. Despite the arrival of reinforcements from the United Kingdom the security situation continued to deteriorate.

Throughout my own time in Aden I was drawn in different directions, including London, the Gulf and even Kenya where I was negotiating the disposal of much of our surplus equipment because, mindful of limiting the cost of our withdrawal to the British tax-payer, prices in Nairobi were much higher than in Aden. While much of my work was involved with current events in Aden, before long it was planning for our withdrawal, coupled with our retention of British interests and presence in the Gulf, which took most of my time, including monthly flights to London. Even so, several stings remained in Aden's tail.

The most significant of these arose out of an unexpected change in policy by a new Labour Government, which announced that Britain would not, after all, maintain a military presence in Aden after independence. This infuriated the Federal rulers, who had only agreed to take over the government on the understanding that Britain would ensure their security. Both major terrorist organizations took advantage of the opportunity to make trouble and declared 11 February as 'The Day of the Volcano'. However, the Aden Brigade, by then four battalions strong, including 1 RNF, managed to thwart them. Nevertheless, trouble from several directions was on the increase and, after a terrorist bomb had killed nine children and wounded fourteen others, all remaining British service families were encouraged to return home.

On 24 May the 1st Battalion The Parachute Regiment entered the fray and inflicted many casualties on NLF bombers and snipers, at a cost to themselves of one killed and four wounded. However, no one foresaw a serious mutiny by the South Arabian Army (formerly the

Federal Regular Army). This erupted suddenly on 20 June and rapidly got out of hand. After the trouble had spread to the police in Crater a truck load of men from the Royal Corps of Transport was ambushed, resulting in eight killed and as many wounded. 1 RNF were in the process of handing over to the Argyll and Sutherland Highlanders and a combined party from the two regiments, mounted in two Land Rovers, came under heavy fire without warning at very short range from the Police Barracks. Major John Moncur and Second Lieutenant John Davis of the Fifth Fusiliers and Major Brian Malcolm of the Argylls, together with six soldiers, were killed. In due course order was restored and the offending police were suitably dealt with. However, it came to the attention of 'higher authority' that his involvement in these events appeared to have gone to the head of Lieutenant Colonel Colin Mitchell who, at the time, was commanding the Argylls. He was indiscreet, or stupid, enough to disagree openly with Major General Philip Tower, who by then had succeeded John Willoughby, and his inflated sense of his own importance also ensured that he always had members of the press corps in tow. When it became clear that he had already overstepped the mark he was imprudent enough not to apologize when taken to task by Philip Tower and I was appointed as his escort when he was marched in front of the Commander-in-Chief. Admiral Le Fanu was very explicit and I formed the impression that from that moment Mitchell's military career was blighted.

The same day that John Moncur and his men were killed, further loss of life was averted by the calmness and determination of Fusilier John Duffy of 1 RNF, who was one of a small picquet observing Crater from Temple Hill. As they were being withdrawn by helicopter it came under fire and the pilot was wounded, causing him to lose control of the aircraft, which crash-landed and caught fire. Duffy's corporal was severely wounded and knocked unconscious, but Duffy, although himself injured, proceeded to drag first him and then the pilot out of the burning wreckage, thereby saving both their lives. He returned to the aircraft for the third time to retrieve his radio in order to contact his base, which enabled the three of them to be evacuated. For his gallantry he was awarded the Distinguished Conduct Medal, in military awards second only to the Victoria Cross.

Within the wider scene, events in Aden moved into less stormy waters as we approached the deadline for our withdrawal, which had been brought forward from the original date of 9 January1968. However, it was particularly unhelpful of our politicians to delay giving any guidance over the timetable or actual date of completion. It

219

certainly made our job in Aden much trickier than it need have been and put us at a disadvantage in planning the overall movement to the United Kingdom and the Gulf.

In the end it was not until 2 November that the Foreign Secretary, on the High Commissioner's recommendation, announced that British troops would leave by the end of the month. The previous year there had been 23,000 British troops and families in Aden; when the announcement came only 6,000 were left.

As time passed, planning and preparations for our departure intensified and I had regular meetings with the High Commissioner, Sir Humphrey Trevelyan, in my new capacity as Joint Service administrative coordinator. He was still striving to achieve what at times looked too much to hope for – a systematic withdrawal of all personnel with our vehicles, stores and equipment, to be achieved with minimum casualties. For five months he negotiated with one faction or another as they sniped at us and fought each other almost incessantly.

One of my lasting memories of Aden concerns the mounting number of casualties during our final year. The military cemetery in use was named Silent Valley, situated some twenty miles from the town in that part of the colony known as Little Aden. As I was responsible for the operation of the cemetery, and also because I often represented my superiors, I attended many of the sixty-six burials that took place in 1967, including those of John Moncur, John Davis and their fusiliers. Silent Valley was closed as we left and remained, lonely and impressive.

Towards the end of our time in Aden we were visited by General Cassels, then Chief of the General Staff, who wished to see the situation for himself. At the same time he took the opportunity of meeting individually all members of the brigadiers' foursome. To each of us in turn he mentioned that we had been selected for promotion to Major General and told us of our appointments. Mine was to be District Commander of the South East District in Colchester but, as the post would not become vacant until well into the following year, he advised me to think of something useful to do in the meantime, or the Army would suggest something less interesting – like President-on-call for Courts Martial and high level Boards of Inquiry. When I had given it due thought I submitted a request to the Director of Land/Air Warfare, Major General Frank King, that I should learn to fly, on the grounds that not enough senior Army officers were familiar with the Army's role in land/air warfare, and this was approved.

As a postscript to Aden it is worth mentioning that, in the intervening years, it became clear to those who returned, for one reason or another, that the older Adenis were looking back on the days of British rule with affection. Retired soldiers, and families, who made the pilgrimage to Silent Valley found it in good order and still tended with care. By contrast, many of the British who left so abruptly felt our Imperial farewell to be a shabby affair, although at the time there were few, if any, soldiers who regretted our departure.

However, whatever the prevailing view may then have been, there was no doubt in any quarter that the large Naval Task Force which was assembled for review by the High Commissioner on 25 November 1967 was highly impressive. Three days later his own departure from RAF Khormaksar, accompanied by Admiral Le Fanu and other senior officers, went as smoothly as could have been hoped and for those of us who were privileged to accompany him it was a memorable occasion. The Comet closed its doors at 1200 hours and the Royal Salute followed.

Chapter Twenty-One

Army Aviation spreads its Wings

Young and lusty as an eagle.

Psalm 103 v 5

As soon as the RAF Comet had landed in the United Kingdom, I travelled to Aldershot. The advance party returning home had established themselves there and I joined them for a while to deal with residual problems. Christmas and home leave followed and then, early in 1968, I was requested to visit RAF Biggin Hill for Pilot Aptitude Tests and Medical Examination. These were successfully completed and soon I was in the hands of the Army Aviation Centre at Middle Wallop, where I joined a course consisting of captains, lieutenants and sergeants. In no time a strong course spirit emerged, as the rest of them took in their stride a stray brigadier among them. I was twenty-five years older than most of them and found myself having to work very hard in the classroom to keep up with some of the advanced theory and technicalities of flight.

Flying instruction was in two stages, the first relating to fixed wing aircraft, which in our case was the Chipmunk. This proved to be a very forgiving aircraft, almost as though it was assisting novice pilots to do the right thing. Helicopters, on the other hand, played it their own way if given half a chance and were much more demanding.

My course ended on 12 July 1968, when we received our 'flying wings' from General Sir Hugh Stockwell, who was then Colonel Commandant of the Army Air Corps. One day during the week following the completion of my training I was flying a helicopter solo back to London to attend a meeting after visiting a unit in Surrey. While I was over Richmond Park, heading for Battersea heliport and under control of London Airport, my radio developed a fault and I was unable to transmit. Soon the controller was showing concern with repeated calls, prompted, no doubt, by my proximity to the Heathrow

222

approach. The situation worsened when my radio ceased to function altogether, followed by several other electrical circuits, making it necessary for me both to land as soon as possible and to find a telephone so that I might placate air traffic control and summon assistance from Middle Wallop. Looking down, I saw a scattering of large houses, one of which appeared to have a paddock suitable for landing in emergency, and this was accomplished without further problems.

As I closed down the engine I saw an elegant woman crossing the garden towards me and by the time I was out of the aircraft she had joined me. With my mind on the priorities facing me I was considerably taken aback when I recognized my companion as HRH Princess Alexandra and realized that of all the houses from which I might have made my choice I had selected her home at Thatched House Lodge. It was an embarrassing moment, but she could not have been more welcoming and helpful in response to my apologies. After listening to my problems she took me into the house to use a telephone and thereafter it was a matter of waiting for assistance, but at least I was able to show her children over the aircraft and answer their numerous questions.

On 2 August, in the midst of my preparations for moving to Colchester, I received a letter from the Military Secretary informing me that my appointment as General Officer Commanding Eastern District had been cancelled and instead I would take over from Frank King as Director Land/Air Warfare, because he was urgently needed elsewhere and I, as an already qualified pilot, was the obvious choice to fill the unexpected vacancy. Three days later I began work in the old War Office building overlooking Whitehall, where I was soon dealing with the prospects and problems of Army Aviation and Airborne Forces.

Most appointments such as my own had as their back-drop the Cold War and the Vietnam War. Among the major issues arising from the Vietnam War was the advent of the armed helicopter. The terrain in Vietnam and the threat posed by elusive infantry to movement in vehicles in close country made the helicopter a key element of army operations throughout the war. They were used extensively for troop deployment, casualty evacuation, re-supply, reconnaissance, direction of fire and a host of other tasks. However, experience showed that unarmed helicopters operating at low level in close contact with the enemy proved to be vulnerable to small-arms fire and a wide variety of weapons were urgently adapted for helicopter use, including machine guns, rockets and anti-tank missiles, which were also effective when used against bunkers. As a result, the armed helicopter emerged as a strikingly effective weapon system, which was only slowly introduced into British service because of high-level indecision before it was placed in the hands of the Army. As a close air support system integral to the conduct of a land battle, it was, arguably, unhelpful of the Royal Air Force not to concede that its rightful place was with Army Aviation, although this position was later firmly established.

In the meantime, many organizational changes were pending as a result of intensive studies affecting the role of British Army Aviation. An early step was to centralize within divisions the air platoons and troops of helicopters previously assigned to individual regiments, a necessary stage which was resented by them, but led to a much sounder organization. This and other domestic problems had to be settled before we could participate in the more interesting doctrinal aspects with our American, French, German and Italian allies. The main purpose and urgency behind our thinking was the necessity at that time to improve our ability to withstand Soviet Union aggression in Europe. Few things in our lifetime will prove to be of greater significance than the fact that we were never put to the test we prayed so hard would not occur. On the positive side, one of the most gratifying aspects that emerged from allied interchanges was the excellent relationship we established among ourselves. Before long, the allied senior army aviators were all on first name terms and this warmth extended beyond the military sphere. Two friendships I particularly valued in this field were those with Sergei Sikorsky, one of the talented sons of the great helicopter designer, and Alan Bristow, the dynamic founder of Bristow Helicopters.

One day I was telephoned by Tony Deane-Drummond, at that time Assistant Chief of Defence Staff in the MOD, who asked for my views on a visit to the war zone in Vietnam, to see for myself anything which might be relevant to our interests within the field of Army Aviation. I enthused, from a professional viewpoint, at the prospect of such a visit and, in due course, was joined by Brigadier Peter Whiteley, then commanding 3 Commando Brigade. (Later, as a full general, he become C.-in-C. Allied Forces, Northern Europe.) Before that stage, however, came my briefing at the Ministry of Defence, covering all aspects of the mission. One of those I met was James Boyden, MP, the Parliamentary Under Secretary (Army), with a background of teacher, lecturer and barrister. He was at pains to impress on me the sensitive side of sending a senior British Army officer to observe the war in Vietnam. The Government's policy was to keep at arm's length from all active operations and for that reason our overt interest had been, and would remain, minimal. According to him it was with some reluctance that the Foreign Office had agreed to authorize my visit, and then only on the strict understanding that I should be briefed to keep the lowest possible profile. Mr Boyden hoped he had made this reservation quite clear. I unhesitatingly agreed, with the feeling that to have raised with him any point at all concerning where I might go when I found myself in the hands of an American Army escort might have endangered the whole mission. I did not think that anyone who listed 'Local Government' as one of his interests in *Who's Who* was likely to encourage much independence of outlook. As it was, my interview came to a perfunctory end, without even some expression akin to bon voyage.

On 8 April 1969 Peter Whiteley and I left Heathrow for Singapore on the first leg of a round trip lasting twelve days. I had first met Peter in 1954 when he was attending the Staff College, where he was regarded as one of the brightest students. As I was about to discover, he was also a refreshing companion. We spent two days in Singapore where we were thoroughly briefed on the relevant background to our respective interests, Peter as a Royal Marine and I as a soldier interested in aviation, before flying on to Saigon. I was keen to take advantage of this visit for two reasons. The first was to see in practice the latest advance in modern warfare – air mobility – and the second was to learn all I could about the performance and reliability of the four types of helicopter in active service in Vietnam. These were the Huey utility, the Cobra attack, the Chinook cargo and the Cayuse light observation helicopter. My particular interest lay with the Huey armed variant and the Cobra, both of which were classified by the Americans as 'gunships'.

For several years air mobility had been discussed and studied in countless conventions and study days at home within all three services, but in spite of this I was not fully prepared for what lay in store for us as we landed in Saigon. As we emerged from the aircraft we were assailed by the background resonance from all directions of countless helicopters in the sky. It was not even possible to single out a particular aircraft unless it was in close proximity and this continued by day and night wherever we went for the next week. I doubt if anyone knew at any time how many helicopters there were operating in Vietnam, but according to published figures the 1 Aviation Brigade mustered 4,230 aircraft and helicopters and 101 Airborne Division had 422 helicopters. After a while one became more or less acclimatized to the continuous noise, although it remained as an irritant to some. What mattered was the achievement it represented. Here was an army largely free from the trammels of fixed lines of communication, which otherwise would have been highly vulnerable to attack by guerrilla forces. Even so, a significant number of US helicopters was being destroyed and damaged by enemy ground fire from the communist Viet Cong forces. During our briefings, we learned that in one week twelve helicopters had been shot down and a further fourteen damaged, plus nine fixed-wing aircraft lost. In a month the overall total of lost and damaged aircraft came to 136. By now, the Vietnam War has receded from many memories and is a matter of little consequence to later generations other than in the countries involved, which include Australia. Nevertheless, throughout its ten-year duration, and for long after, it cast a shadow over much of Asia, as it came to be regarded as one of the costliest wars of all times.

Reverting to our own visit to South Vietnam, in practical terms it gave us an insight into three very different aspects of the changing scene. The first became apparent as we flew over much of the ground where the tides of war had either passed or were still flowing. It was an awesome sight, revealing a degree of destruction comparable in some ways with that in Flanders during the First World War. The total devastation of all natural vegetation over large areas reflected the huge scale of bombing and massive use of chemicals in earlier years and the intensity of the ground fighting that followed. The second came as we visited a number of defended localities during the course of our tour and I gained the impression, later verified, that little, if any, night patrolling took place. In this regard there appeared to be a significant difference in outlook and practice between our two armies as, indeed, there was when it came to the retrieval of bodies from no man's land. The Americans appeared determined to recover their dead at all costs for later return to the USA, even if in doing so they risked adding to them. As an observer, I felt that the British view would have been more pragmatic and that we would have endeavoured to restrict any further loss of life by putting the clearance of ambushes before the recovery of bodies.

The third insight was directly related to the main purpose of my visit and could hardly have been more convincing. In the course of a tour of headquarters and actively engaged units there were several opportunities to view and discuss the Cobra, but none so rewarding as that provided by the 235 Aerial Weapons Company, otherwise known as 'The Delta Devils'. There we were given an excellent briefing on their offensive role, and the capabilities of the Cobra, by their commander, Major Charles Teague. When he had finished he asked if there were any questions and I wondered if it might be possible to have a flight, which was agreed. His briefing was then extended to include the anatomy of the aircraft, its controls and weapons system, before he took off with me in the gunner's seat, in front of and below that of the pilot. I found everything about the aircraft impressive, including the firepower from its six-barrel machine-gun turret and rockets fired in ripple or salvos. After demonstrating its characteristics in flight, he circled round looking for an imaginary target. Having pinpointed one he then simulated an attack, during which I was able to engage the target with the satisfaction of achieving an effective result. After this sortie I was given a sheet from the Army Aviator's Flight Record on which were entered full details of the forty-five minute mission for entry in my log book. I recollect that at some stage I wondered what Mr Boyden would have thought, had it by some means come to his notice, but lost no sleep on that account. In fact the practical experience was worth much more than the best of briefings and I realized that in the interests of both Army Aviation and the Army as a whole I could do no better than encourage maximum thought and effort leading to the introduction of armed helicopters. It proved to be a long haul and it was many years before Army Aviation took possession of the Apache, the most advanced attack helicopter yet to exist (up to 2006).

Later in our programme we were flown into a strong American defence position, which had previously been attacked by Viet Cong on a number of occasions, and I sensed an edginess among some of the younger defenders. In conversation they made little effort to disguise their disenchantment with the policy that had resulted in them being drafted into a highly unpopular war, although the officers and senior ranks I met appeared to be well motivated. Also noteworthy, among those we visited, was the strong Australian Task Force, including 1st Army Aviation Squadron and a squadron of SAS, both of which distinguished themselves.

1 January 1970 marked a significant stage in the recognition of the importance of aviation in the modern British army when my appointment as Director Land/Air Warfare was re-designated Director Army Aviation. At the same time, much to my satisfaction, my headquarters moved from Whitehall to Middle Wallop, although I retained a small office in London. That was the moment when Middle Wallop truly became the Centre of Army Aviation and, as such, it has since gone from strength to strength. Meanwhile, an important agreement had been reached with the French relating to a new family of service helicopters consisting of the Puma, the Gazelle and the Lynx. On the whole they were all successful, although financially the French came out of it better than the British.

The ensuing year was also marked by a succession of aviation visits and conventions, which Frank King had forewarned me of during his handover, including those of the USA, Australia and various European countries. Among international visits there were several memorable highlights, one of which was the opening in September of the City of Bückeburg's new helicopter museum, proudly proclaimed as the first in the world. During the preliminaries the Germans seemed keen to stimulate the involvement of other countries and I felt honoured to be appointed a Vice President. It turned out to be a much more entertaining occasion than I had anticipated, with discussion interwoven with hospitality. My German opposite number, Brigadier General Hans Drebing, I had already found to be warmhearted and generous and there were a number of other distinguished guests present. None was more interesting than Hanna Reitsch, Germany's famous *Luftwaffe* test pilot, who assisted in bringing many types of Second World War aircraft into service despite her diminutive size. We were introduced before lunch, at which we sat together, and I found her delightful as well as modest about her many achievements, for the earliest of which she had been decorated by Hitler with the Iron Cross. During the meal I asked her what, in her career, had given her the most professional satisfaction. After a pause for thought, she answered: 'Flying round the inside of the Berlin stadium.' This was no surprise because at the time it had been hailed by aviators as quite a feat, bearing in mind not only the restricted space, but the consequences if it had failed to go according to plan. At the time the stadium was crowded during the 1936 Olympics and Hitler was present. Thereafter, she added many peacetime and wartime achievements as a test pilot, although she never flew in combat. She was, without doubt, exceptionally talented and after the war she established more than forty endurance and altitude records for powered and motorless flight, but when we met she was just as happy talking about art and music. To my regret I never met her again.

Earlier in the year, on 2 May, I had flown to Alnwick Castle to assist in the ceremony of laying up the Colours of the 1st Battalion Royal Northumberland Fusiliers, which I handed over to 'Hughie', the 10th Duke of Northumberland. He had always been a strong supporter of the regiment and had generously made the Abbot's Tower available for use as our regimental museum. It was officially opened on that day and the Colours were carried into it for safe keeping. Every year the museum attracts a growing number of visitors, including former members of the regiment, and continues to enjoy the support of the current Duke, Hughie's son Ralph.

During the last of my three years as Director I was fortunate in having more than a few attractive invitations that took me overseas, to discuss mutual problems with others, to offer advice or in return for hospitality already given. In October 1970 I flew via Cairo, Karachi and Colombo to Singapore and thence to Perth, Western Australia.

During a week of engagements, I visited the Australian Royal Air Force Base at Amberley in Queensland and was able to present an Auster to the Australian Army Aviation Corps, who had been seeking one for their collection. With the comparatively recent emergence of Army Aviation within NATO armies and the importance of its potential anti-armour capability, conferences and conventions flourished as research intensified. Early in May we hosted an international helicopter anti-armour convention at Middle Wallop, attended by all our principal allies. The convention turned out to be a great success and much enjoyed by all participants, many of whom already knew one another. Indeed, it was recorded as a notable event at which for the first time the directors of Army Aviation of the UK, France and Italy and representatives of the directors of the USA and West Germany had been able to gather in one place to discuss the role and tactical concepts of the helicopter against armour. Our allies had already recognized that modern armies must have their own fully integrated aviation arm, while we were still fighting our corner. In spite of growing pains, however, we were proving our case for independence and soon the Army Air Corps took its place as a conventional arm of the service, with direct recruiting and all the attendant advantages.

The next few months, leading up to my retirement from the Army in the middle of August, were filled to capacity with work at home as well as abroad. On my last day, after a memorable lunch in the officers' mess, I was taken to the front door, outside which was a vintage helicopter. I was invited to sit in this while it was pulled by colleagues to another aircraft, fully serviceable, in which I was flown home to Exmoor.

Over that period I received more letters and messages of goodwill than I felt I deserved. One came from Hans Drebing and I kept it as a sprig of laurel from a thoughtful, albeit overgenerous, friend:

> ...We German Army Aviators can be proud of knowing you and of your interest in us. As a parachutist known throughout the World and as an international figure in the fields of Army Aviation and the airtransportability of Land Forces, your authority as an expert is a lesson to us in many ways.

229

Please accept, dear General, the heartiest greetings of German Army Aviators and my personal best wishes for the future of British Army Aviation and for your personal well-being.

To you, General Wilson
'Hals und Beinbruch!' *
Yours sincerely,
Hans Drebing.

* Traditional German pilot's 'Good Luck' wish – literally translated: 'Broken neck and bones!'

My retirement, however, did not mark the end of my service flying. A few weeks earlier, I had taken a telephone call from a senior RAF officer whose staff in the Ministry of Defence and mine had a good working relationship. He had enquired whether I would be interested in joining a Transport Command crew who were due to make a route familiarization flight to the West Indies via Newfoundland during the first week of September. It was a most thoughtful gesture and I accepted his invitation with gratitude. A few weeks later, I reported to RAF Lyneham for a 14,000 mile journey, involving two crews, which took in Newfoundland, Bermuda, Coolidge (USA), St Lucia, Montego Bay, Acapulco, Washington DC, Gander and back to Lyneham. I was the only passenger throughout the trip and spent much of the time on the flight deck. In what nicer way, I asked myself, could the RAF have marked the end of anyone's association with them during a period of over thirty years.

I returned to Exmoor to resume my retirement, but although my service career had come to an end this was by no means the end of my association with Army Aviation and the SAS or, for that matter, with Old Comrades of the Fifth Fusiliers and 3 Recce Regiment. I keep in regular touch with them all, not infrequently visiting Middle Wallop, Northumberland and Hereford. Indeed, for some years I returned to the latter at regular intervals to talk to cadres of NCOs about the regiment's early days in Hereford and the evolution of some of its current roles. I have never needed an excuse to visit Northumberland as often as the distance from Exmoor permits and eventually took on the responsibilities of honorary colonel of what had been my parent regiment. The bonds with all six of the regiments with which I have been involved remain durable with the assistance of Old Comrades' organizations, and the opportunities for the renewal of old friendships are frequent enough to keep them alive.

Quo Fata Vocant.

Chapter Twenty-Two

New Horizons

The Country Life is to be preferred for there we see the works of God, but in the cities little else but the works of men.

William Penn, 1644-1718

My career in the Army spanned thirty-three years. Even longer has elapsed since the end of it and some might say that these years have been almost as eventful. Within three months I had returned to Cambridge, as an undergraduate, to complete the degree interrupted in 1939, and there I met Sarah. We were married in 1973 in St John's College Chapel by my wartime padre, The Venerable George Fox, with the choristers and choral scholars, under the direction of George Guest, excelling themselves. Chips Jewell was my best man.

In 1974 my degree in Land Economy and my long-standing interest in national parks worldwide led to further employment when I was gratified to find I was chosen out of 360 applicants to become the first National Park Officer for Exmoor. Initially we were a team of four, with Jim Collins as warden, John Essen in charge of administration and the inimitable Birdie Johnson as my secretary. The job was extremely interesting, if sometimes frustrating, and I was able to take on more staff as our responsibilities increased. By 1978, in the knowledge that the fledgling organization was firmly established and having already been invited to become a consultant to the European Federation of National Parks and an accredited observer for the International Union for the Conservation of Nature, I decided to retire for the second time so that I could occupy some of my time lecturing. During my service career I had taken opportunities to visit fourteen national parks in North America and several in Africa and Australasia. More recently I had been to some of the remotest in Europe. As well as visiting Turkey and what was then Czechoslovakia, I had enjoyed two 'working holidays' with Sarah, one north of the Arctic Circle and the other from northern Italy to the Spanish Pyrenees. All this gave me plenty of material and hundreds of slides to illustrate my lectures, which I was able to do in both the USA and this country.

There was also always plenty to do looking after the farm and woodlands at home and being involved in the local community. In 1979 I succeeded John Gooding, who had been a churchwarden of St George's Church, Morebath, for forty-seven years and for thirteen years I worked in a harmonious partnership with the other church-warden, Bill Payne, who himself completed twenty-five years. For eight successive years we held the Morebath Easter Music and Flower Festival, which raised thousands of pounds for the Church and Save the Children Fund jointly. During this time our sons, Alexander and Peter, were born and my travelling changed to take account both of the family and other responsibilities. These included officers' and old comrades' associations of the six corps and regiments with which I had been associated. Most prominent among them has been my parent regiment, the Fifth Fusiliers, where I stepped into the shoes of the late Major General Roger St John, by acting as the equivalent to Colonel of the Regiment, with a remarkable number of, mostly Geordie, old soldiers. Other ties not only exist but, in some cases, have gained strength. The SAS record-breaking free fall parachute team of 1962 now reassembles, close to its original strength, for an annual reunion lunch, and the remnants of 3 Recce Regiment still forgather at Hexham to worship in the Abbey on Remembrance Sunday. Friendship, of course, knows no bounds, often starting early and enduring into later life. As well as friends from my military career and from living in the same beautiful part of England since soon after the war, I count myself fortunate in having been able to keep in touch with the survivors of a group of contemporaries from my schooldays at Shrewsbury and we still meet annually.

Through all my life I have been sustained by the ties of home, first in the North and then on the fringe of Exmoor. My father and I used to go rough shooting near Dulverton over farmland belonging to a Polish family. There from high ground my eye was repeatedly drawn across a valley to a secluded farmhouse, nestling in its own wooded combe. In due course, when on leave from Germany, I heard a rumour that it might be coming up for sale and was tempted to take a closer look. I arranged to visit, but only when I was on my way did I discover that the track up the combe was impassable except on foot or horseback and as I walked I passed a succession of six derelict cars that had died in the attempt. When I eventually reached the top I was beset by mixed feelings as I found myself surveying the utmost dilapidation, but in a setting that was idyllic. I was captivated and knew that I could not turn my back on it unless I was convinced it was beyond my means to buy and restore. Eventually I took the plunge, realizing that I would always rue the day if commonsense prevailed. The rebuild took eighteen months and it then proved to be ideal for my parents and quite big enough for me to share with them when I was home on leave.

In 1971, the Polish family decided to sell their small farm and my father and I bought it together. We engaged a splendid bailiff, Cecil Crudge, to farm the land on both sides of the valley as one and he and his wonderful wife, Mildred, moved into the farmhouse with their family. The house was larger than they needed so when my batman, Jimmy Shannon, left the Army the same day that I retired, there was room for him and his wife and two small daughters to live in part of it. However, they were a true Geordie couple and the call of the North proved too much, so after two years they moved, just in time for Sarah and me to take their place after our wedding. It proved to be a happy home for three years until my father died, aged ninety-two, and we moved across the valley into the house that had so beguiled me.

Now, looking back, none of my interests has been more compelling than the enjoyment of the home and countryside in which Sarah and I live. Here, with the latest in the line of black Labradors bred from the puppy given to my mother in 1936, we are joined at regular intervals by our two sons. I have had the pleasure of seeing them grow to manhood, with Alexander following me into the Army and Peter coming down from Oxford, ready to embark on his chosen career. Here, from a summerhouse a short walk away through our woods, we can survey much of the ancient parish of Morebath, once owned by King Harold and then by William the Conqueror. With Exmoor to the north, our panoramic views sweep eastwards from the Blackdown Hills, then to the south, down the winding valley of the River Exe, and westwards to Dartmoor in the far distance. The intervening farming scene changes through the seasons with every nuance of weather, while the only sounds that reach us are almost all natural ones and sometimes there is total silence. Life here remains tranquil, while we, the custodians of this gem of unspoilt countryside, give thanks.

Bibliography

Books

Aldrich, Richard J., (ed.), *British Intelligence, Strategy and the Cold War, 1945-51*, Routledge, 1992

Barclay, Brigadier C.N., *History of The Royal Northumberland Fusiliers 1919-1945*, Wm Clowes and Sons Ltd., 1952

Barnett, Corelli, *Engage the Enemy More Closely, The Royal Navy in the Second World War*, Hodder & Stoughton, 1991

Butler, J.R.M., *History of the Second World War, Grand Strategy Vol II, September 1939 – June 1941*, HMSO, 1957

Carew, Tim, *Korea – The Commonwealth at War*, Cassell and Co. Ltd., 1967

Denning, Lord, *The Family Story*, Butterworths, 1981

Doherty, Richard, *Only the Enemy in Front – The Recce Corps at War 1940-1946*, Tom Donovan, 1994

Fox, George, *Diary of The Reverend George Fox, MC (June 16th 1944 - June 6th 1945)*, published privately, 1998

Graham, Dominic and Shelford Bidwell, *Tug of War, The Battle for Italy 1943-45*, Hodder & Stoughton, 1986

Hickey, Michael, *The Korean War*, John Murray, 1999

McManners, John, *Fusilier – Recollections and Reflections 1939-1945*, Michael Russell (Publishing) Ltd., 2002

Miller, Edward, *Portrait of a College, a History of The College of St John the Evangelist in Cambridge*, The Cambridge University Press, 1961

Perrins, Anthony, (ed.), *"a pretty rough do altogether"*, *The Fifth Fusiliers in Korea 1950-51*, The Trustees of the Fusiliers Museum of Northumberland, Alnwick Castle, 2004

Scarfe, Norman, *Assault Division, A History of the 3rd Division from the Invasion of Normandy to the Surrender of Germany*, Collins, 1947

Smyth, Brigadier Sir John, VC, *Bolo Whistler, The Life of General Sir Lashmer Whistler*, Frederick Muller, 1967

Wilson, Major R.D., *Cordon and Search, With 6th Airborne Division in Palestine, 1945-48*, Gale and Polden, 1949 and Battery Press, Nashville, Tennessee, USA, 1984

234

Other Sources

21 Army Group Internal Memorandum. PRO Ref: WO 205/139.

3 Reconnaissance Regiment (NF) RAC War Diary. PRO Ref: WO 171/4133.

3 Reconnaissance Regiment (NF) War Diary. PRO Ref: WO 171/418.

3rd Division Intelligence Summary No. 205, Part I, based on information received at 2100 hours, 28 January 1945. PRO Ref: WO 171/4133.

8 RNF War Diary, 23 March 1940. PRO Ref: WO 166/4576.

Account of Movements and Actions fought by 1st Battalion Welsh Guards in France and Flanders from 17 May to 1 June 1940. PRO Ref: WO 167/696.

Agenda for Directors' Meeting. PRO Ref: CAB 159/9 Part 1.

Appreciation by GOC Palestine (Lieutenant General G. H. A. MacMillan of MacMillan) dated 5 August 1947 (Ref DS/MISC/15 GMM 8) lodged with the Documents Department of the Imperial War Museum.

Cambridge Daily News, 20 May 1939.

Churchill Archives, Ref. CHAR 9/137.

Dictionary of National Biography 1971-1980.

Handley Page *Report on High Altitude Paratroop Drop* by Squadron Leader Hazelden, dated February 1962.

History of 3rd Reconnaissance Regiment (NF) in the Invasion and Subsequent Campaign in North West Europe, 1944-45. Edited by Major J. K. Warner.

HQ 3rd British Infantry Division War Diary. PRO Ref: WO 171/412.

JIC (51) 1/1 (Final) dated 1 February 1951. PRO Ref: CAB 158/12.

Keesings Contemporary Archives, 23 August 1938.

Medical Diary ADMS 3rd Division, 1-31 October 1944. PRO Ref: WO 177/377.

Military Review, January 1989.

Nichomachean Ethic iii, by Aristotle, c. 340 BC.

Notes on Proposed Raid over R. MAAS addressed to Major R. D. Wilson, WILFORCE. Dated 23 January 1945. PRO Ref: WO 171/4133.

Prime Minister's statement to the House of Commons. Hansard, 26 March 1981.

Programme of the Commemoration of the Battle of Overloon. Published by the Municipality of Vierlingsbeek, 1994.

Report by Neville Gill to Colonel Clarke dated 21 June 1949, lodged in RNF Regimental Archives, Alnwick Castle.

Report on the Patrol Crossing of the R. MAAS near SAMBEEK on 27 January 1945. PRO Ref: WO 171/4133.

Soldier, Volume 23, Number 11, HMSO for the Ministry of Defence, November 1967.

St George's Gazette, issues for September 1958, Volume LXXVI and May 1967, Volume LXXXV.

The British Part in the Korean War Volume II: *An Honourable Discharge* by General Sir Anthony Farrar Hockley, HMSO for the Cabinet Office.

The Denning Report on 'The Profumo Affair', Pimlico Edition. Reprinted by Hutchinson by permission of the Controller of HMSO, 1992.

The Record of the 8th (M.C.) Battalion The Royal Northumberland Fusiliers from 17 May to 31 May 1940. PRO Ref: WO 167/802.

War Diary of 48th Battalion Royal Tank Regiment for 23-26 August 1944. Quoted by courtesy of the Librarian, The Tank Museum, Bovington, Dorset.

Index